Reason and Morality

BY THE SAME AUTHOR

Metaphysical and Epistemological Problems of Perception

Reason and Morality

A Defense of the Egocentric Perspective

Richard A. Fumerton

Cornell University Press

ITHACA AND LONDON

First published 1990 by Cornell University Press.

International Standard Book Number 0-8014-2366-X
Library of Congress Catalog Card Number 89-38801

Printed in the United States of America

Librarians: Library of Congress cataloging information
appears on the last page of the book.

∞ The paper used in this publication meets the minimum
requirements of the American National Standard for Permanence
of Paper for Printed Library Materials Z39.48–1984.

For Patti

Contents

ALICE: "Would you please tell me which way I ought to walk from here?"

THE CHESHIRE CAT: "That depends a good deal on where you want to get to."

LEWIS CARROLL, *Alice's Adventures in Wonderland*

Preface

This book deals with some of the most ancient questions in philosophy. In it I seek to uncover the conceptual connections between morality and practical rationality. It is therefore an exercise in metaethics and metarationality, but it is not an exercise narrowly confined. My background is in epistemology, and my interests in these questions grew out of my concern with epistemic concepts upon which, I am convinced, the concepts of practical rationality and morality are parasitic.

After well over two thousand years of philosophical reflection on the nature of morality and its place for the rational person, it would be foolish to suppose that the views I defend are in their basic structure entirely original—indeed, it seems to me that the right answer to the most fundamental question concerning what we ought to do is essentially the Cheshire Cat's. In fact, one of my primary reasons for writing this book is my concern that philosophers too often stray from the most obvious approach to understanding the concepts of morality and rationality.

I characterize my stand as a defense of the egocentric position. Although the Copernican revolution succeeded in establishing that our earth is not at the center of the universe, I argue that each person's values are at the center of that person's universe of rational and moral thought. It is through what *I* value intrinsically that I assess the rationality and morality of my actions. The fact that *I* take an intrinsic interest in certain things always in part determines what is rational for me to do, what I morally ought to do. The account given here is egocentric in yet another way in that the possibility and probability of consequences relevant to my making a decision are those possibilities and probabilities relative to *my* body of evidence. What is likely relative to my evidence may not be likely relative to your evidence, and even if we value the same things this difference in epistemic perspective may well affect the rationality and morality of our respective actions.

The consequences relevant to defining rational and moral action are the possible consequences of the specific act in its specific set of circumstances—the view I defend is a version of *act* consequentialism. In calculating what is rational or moral for me to do, I worry about the effects or possible effects of *my particular action*. I do not concern myself with rules (except insofar as their violation determines the effects of my action) or hypothetical questions about what would happen if other people acted in a similar way.

There is a sense, then, in which I am interested in defending a "crude" (extreme) relativistic act consequentialist approach to understanding rational action and an equally "crude" approach to understanding the conceptual connections between acting rationally and acting morally. I worry that philosophers, particularly philosophers who write in this field, are too frequently eager to compromise the most straightforward answers to certain questions in order to accommodate so-called intuitions about how people morally and rationally ought to behave. Ironically, however, a convincing defense of this "crude" approach requires us to recognize some rather sophisticated and subtle distinctions and ambiguities that are often or, in some cases, always ignored. When these distinctions and ambiguities are overlooked, a basically sound approach to understanding rationality and morality can easily appear to be oversimplified.

In the discussions that follow I try to address in a comprehensive way what I take to be the fundamental issues in metaethics and metarationality. For reasons that will become evident, I think it is a mistake to try to work in ethics without considering questions of rationality. And given the historical dominance of ethical theory in philosophy, I think it is equally problematic to discuss issues in practical rationality without considering their implications for ethical theory. The scope of this book, then, is very broad, and since I also wanted it to be accessible to as wide an audience as possible, it seemed obvious to me that I could keep my project manageable only through a highly selective discussion of the voluminous literature. I have tried to focus on what I take to be the most important alternatives and objections to the views I defend, and there are many extremely valuable contributions to both ethical theory and the theory of rational action which I treat all too briefly or ignore completely. I apologize in advance to the many philosophers whose writings I do not consider but whose work has helped build the tradition out of which this book has grown.

Many people over the years helped me develop the views I defend here. I particularly thank my colleague Scott MacDonald, who looked over a rough draft of the manuscript and made many valuable suggestions. I also thank Richard Foley, Richard Feldman, Robert Audi, and an anonymous referee for Cornell University Press, all of whom offered insightful comments, criticisms, and suggestions on earlier versions of the manuscript. The many philosophical discussions I have had here at Iowa with my colleagues and with graduate students have also helped to shape my views, and I especially thank the graduate students who participated in a seminar I taught dealing with a rough draft of the manuscript. Many raised very useful questions or objections, but I am particularly grateful to Grant Sterling and Xiaohua Mu.

On a more personal level, I thank my parents for their constant support. At least some of this manuscript was written in their company, and there is no way of estimating the contribution of summers spent fishing to the kind of contentment that makes it so much easier to research and write. In the same way, it is difficult to imagine doing anything in life without the pleasure that my wife and children bring me. Their mere presence makes everything easier, and that certainly includes the work on this manuscript.

Much of this book was written on a developmental leave provided by the University of Iowa.

RICHARD A. FUMERTON

Iowa City, Iowa

Reason and Morality

CHAPTER I

Introduction

In this book I am interested in discovering the nature of morality, the nature of practical rationality, and the relations that exist between moral action and rational action. Philosophers who carry out investigations into "natures" often proceed with radically different metaphilosophical presuppositions with respect to the nature of philosophical investigation. Although I shall not ask the reader to accept the details of my own metaphilosophical views here, I should point out that I approach an inquiry into the nature of morality presupposing a very traditional (but now less commonly accepted) distinction between metaethical questions and normative questions. My dominant concern is with metaethics, although I discuss some normative ethical issues primarily as part of an attempt to avoid confusing certain normative controversies with both metaethical issues and issues concerning the nature of rational action. There is no commonly accepted terminology to mark the analogue of the metaethical/normative distinction in ethics for the study of practical rationality, but it seems obvious that if the distinction can be made in ethics, one can make a metarationality/normative rationality distinction in the study of rational action. And here, too, my primary concern is with metarationality. Normative issues are discussed, but mainly in response to certain objections to the radical conception of practical rationality that I shall be defending.

Many different questions fall within the scope of metaethics and metarationality, and part of the task of discovering answers to these questions involves deciding which answers are parasitic on others. Certainly, before we are finished, I want answers to the following two questions:

(1) What does it mean to say of someone that he (morally) ought to take some action X?

(2) What does it mean to say of someone that it would be rational for him to take some action X?

To put these questions as questions about *meanings* (vague as the notion of meaning is) may at least prejudice some of the metaphilosophical issues I alluded to earlier and on which I would like to remain as neutral as possible. For my present purposes, you can reformulate (1) and (2) in any of the following ways:

(1a) What is the meaning of the sentence "S (morally) ought to do X"?

(2a) What is the meaning of the sentence "It would be rational for S to do X"?

(1b) What is the correct analysis of the proposition expressed by the sentence "S (morally) ought to do X"?

(2b) What is the correct analysis of the proposition expressed by the sentence "It would be rational for S to do X"?

(1c) What would make it true (if such statements have a truth value) that S (morally) ought to do X?

(2c) What would make it true (if such statements have a truth value) that it would be rational for S to do X?

(1d) What is the correct analysis of the state of affairs that S (morally) ought to do X?

(2d) What is the correct analysis of the state of affairs that it would be rational for S to do X?

(1e) What is the correct analysis of the fact that S (morally) ought to do X?

(2e) What is the correct analysis of the fact that it would be rational for S to do X?

Obviously, each way of putting the question carries its own ontological commitments and therefore involves the metaphilosophical task of explaining and justifying reference to the respective problematic categories of meanings, propositions, truth conditions, states of affairs, and facts. The formulation I feel most comfortable with is (1b) and (2b), and I have defended in some detail the conception of philosophical analysis and the metaphysical categories it presupposes elsewhere.[1] Again, however, I do not think the reader needs to accept the details of my metaphilosophical account to accept the views defended in this book. The reader who prefers an alternative will no doubt be able to translate my way of putting things into that preferred account.

In addition to the different ways of paraphrasing (1) and (2) which emphasize alternative metaphilosphical presuppositions, one can find alternative ways of putting the questions that substitute relatively uncontroversial synonyms for the problematic phrases referring to ethical concepts and the concept of rationality. Thus, to consider just one example for each question, instead of asking (1), we could worry about what it means to say that some action X was the morally right thing for an agent to do, and instead of asking (2), we could worry about what it means to say of someone that he had more reason to choose X than any of its alternatives. The nature of philosophy being what it is, however, apparently innocent attempts at paraphrase can become philosophically controversial very quickly. Although the notions of virtue, duty, and obligation, for example, are obviously paradigm ethical concepts, it is not altogether clear what their conceptual connections are to the concept of what it would be right for someone to do.

The Philosophical Priority of Metaethics and Metarationality

My reasons for focusing on questions of metaethics and metarationality are two. First, it seems obvious that one is hardly in a position to decide either general normative questions about kinds of actions (e.g., Is it always wrong/irrational to lie, break promises, value one's own well-being more than another's?) or particular normative questions about specific actions (e.g., Was it wrong/irrational for me to lie to

1. See Fumerton 1983 and 1985, chap. 2.

Smith yesterday, break my promise to Jones on Tuesday, put my well-being above yours last Thursday?) until one has a clear understanding of the subject matter of such questions, that is, unless one has answers to questions of metaethics and metarationality. It would be like going on safari to hunt a rhinoceros without knowing what a rhinoceros is.

Plausible as this argument seems, one can certainly object if it is intended to demonstrate the necessity of addressing metaethical questions first. We may lack adequate *philosophical* analyses of the fundamental concepts of ethics and rationality, but it hardly follows that there is no sense in which we understand these concepts prior to our philosophical investigations. If my friend asks me if the movie I saw was good, she will be justifiably put off if I claim that we really should not discuss such matters until we first address the question of what it means to say of something that it is good. The well-known paradox of analysis just is the puzzle of how philosophers who at some level seem to have no trouble understanding each other when they talk about good movies can end up with such radically different accounts of what they were talking about. Whatever the solution is to the paradox of analysis,[2] at least some ethical philosophers impatiently demand that we stop the endless "logic-chopping" preoccupation with philosophical analyses in ethics and rationality and start addressing the pressing issues about what we ought to do in a world that faces one crisis after another. To insist that these normative investigations should await the results of our meta-investigations is no more reasonable than to insist that the dry cleaner not do anything with my shirt until we have an adequate philosophical analysis of the physical world.

It must be said that there is at least something to this reply. *Nonphilosophers* certainly don't need to engage in metaethical inquiry before they decide whether or not they ought to give to charity. But then nonphilosophers are not expected to arrive at their conclusions philosophically. The very essence of philosophy includes a willingness to address questions that most people don't ask, to view as problematic assumptions that most people unreflectively make, to ask for justification and argument where normally no justification or argument is sought. And in the context of a *philosophical* effort to make explicit the reasons we have for concluding that we morally or rationally ought to

2. I have presented my solution to the paradox in Fumerton 1983 and discuss the paradox in more detail when we examine Moore's open question argument.

do something, I think one does need a *philosophical* account of the subject matter of these judgments. The dry cleaner doesn't need a philosophical account of the external world because no one is likely to ask him, and he is not likely to ask himself, whether he really knows that there exists a shirt he is trying to clean. But if he were to consider such a question, he would be hard pressed to answer it without the aid of philosophical analysis. In our culture, no one is likely to ask, outside of a philosophical context, whether anything but happiness is intrinsically good—the question just doesn't come up. When the philosopher asks it, by way of trying to get to the bottom of normative disputes, she will be hard pressed to answer it without getting clear about the meaning of intrinsic goodness.

In arguing that metaquestions have philosophical priority over normative questions, I haven't yet endorsed the extreme positivist position that the *only* appropriate philosophical questions in ethics and rationality are metaquestions. We live in an age of philosophical tolerance. We are encouraged to bridge the analytic/continental divide, and we are certainly encouraged to view as philosophically respectable the expansion of moral philosophy into such clearly normative areas as business ethics, environmental ethics, and medical ethics. A glance at the course offerings of most major philosophy departments indicates that courses on contemporary normative ethical issues are at least as common as courses stressing the classical issues in metaethics. Rumor has it that some ethical philosophers are on the staffs of major hospitals and wear "beepers" ready to respond with their expert advice on the next ethical emergency (Who should get the liver—eight-year-old Billy or Betty, the seventy-year-old genius?).

At the risk of alienating many of my readers, however, I would like to make a plea for a certain amount of intolerance, or at least extreme skepticism, with regard to the respectability of the current emphasis on normative issues in philosophy. And this brings me to the second of my reasons for focusing on questions of metaethics and metarationality. To be blunt, it seems to me that on almost any metaethical theory, philosophers are simply not particularly qualified to decide normative controversies. It is true that somebody has to decide whether Billy or Betty gets the liver. Somebody has to decide whether cigarette advertisements ought to be made illegal, whether we ought to develop and deploy the "Star Wars" defense shield, whether we ought to go ahead with the development of nuclear energy. These are enormously difficult and important questions. But on the metaethical views I shall defend and, indeed, on any of the consequentialist views I talk about in the next chapter, these are enormously difficult *empirical* questions.

On some metaethical views, the answers to these questions depend in part on the actual, probable, or possible *causal* consequences of the particular act in its particular set of circumstances. On other metaethical views, one must consider even more complicated hypothetical questions about the causal consequences of people generally acting in a certain way. And the philosophers I know are not particularly good at answering these sorts of *empirical* questions. Philosophers typically lead rather sheltered lives, far removed from the harsh realities of the outside world and the kind of knowledge exposure to that reality brings. If, on the other hand, consequentialism is false and some extreme form of intuitionism, for example, is true—one simply intuits immediately the rightness and wrongness of actions—it is again difficult to see what a philosopher has to contribute to normative controversies. I can't really say because I have no idea what these intuitions are supposed to be, but I gather that even those who think they have them do not usually claim to be better than others at intuiting what we ought to do.

But surely one will object that all this overstates the case. Philosophers can, after all, learn the relevant facts necessary to make ethical and rational decisions in various fields, and they have the added qualification of being aware of the metaethical controversies. How does being aware of the metaethical controversies, however, help us become expert at resolving normative issues? The philosopher knows the distinction between act and rule generic utilitarianisms (discussed in the next chapter). But when he gets called into the operating room for his "expert" ethical advice, does he offer it as an act utilitarian, a rule utilitarian, or neither? How do hospital administrators decide whom to hire in the first place? Do they make up their minds that they want a nonrelativist, objectivist, actual consequence rule utilitarian, or do they just keep their fingers crossed and hope that the philosopher they hire doesn't think within the framework of a mistaken metaethical theory?

Philosophers, qua philosophers, obviously do have something to contribute to the resolution of normative issues. But what they have to offer just is their metatheories. Qua philosophers, we can make people aware of the different metaviews of ethics and rationality and their sometimes dramatically different consequences. People who know the relevant facts can then "plug them in" to the metatheory they end up accepting in order to generate their normative conclusions. In addition to pointing to the value of their metaskills, I might also admit that good philosophers are often handy to have around, regardless of the issue being discussed, for their special skills at analyzing, making clear distinctions, and recognizing fallacious argument. But these skills define the concept of a good philosopher. They don't define the concept of an expert on normative controversies.

As I have said, I discuss certain very general normative issues by way of explicating at least hypothetical consequences of my metatheories of morality and practical rationality and by way of addressing those who object that my metaviews have counterintuitive normative consequences. The reader gets very little advice with respect to what we ought to do in life, however. It should become clear from my philosophical views why, qua philosopher, I am not in a position to offer such advice.

MORALITY AND RATIONALITY

If we get adequate philosophical answers to questions concerning the subject matter of judgments about morality and practical rationality, I assume we should then be in a position to answer the ancient question concerning the relationship between morality and rationality. That question has been put many different ways, but the most straightforward one is perhaps the best:

What is the connection between X's being something I morally ought to do and X's being something that it would be rational for me to do? Put another way, what reason do I have for doing what I morally ought to do?

The question is sometimes put in the more provocative form: Why should I be moral? a question that in turn can be expanded to read: Why should I do what I morally should do? This way of putting the question is provocative for it already suggests that morality and rationality are at least conceptually distinct. The fact that the question "Why should I be moral?" strikes most people as a perfectly sensible and, indeed, *significant* question strongly suggests that the first "should" in the question "Why should I do what (morally) I should do?" cannot be the "should" of morality. If it were, then the question "Why should I be moral?" would presumably reduce to the question "Morally speaking, should I do what morally speaking I should do?" a question we need hardly rack our brains trying to answer.

If I am right, then the ancient question "Why should I be moral?" is essentially a question that asks about the *rationality* of acting morally, of doing the morally right thing. But if this is so, words like "ought" and "should" would appear to be ambiguous, at least between the "should" and "ought" of rationality and the "should" and "ought" of morality. To keep open the possibility that even after philosophical analysis there will remain an ambiguity between two fundamentally different uses of "should", in what follows I shall try to avoid confusion by always prefacing words like "should" and "ought" with the adverbs "morally" or "rationally". In doing so, I am *not* taking for granted that there *is* a distinction between the concept of what one morally ought to do and the concept of what one rationally ought to do. Indeed, as will become evident, I am most sympathetic to an identification of morality and rationality. At least part of the task of defending such a view obviously involves trying to account for the apparent significance of the question "Why should I be moral?" Distinguishing between morality and rationality allowed us a way of understanding that question which made it significant. If one collapses practical rationality and morality, if one views "should" as univocal in meaning, one is obviously in danger of relegating what appears to be a perfectly sensible, perhaps even profound, question to one that is trivial or at least one whose answer is an analytic truth.

Before concluding these introductory remarks on the nature of my understanding of the question "Why should I be moral?" I might simply note in passing that at least some philosophers who allow the significance of the question attempt to understand it as a question about the relationship between *egoistic* action and moral action. More specifically, they would understand the question "Why should I be moral?" as a question that asks for self-interested reasons to do what morally one should do.[3] This would constitute an interpretation different from my own only on the supposition that the concept of practical rationality is a concept distinct from the concept of egoistic action, a supposition that is nevertheless true and that I shall defend in more detail later in the book as part of the task of clarifying my conception of rational action.

3. See, for example, Hospers 1961, Nielsen 1970, and Baier 1958.

We are going to begin, then, our attempt to understand morality and rationality leaving open the question of how they are conceptually linked, and in order that our terminology will not beg questions, we shall continue to distinguish between the "should" of morality and the "should" of rationality in the way indicated above. We may, of course, end up distinguishing still other "shoulds" and "oughts". Thus, for example, in addition to the "should" of morality and rationality, there may be a legal "should" and a "should" of etiquette designed to describe the latest dictates of Emily Post or whoever lays down the laws of etiquette these days. There may even be more specialized "shoulds" relating to the rules and regulations of particular games or subcultures. These other putative uses of "should" may well be useful to consider in trying to understand the connection between the "should" of morality and the "should" of rationality. They might well provide a model that will help us understand how the question "Why should I be moral?" might be significant even within the framework of a view attempting to identify the fundamental concepts of morality and practical rationality.

I said that before we are finished I wanted answers to questions (1) and (2). I want to know what it means to say that one morally ought to take some action X, and I want to know what it means to say of some action X that it would be the rational course of action for someone to take. When I single out these questions in this way, there is certainly a sense in which I am implying that they are fundamentally important. But I do not mean to imply that these questions are philosophically fundamental in the sense that they are the questions in metaethics and metarationality which need to be answered first. In fact, I think they are not. With G. E. Moore, whose views I shall examine in some detail shortly, I take the concept of intrinsic goodness to be the most fundamental concept in ethics. And that is because, like the Moore of *Principia Ethica,* I believe one can analyze the concept of what one ought to do (the concept of right action) only if one has a prior understanding of the more fundamental concept of intrinsic goodness (badness). Specifically, I think one ought to define the ethical concept of right action in terms of epistemically rational belief about intrinsically good and bad consequences. The details of that account await the more complete discussion of practical rationality in Chapter 4. Since I am interested in pushing as far as possible an identification of morality and practical rationality, I obviously need to find in the concepts of practical rationality a structure that parallels the relationships between right action and intrinsic goodness—I need to find something in the analysis of rational action which fulfills the role of intrinsic goodness. That concept is the concept of an end or goal, and the identification of morality and practical rationality must, I believe, be built on the well-worn, much maligned, but basically correct idea of identifying intrinsic goodness with goals or ends.

There are, of course, all kinds of objections to attempts to identify goodness with ends, and an equally impressive array of objections to consequentialist views in both ethics and practical rationality, particularly the extreme sort of act consequentialist views I am interested in defending. My presentation of and response to at least some of these objections follows the more detailed discussion of the egocentric act consequentialist conceptions of rational action and morality which I defend later in the book. I shall, however, have more to say about consequentialism, still of a very introductory nature, in the next chapter.

NONMORAL USES OF VALUE TERMS

One of my reasons for singling out metaquestions about the concepts of morally right and rational actions as questions we ultimately want answered is to emphasize that the concept of *goodness* I am primarily interested in is the one that is conceptually linked to the concept of right action. The term "good", however, is used in a wide variety of contexts, many of which don't seem to have anything to do with ethics. We talk about good can openers, good knives, good movies, good arguments, good thieves, good poisons, for example, and it seems relatively clear that these uses of the term "good" are rather far removed from anything that is of fundamental concern to an ethical philosopher. Still, it is the same word "good" used in describing both charity and can openers, and a philosopher needs to say *something* about the relationship between the uses of "good" in these widely differing contexts. Although it is theoretically possible that we would conclude that the term "good" is completely ambiguous as between its use in describing charity and its use in describing can openers, it seems to me that it is a desideratum of a plausible mataethical theory that it exhibits at least conceptual *links* between the different uses of "good". I shall argue that it is a virtue of the view defended in this book that we can understand clearly the relationship between the goodness that is conceptually linked to morality and the goodness a can opener has by virtue of the ease with which it opens cans.

EPISTEMIC RATIONALITY AND PROBABILITY

I have said that I will be defending act consequentialist accounts of practical rationality and morality. More accurately, I will be defining rational action and moral action in part by reference to rational belief about the consequences of action. My account of morality and practical rationality, then, presupposes an understanding of rational belief.[4] It presupposes an understanding of epistemic rationality and (what I take to be one of the two fundamental concepts in epistemology) the concept of one proposition being epistemically probable relative to a given body of evidence. It would seem, then, that I owe the reader an account of epistemic rationality and its relation to practical rationality, and to avoid a digression later in the book I will say what I have to say about epistemic rationality here.

As will become evident, I take the concepts of practical rationality and morally right action to be parasitic on the concepts of epistemic rationality. And this is so because what is rational or right to do is in part a function of what is epistemically possible and probable relative to one's evidence. I defend in more detail an analysis of the fundamental epistemic concepts elsewhere,[5] so I only briefly summarize the main ideas here. I defend a widely rejected version of radical foundationalism which takes as one of the most fundamental epistemic concepts the concept of being directly acquainted with a fact. One has noninferential knowledge that P when one is directly acquainted with the fact that P, the thought that P, and the relation of correspondence that holds between the thought that P and the fact that P. A defense of this view obviously requires a defense of the theory of truth it presupposes, but I must again refer the reader to the more detailed discussions of this question in Fumerton 1985. The concept of something being epistemically *possible* or *probable* is always the concept of some proposition asserting some fact being possible or probable relative to a given body of evidence. Given the version of foundationalism I defend, what is possible or probable is possible or probable only relative to what one is

4. In *The Theory of Epistemic Rationality*, Richard Foley *initially* appears to argue that epistemic rationality and practical rationality are both species of a more general concept of rationality defined in terms of means and ends. The difference between different kinds of rationality is a function of the different *goals* that define species of rationality. I think this view is mistaken, for means/ends conceptions of rationality are plausible only if the rationality is a function of the agent's *rational* beliefs about means and ends. In fact, I think Foley eventually comes to this conclusion himself. See p. 121.

5. See Fumerton 1985, chap. 2.

noninferentially justified in believing. Noninferentially justified beliefs constitute the source of all epistemic possibility and probability and end the regress that has so troubled epistemologists. If all justification were inferential and if only justified beliefs can justify other beliefs, it is difficult to see how one can avoid foundationalism without embracing skepticism, the implausibility of a coherence theory, or the abandonment of commonsense intuitions implicit in externalist epistemologies (more about that in a moment).

The principle that only justified beliefs can justify other beliefs is one part of what I call the *principle of inferential justification*. The other part of that principle maintains that one can be justified in believing one proposition P on the basis of another E only if one is justified in believing that E makes P probable. One is justified in believing that one proposition P has a very low epistemic probability relative to one's evidence E only if one is justified in believing that E makes P unlikely. One is justified in believing that P is possible relative to one's evidence E only if one is justified in believing that P is logically compatible with one's evidence E. If we accept the principle of inferential justification, we are obviously threatened with not just one but an infinite number of infinite regresses. To block all of these regresses as foundationalists accepting the principle of inferential justification, it would seem as though we must find, among the propositions we are noninferentially justified in believing, propositions of the form E makes probable (improbable) P. Whether or not one can be noninferentially justified in believing assertions describing relations of probability between propositions obviously depends on how we understand the second most fundamental epistemic concept, the concept of one proposition making probable (to some degree or other) another. How are we to understand this concept?

One of the most commonly accepted and more plausible theories of probability is the so-called relative frequency theory. There are many variations on the view, but all hold that when a meaningful probability assertion is made there is always implicit reference to a reference class. Thus, for example, if I assert that it is likely that Jones will live to be sixty, and my assertion is to have a truth value, I must, on this theory, view that assertion as (1) assigning Jones to a certain class of people and (2) making a certain statistical claim about the percentage of people in that class who live to be sixty. Sometimes the context makes fairly clear what reference class is presupposed by the assertion of probability, but often there is no way to determine the content of a probability assertion other than to ask the person making the claim to make explicit the assumed reference class. In summary, as the name of the theory implies, probability is always construed as a *relative* notion. A thing's having one property is probable only relative to its having some other properties. And to say that it is likely that the thing has the former property relative to its having the latter properties is to say, roughly, that most things that have the latter have the former. Despite the fact that there are all kinds of problems facing a proponent of a relative frequency theory of probability,[6] it seems to me that some version of the theory does capture *one* sense of probability. But can the frequency conception of probability be employed in trying to understand the concept of one proposition being probable relative to another?

It is not easy to see how this would work. In saying that P is probable relative to Q, we certainly are relativizing the probability, but we do not seem to be assigning the proposition P to a reference class. If we say that the proposition that this is black (P) is likely to be true relative to the proposition that most observed ravens have been black and this is a raven (Q), in what sense has the proposition P been assigned to a reference class? The only class of propositions Q might seem to implicitly refer to is the class of propositions having the form, —— is a raven and —— is black, which have been observed to be true, and P is not even a member of *this* class.

The idea of employing the notion of relative frequency in trying to understand the concept of one proposition E making probable another P is not, however, completely hopeless. One can borrow at least the spirit of the relative frequency analysis of probability in developing the following view. We could suggest that in claiming that P is probable relative to E, we are simply asserting that E and P constitute a pair of propositions, which pair is a member of a certain class of proposition pairs such that, usually when the first member of the pair is true, the other is. Thus, in saying that a's being G is probable relative to its being

6. The most serious is the problem of distinguishing between accidental or coincidental statistical correlations and the kind of statistical correlation that would support a statement of relative probability (a problem directly analogous to the problem of distinguishing accidental generalizations from laws of nature). One can always try to solve the problem by turning to subjunctive conditionals (a's being F is probable relative to its being G if and only if, *were* we to produce an indefinite number of G's, most of them would be F's), but the concept of a subjunctive conditional is hardly the sort of philosophically innocent concept with which one tries to make clear other concepts.

F and most observed F's being G, I could be construed as claiming that this pair of propositions is of the sort: Most observed X's are Y and this is X / This is Y, and most often it is the case that when the first member of such a pair is true, the second is. Similarly, if I claim that my seeming to remember eating this morning (E) makes it likely that I did eat this morning (P), I could be construed as asserting that the pair of propositions, E / P, is of the form S seems to remember X / X, such that most often when the first member of the pair is true, the second is.

The above view is in some ways attractive, for at least it offers a relatively clear analysis of the concept of one proposition making probable another. It presents, however, enormous epistemological problems for those who wish to escape the regress of justification through foundations and who are committed to the principle of inferential justification, for it is difficult to see how on this interpretation of "makes probable" we could be noninferentially justified in believing any proposition of the form E makes probable P. In the example given above, it would seem to be a straightforward contingent fact that, usually when the first member of such a pair is true, the second is. Moreover, the contingent fact seems to be of a sort that would preclude direct acquaintance with it. To be directly acquainted with such a fact, one would presumably need to be directly acquainted with indefinite numbers of facts in the past, present, and future. Yet without noninferential justification for believing at least some propositions of the form E makes probable P, we cannot block a regress arising through the attempt to satisfy the second condition of the principle of inferential justification. And certainly if we later use *this* concept of probability in our analyses of rational and right action, these same insuperable (from a foundationalist's perspective) epistemological problems will arise in connection with knowing what it would be rational and right to do.

In any event, perhaps we should not be overly concerned with these epistemological problems, for I would argue on other grounds that one cannot define *epistemic* probability in terms of the sort of frequencies sketched above. In fact, it seems clear to me that there is no inconsistency in the hypothesis that one proposition E makes probable another P, even though the pair they form is of a sort such that the second member is almost never true when the first is. Suppose, for example, that we were all created a minute ago complete with nonveridical memory experiences of a long and complicated past. Suppose, further, that we are destroyed a minute later and that in our brief existence most of what we seemed to remember was false. In such a hypothetical situation it would be false that when a proposition of the form *S* seems to remember *X* is true, it is most often also true that *X*. But it is certainly not obvious that in such a situation our beliefs about the past based on memory would be unjustified. It is not obvious that propositions describing our memory experience would not make likely for us the truth of propositions about the past. Old philosophical views have a habit of resurfacing under new labels. Philosophers who used to try to define epistemic probability in terms of frequency[7] have been replaced by epistemologists trying to externalize fundamental epistemic concepts.[8] It should come as no surprise that the above objection to defining epistemic probability in terms of frequency is the basis for attacks on externalist analyses of justification.[9]

If we do not define epistemic probabilities in terms of frequencies, how should we understand the concept? Our options are limited.

Dialectically, I think the most attractive view is to take "makes probable" as a sui generis internal relation holding between propositions, analogous to logical relations, and discoverable through direct acquaintance.[10] Unfortunately, to embrace the view honestly, one must convince oneself that one is phenomenologically acquainted with the sui generis relation of making probable, and I can certainly sympathize with the Humeans who cannot find such a relation no matter how hard they "look."

Another, rather radical approach would be to offer a subjectivist analysis of making probable analogous to Hume's famous subjective definition of cause. One could argue that the idea of *E*'s making probable *P* is just a (perhaps confused) recognition that the mind is conditioned to believe one sort of proposition when it accepts another. There is no more cognitive content to the idea of one proposition's making probable another than this habit of mind. This view, however, seems mistaken for a reason similar to the problem mentioned with the frequency theory. The supposition that we might all be irrational (conditioned, perhaps, by some Cartesian evil demon to make unreasonable

7. See Russell 1948, part 5, in which he repudiates reliance on a sui generis concept of epistemic probability.
8. See, for example, Goldman 1979, Dretske 1969, Armstrong 1973, and Nozick 1981.
9. See, for example, Foley 1987 and Chisholm 1989.
10. Though he might not like the notion of acquaintance, I take this view to be essentially the one defended by Keynes (1952) and by Chisholm (1988), although Chisholm would refer to the relevant relation as tending to make probable.

inferences to false propositions) strikes us as wildly implausible but not contradictory. Yet it is only if such a hypothesis is contradictory that we can maintain that probability relations are just habits of inference.

A view closely related to the one above and even more extreme places the emphasis on *confused* in characterizing the concept of 'makes probable' as the recognition of the mind's habit of inference and goes on simply to deny that there is any genuine concept of one proposition's making probable another. And in the final analysis, I suspect that this view and the view that the concept is primitive are the two most likely alternatives.

This conclusion might strike the reader as particularly odd, given that I have already announced my intention to make full use of the concept of epistemic probability in analyzing fundamental concepts of morality and rationality. How could I even consider the possibility of employing a concept that might be utterly confused in analyzing other concepts? Reflection on this question, however, should reveal that there is nothing paradoxical about this move at all. The only crucial presupposition for the analyses that will be offered later in the book is that we (ordinary people in their nonphilosophical thought) *think* we understand perfectly well the concept of one proposition's making probable another. Quite literally, no one outside of a philosophical context, for example, doubts that our memory experiences make likely for us truths about the past. And as long as we feel perfectly comfortable employing a concept, there is no reason for the philosopher who is *philosophically* suspicious of it to deny that it is a concept that pervades our conceptual framework. It is equally obvious that one needn't accept the epistemological views that I have ever so briefly sketched in order to accept the analyses I shall offer which make use of the concept of epistemic probability. Externalists in epistemology are invited to translate my reference to possibilities and probabilities into the terms of their analyses, although as I indicated, they will surely inherit more than their share of epistemological problems concerning knowledge of right and rational action. Torn between sidestepping the issue entirely and developing and defending a detailed epistemological view, I decided that it would be best simply to indicate as briefly as I could my position with respect to the critical epistemic concepts that, I shall argue, the subject matter of this book presupposes.

The book is structured as follows. I begin with the metaethical investigation into the nature of fundamental ethical concepts. And by way of a metaethical introduction, I discuss in a very preliminary and abstract way some fundamental metaethical questions. My aim is primarily to make clear my understanding of these controversies, but in some cases I shall attempt to arrive at some cautious conclusions concerning the prima facie plausibility of some of the views discussed. This abstract discussion leaves hanging a number of crucial issues, issues that are discussed in the context of a consideration of specific metaethical theories. In Chapter 3, using Moore as a foil, I argue that there is a fundamental dilemma facing a wide range of metaethical views concerning the implication of these views on the connection between morality and practical rationality. Evaluating this dilemma requires that we turn our attention to the concept of practical rationality (Chapters 4 and 5). In Chapter 6 I consider some of the main objections to the egocentric act consequentialist account of rationality I defend and to an analogous theory of what makes actions morally right. I am particularly interested in objections that focus on alleged counterintuitive consequences of *act* consequentialism. Finally, in Chapter 7, I return explicitly to a discussion of the conceptual connections between morality and practical rationality.

CHAPTER 2

Fundamental Metaethical Controversies

The purpose of this chapter is to, first, outline in abstract form some of the main metaethical controversies and, second, evaluate at least some of the prominent arguments advanced to decide some of these controversies. There is a very real danger in trying to carry on a metaethical inquiry at this abstract level. All the dialectical arguments for cognitivism, subjectivism, relativism, consequentialism, and so on are for naught in the absence of concrete, detailed, and plausible analyses of the fundamental ethical concepts. The history of philosophy is littered with the remains of philosophers who have quite persuasively argued, for example, that we must adopt a regularity theory of causation, a phenomenalistic analysis of the external world, a Humean bundle theory of the self. But unless these philosophers deliver the goods in the form of specific analyses that survive objections, we must remain at least skeptical of their initially persuasive arguments. I expect, then, any conclusions I reach in this chapter to be taken with a grain of salt and to be viewed as merely preliminary. Their ultimate test involves the plausibility of the specifics offered later.

THE COGNITIVISM/NONCOGNITIVISM CONTROVERSY

The *cognitivism/noncognitivism* debate in metaethics is, at least superficially, one of the most dramatic of the metaethical controversies because the respective views seem so diametrically opposed. The disagreement is, of course, initially easy to define. The cognitivists take moral statements (in the indicative mood) to have a truth value. The noncognitivists deny that such statements (perhaps it would be better to say utterances) have a truth value. Some qualifications, however, need to be made. Certainly some noncognitivists would restrict their thesis to paradigmatically *normative* ethical statements. Hare, for example, would allow that one *can* use ethical sentences in the indicative mood to give anthropological descriptions of a culture's ethical views,[1] and it seems to me that he is quite correct both in allowing this and in insisting that these uses of ethical statements are not paradigmatically normative.[2] Thus when we say that in certain Eskimo cultures a husband ought to offer his wife to a guest, we are presumably intending only to describe the fact that (most? many?) male members of that culture accept this as one of the things they ought to do. We are not necessarily endorsing their view that they ought to behave in this way, nor has anything been said by way of analyzing the ethical judgment that these Eskimos apparently accept.

Assuming that one can identify a class of paradigm first-order moral judgments, the noncognitivist holds that *these* lack a truth value. Although the vast majority of noncognitivists would take their thesis to apply to all paradigm normative ethical judgments, it is, of course, formally possible to allow that some ethical statements have a truth value while others lack one. Such a view would be unusual primarily because it is initially difficult to see what would justify treating some ethical statements so differently from others. Nevertheless, given some important differences that I emphasize in later chapters between first-person and second-/and third-person value judgments, a mixed cognitivism/noncognitivism view is a possibility that we shall at least seriously consider.

In explaining their view, the noncognitivists will sometimes try to make it more precise by saying that ethical statements lack the kind of truth value that other paradigmatic *descriptive* statements have. And, indeed, given plausible views of truth, cognitivism in ethics is essentially indistinguishable from *descriptivism* in ethics. Noncognitivism entails

1. Hare 1952, p. 167.
2. The distinction between descriptions of a culture's norms and normative ethical judgments may presuppose the implausibility of certain sorts of metaethical relativism. Specifically, it may presuppose that ethical statements are not descriptions of values relativized to community standards.

the rejection of descriptivism. The descriptivist (as the label implies) takes paradigmatic normative ethical statements to describe some feature of reality, and such statements are presumably true when reality is as described, false when the relevant reality fails to obtain. All of this smacks of a realist, correspondence theory of truth, and in these days of rising antirealism some might find this way of putting the cognitivist/descriptivist commitments disquieting. In fact, I don't think there is any intelligible alternative to a correspondence theory of truth and the realism that it implies,[3] but I take it that even an extreme metaphysical antirealist will be able to find *some* way of characterizing the cognitivist/noncognitivist, descriptivist/antidescriptivist metaethical controversies within the framework of that view. The metaphysical antirealist who takes all of reality to be in some sense existentially dependent on our representations of it (even representations on metarepresentations?!) will presumably want to acknowledge (with an antirealist interpretation of that acknowledgment) that we use the predicates "true" and "false" to characterize some meaningful utterances and not others (imperatives, questions, interjections), and again giving the question his antirealist spin, he can raise the issue of how we might most perspicuously class moral utterances. As I said, and fortunately don't need to argue here, I don't find even intelligible the more well-known antirealist positions, and in what follows I shall continue to put things in ways that reflect my overall realist biases. Antirealists who are not so put off by the above remarks that they quit reading will no doubt find ways of understanding the distinctions I make within the framework of their antirealism.

In endorsing a realistic, correspondence conception of truth, I trust it is clear that I am not presupposing what is sometimes called *moral realism*. The expression "moral realism" is one I shall avoid because it has too many different connotations to be useful. At the one extreme, one can simply identify moral realism with cognitivism—there are truths (realistically understood) about what is good and bad, right and wrong, about what people should and should not do. More often, however, what people seem to have in mind by "moral realism" is a more specific form of cognitivism, namely some nonrelativistic form of objectivism (I'll have more to say about these concepts shortly).

As I use the terms, *metaethical noncognitivism* must not be confused

---

3. I present and defend a specific theory of truth in Fumerton 1985, chap. 2.

with *moral skepticism*. The most sensible interpretation of moral skepticism is simply epistemological skepticism with respect to knowledge of, or justified belief in, ethical truths. Far from presupposing noncognitivism, moral skepticism might better be thought of as implying metaethical cognitivism. It would be at best highly misleading for a noncognitivist in ethics to endorse a skepticism with respect to questions about what is good or bad, right or wrong. It would be as inappropriate as a philosopher who professed to be a skeptic with respect to imperatives, meaning by that only that one cannot know an imperative to be true. An endorsement of skepticism in some area seems to me to presuppose a context in which there is some truth or other about which we might be ignorant.

Now skepticism, in general, is a much maligned philosophical position—some philosophers refuse even to consider it as a serious option.[4] I have maintained elsewhere (Fumerton 1985, chap. 1) that one should not shape one's metaphysical views solely with the goal of avoiding skepticism, and I would certainly extend that thesis to the field of metaethics. I have argued, however, that if people *think* they have justified beliefs in a given field one might have a philosophical obligation at least to account for this metabelief. Nonetheless, accounting for this metabelief isn't the same thing as showing it to be justified. We can account for a belief by pointing out that it is just what one would expect people to believe given their other, perhaps mistaken, beliefs about what yields epistemic justification. I emphasize these matters here because at least one objection to the kind of consequentialist views of value judgments I shall defend attempts to tar the view with the brush of an unpalatable skepticism. In replying to this objection, I try to deflect its force by relying on the considerations briefly sketched above.

Once one defines noncognitivism clearly, and sharply distinguishes it from ethical skepticism and more global (and for that reason irrelevant to our present concerns) antirealism, metaethical noncognitivism seems to be prima facie a highly implausible view, so implausible that it is difficult to find reasons to take it seriously. Certainly the many undergraduates in our classes who start out confirmed noncognitivists usually hold the view because they don't feel comfortable claiming to *know* right from wrong. We live in an age and a culture in which cultural chauvinism is generally frowned on, and given the fascinating array of ethical

4. Chisholm 1977, chap. 7.

views held by apparently intelligent people in different cultures as to what is right and wrong, it does take more than a little nerve to proclaim oneself a beacon of ethical light, a bearer of moral wisdom and truth. Still, despite the fact that even some philosophers have tried to make noncognitivist hay out of the familiar facts of cultural relativism, there is surely no good *argument* that establishes a noncognitivist position from premises describing the fact that there appears to be widespread disagreement between people on issues of right and wrong.

I suppose that those who think that the existence of this kind of ethical disagreement tells against ethical cognitivism do so because they think that, if there were ethical truths, societies made up of intelligent people would eventually evolve so as to discover them. Proponents of such a view have far more faith in human rationality than I have, and in any event it is easy to offer analogies that argue against the conclusion. One can find the same sort of cultural disagreement that exists in ethics in areas where it seems clear that the disagreement concerns *matters of fact*. Thus, for example, the nonethical components of religious belief seem to vary from culture to culture just as much as, and in a very similar way to, ethical belief. The religious beliefs of people seem causally conditioned by the cultures in which they are raised in the same way as do ethical beliefs. And yet if we put aside misguided positivist concerns about the intelligibility of the supernatural, it seems to me foolish to deny that Jones's belief that there is one God who arranges for us an afterlife is a belief that lacks a truth value. Indeed, the existence of culturally conditioned disagreement in ethics seems to me no more relevant to the cognitivism/noncognitivism debate than is the existence of different schools of economics with their differing economic forecasts, vis-à-vis the question of whether propositions about the economic future have a determinant truth value. As long as we assume that it is *difficult* to arrive at ethical conclusions (and God knows we agonize enough about what we ought to do), we should surely not be surprised to find a great deal of ethical disagreement. And as long as we assume that people influence each other, we shouldn't be surprised to find that the disagreement is often along cultural lines. All this presupposes that there really is a significant amount of cultural disagreement with respect to ethical matters, and though I think there is, we shall have to consider the matter more carefully in exploring the implications of cultural disagreement for the subjectivist/objectivist and relativist/nonrelativist metaethical controversies.

Is there anything that can be said to offer prima facie support for the noncognitivist's position? Ironically, many noncognitivists give at least an approving nod to Moore's famous open question argument and the naturalistic "fallacy" it was supposed to establish. I say ironically because Moore's ethical views are in other respects a model of the kind of descriptivism that noncognitivists reject.[5] Frankly, I'm not sure whether the noncognitivists who cite Moore's arguments with approval really think they are good arguments or are simply prepared to reap the antinaturalist benefits that grew from the inexplicable widespread acceptance of Moore's charges against naturalism. In fact, the noncognitivist would be wise to remember that Moore's open question argument was an argument designed to attack *all* analyses of the fundamental ethical concept, not just naturalistic analyses. And if there were anything to the argument, it seems to me that it would tell equally well against the noncognitivist analyses of ethical terms. Since we are going to be looking at Moore's views, and his open question argument in particular, more closely in the next chapter, we shall postpone a more detailed evaluation of the argument as a potential source of support for noncognitivism. Certainly, *if* the noncognitivist can (a) establish that there is a naturalistic fallacy and (b) refute descriptivist nonnaturalism, some version of noncognitivism might be offered as a viable alternative.

I take establishing (a) and (b) above to be *prior* to establishing that other theme common to noncognitivist ethical theories, the proposition that you can never be logically forced to a moral conclusion by your acceptance of purely factual (descriptive) propositions. It may be that this is so, but it will be true only if descriptivism is false, and to *argue* for this gap between descriptive premises and moral conclusions, one must argue against descriptivism in either its naturalistic or nonnaturalistic form.

Aside from the above considerations, it seems to me that the most promising source of argument for noncognitivism is simply the support specific versions of it might seem to get from the apparent interchangeability of sentences containing value terms and utterances that obviously do seem to lack a truth value. The two principal models of meaningful noncognitive discourse to which noncognitivists in ethics have appealed are, of course, interjections ("terrific!", "hooray!",

5. One would be reluctant to view Moore as a descriptivist only if one confuses descriptivism with naturalism. I characterize Moore's views in much more detail in Chapter 3.

"damn!", etc.) and imperatives. The earliest (and most primitive) versions of emotivism emphasized the former. The prescriptivists (best exemplified by the Hare of *Language of Morals* and *Freedom and Reason*) emphasized the latter. But even early versions of emotivism allowed for a "quasi-imperative" aspect to moral pronouncements.[6] Although this oversimplifies matters somewhat, I think it is fair to say that both models are at least initially attractive to noncognitivists in part because they can find *contexts* in which the paradigm value terms are *used* much the way interjections and imperatives are used. This is particularly plausible in situations that are not paradigmatically moral, but if the view works in these situations, it suggests the possibility of generalizing. When the child learns that he is going to the zoo and shouts "Oh, good!" it certainly does seem as though "good" here is functioning much the way the interjections "Terrific!", "Fantastic!", and "Oh, boy!" function. And, indeed, these other expressions could just as easily have been used by the child to accomplish the same linguistic ends served by "good". It seems natural, then, to conclude, minimally, that "good" *sometimes* functions as an *expression* of pleasure or satisfaction. And this distinction between *expressing* and *describing* attitudes is precisely the distinction the emotivist wants to emphasize and generalize in explaining his alternative to understanding value judgments as descriptive judgments.

Now one might worry about trying to make clear this distinction between expressing and describing our attitudes. I said at the beginning of this section that the cognitivist/noncognitivist debate appears to be dramatic in part because of what seems to be a radical disagreement over how to understand ethical discourse. There are, however, versions of noncognitivism which are only ever so subtly distinct from versions of cognitivism. Specifically, it is difficult to see that a lot hinges on whether we take ethical statements to describe or express the attitudes of the person making the statement. I suppose we can get a feel for the distinction in the usual way by contrasting statements like "I am in severe pain" with utterances like "Ouch!" The former does seem to function more or less unproblematically as a description with a truth value, and it would be at least odd to characterize my *expression* of pain "Ouch!" as being either true or false. But note that even with this example, we can certainly wonder whether someone's use of "Ouch!"

6. See, for example, Ayer 1952 and Stevenson's "The Emotive Meaning of Ethical Terms."

was sincere or insincere. And without damaging the English language too violently, we might even characterize that "Ouch!" as a calculated *false* expression of pain. Moreover, I am not sure anything philosophically important depends on the distinction between false descriptions and false expressions of emotions or attitudes.

If there is a significant distinction between describing and expressing attitudes, it seems to me that one of the defining characteristics of *paradigmatic* interjections is a kind of *spontaneous* character to their use. "Ouch" is, of course, conventional and learned just as many physical expressions of pain are learned, but when it functions in what might reasonably be called a nondescriptive way, it is more like a conditioned response to a given stimulus than a conscious, deliberative attempt to describe oneself. But insofar as this is true of paradigm *expressions* of attitude, it is obviously a serious mark against the attempt to model most ethical judgments on this use of language. Most ethical judgments are patently *not* expressed as a kind of unreflective response to a given stimulus. We deliberate long and hard over what it would be good for us to do; we agonize in difficult situations over what course of action would be right for us to take. And all this seems very far removed, indeed, from that child spontaneously expressing his joy with the outburst "Good!"

The above argument is, of course, in some ways a serious injustice to the sophisticated emotivists like C. L. Stevenson. It is something of a caricature of his conception of the quasi-interjectionary character of ethical judgments. The injustice lies in not recognizing that Stevenson has a detailed theory of meaning as use underlying his metaethical view. A proper evaluation of his metaethics would involve a thorough examination of that theory of meaning. This, however, I cannot properly do in this necessarily brief sketch of an initial reservation about this version of noncognitivism. Nevertheless, in evaluating the prescriptivist's view below, I argue against reaching incautious conclusions about meaning based on observations about use.

As my own view emerges, I trust it will become clear that I am often highly sympathetic with many of Stevenson's views, particularly with what I take to be his Humean rejection of objectivism in ethics and his emphasis on the need to tie the meaning of at least *some* ethical judgments to the psychological states of the person making the judgment. The crucial problem is to do it in a way that accounts for the deliberation, reservations, and, indeed, concern that one has reached incorrect, false conclusions which often characterize our judgments about what we ought to do.

It should also be emphasized that, although Stevenson is perhaps the most well known defender of emotivism, he placed at least as much importance on what he called the *quasi-imperative* character of ethical judgments, the theme later developed and "universalized" by Hare. Again, the attempt to model an understanding of ethical discourse on the way in which we use meaningful nondescriptive discourse, in this case imperatives, gets some initial support from the way in which *in some contexts* we can apparently substitute imperatives for statements made using value terms without seeming to lose anything. To para-phrase an example of Stevenson's (used for another purpose),[7] we can easily imagine a conversation in which two friends committed to spend-ing the evening together are arguing about what to do. Jones begins the conversation by suggesting that they ought to go to the movies. Smith replies that instead they ought to go to the symphony. Notice that in spite of the fact that they did use the paradigm value term "ought", the conversation could have proceeded just as easily using imperatives. Thus Jones might have said "Let's go to the movies," and Smith might have replied "No, let's go to the symphony." The ensuing argument might swtich back and forth between the making of suggestions using "ought" statements and the making of suggestions using imperatives, and certainly someone listening to the conversation wouldn't be struck with the thought that these two people were curiously constantly changing the subject. Again, this conversation doesn't involve a para-digmatically *ethical* use of the value term "ought", but it would be tempting for a philosopher to try to generalize from the use of the term in these sorts of situations to conclusions about the use of the term in moral contexts. If one thinks of meaning as use, and one believes that one has discovered by considering conversations like the above that "ought" judgments and imperatives are often used in the same way, it is not difficult to infer that the kind of meaning certain paradigmatic value judgments have is the same sort of meaning imperatives have. And since the use of imperatives seems a relatively uncontroversial example of meaningful discourse that lacks a truth value, we might seem to have an argument for the conclusion that at least some value judgments lack a truth value.

7. Stevenson 1937.

In evaluating this suggestion, I certainly don't want to go into the details of that hopelessly vague conception of meaning as use. One comment I would make, however, is that one simply cannot infer that two utterances have the same meaning on a given occasion of their use just because they are used the same way in that context. Nor can one infer that two utterances have the same meaning because they are *typically* used in the same way in similar contexts, if by "used the same way" we mean something like "used to accomplish the same goals or ends". Consider, for example, the paradigmatically descriptive statement "The roads are icy" and the imperative "Drive carefully." Certainly if I am seeing a close friend to the door who has a long drive ahead of her, I might well, noticing that the roads are icy, warn her to drive carefully by saying, "The roads are icy." Of course, given the end I was trying to accomplish, I might just as well have said, "Be sure to drive carefully on these icy roads." But despite the fact that in this context the descriptive statement "The roads are icy" is serving the goal or end of advising my friend to drive carefully, it surely loses none of its descriptive character, nor does it lose its truth value. For all I know, it may even be that in the vast majority of cases in which people tell other people "The roads are icy" they do so with the primary intention of warning them to be careful. But even if that were true, it still seems to me absurd to suggest that such a statement would lose its descriptive character and its truth value.

One of the marks of a descriptive statement is surely that it expresses a thought or a proposition that can be *believed* even if one has no intention of, and can think of no purpose for, communicating that belief to anyone else. I can think to myself that the roads are icy without even considering the question of whether I might want to communicate that fact to some other person. A typical imperative like "Shut the door" doesn't express anything when used that can be believed or thought in that way.[8] I certainly think it is true that, in many cases when one tells another person that he ought to behave in a certain way, one is indeed trying to get that person to behave in that way, much as one is sometimes trying to get a person to act in a certain way by using an imperative directing him to behave in that way. Of course, that is not *always*

---

8. There may be descriptive content to imperatives. The imperative "Shut the door!" may carry with it the information that there is a door, but the imperative as a whole doesn't seem to express anything that can be believed or thought.

true. Sometimes we tell people what they ought to do (for that matter, issue imperatives directing them to behave in a certain way) with the primary intention of, for example, annoying them, knowing full well that, if anything, our advice to act in a certain way is more likely to result in their doing precisely the opposite. But if a friend comes to us, faced with an important decision, asking our advice about what to do, we might well respond using either an "ought" statement or an imperative, and using either utterance with the same goal, with the same end, of directing the person to act in a certain way. And it does seem to me that in developing a plausible analysis of "ought" judgments, one certainly should try to account for why we might expect someone to act in a certain way after getting him to agree that he ought to behave in that way. In other words, we should have a philosophically satisfying explanation of why we might reasonably hope to accomplish the goal of directing a person's behavior through the use of an "ought" judgment that we get the person to accept. But what I want to emphasize here is that one can *think* that a person ought to behave in a certain way, one can reach the conclusion that he ought to act in a certain way, without having the slightest intention, the slightest desire, to communicate that information to the person concerned. Again, the point is obvious if we look at the use of "ought" judgments in certain typical nonmoral situations, specifically situations involving competition.[9] When I play tennis, knowing my own game all too well, I often think to myself that my opponents ought to do certain things, but I pray and hope that they will never figure out what those things are. Certainly, I haven't even the slightest intention or inclination to tell my opponents what they ought to do in order to beat me. But this simple and uncontroversial fact, the fact that I can think that somebody ought to do something without using or having any intention of using the sentence "That person ought to do *X*" in any context, is itself a persuasive argument that "ought" judgments express something that can be believed or accepted independently of any considerations about how to use language which might convey that thought. And as I said before, I think the above just is at least one mark of a statement that is descriptive, that has a truth value.

I suppose that in the case of an unuttered, first-person "ought" judgment (my judgment that I ought to behave in certain ways) the prescriptivist might try to understand it as a kind of internal "silent"

9. A point made by Kalin 1970 in his reply to Medlin 1957.

imperative. When someone judges that she ought to quit smoking, she is simply issuing to herself the imperative "Quit smoking," an imperative she might or might not succeed in obeying. But in what sense could my thought that Jones ought to hit to my backhand be construed as an internal imperative directed at Jones to hit to my backhand? Is there the slightest plausibility to the suggestion that, when I think to myself that Jones ought to hit to my backhand, I am thinking to myself "Hit to it, hit to it!"? If anything, it seems to me I am usually thinking to myself, "For God's sake, don't hit to my backhand!"

Again, one cannot do justice to a view as complicated as Hare's and to the many sophisticated variations on prescriptivism in comments as brief as these. My intention is simply to sketch at least my primary reservation about the very idea of trying to model an understanding of ethical statements in particular and value judgments in general on an understanding of imperatives. There are also many aspects of Hare's metaethical theory which can easily be divorced from his prescriptivism, most notably his famous thesis that ethical judgments are universalizable, and this is an element of his theory that I treat later (in discussing objections to egoism, Chapter 5).

When all is said and done, perhaps the most striking prima facie implausibility to noncognitivist views, the thing that ought to make noncognitivists feel the most uncomfortable, is simply that we *do* without any apparent embarrassment use the expressions "true" and "false" frequently in evaluating ethical positions. You say, "We ought to unilaterally disarm," and I say, "I don't think that is true . . . I think that we ought to develop even more weapons." You say people ought to remain celibate until they get married, and I say that I don't *believe* that there is any truth to that idea. Now, to be sure, the noncognitivist can take these uses of the expressions "believe" and "true" and construe them as functioning in some nontypical way. To say of someone's (grammatically disguised) imperative that it is true might just be a way of saying I'll do it—that is to say, act, or support others who are acting—in the way prescribed. If I am an emotivist, I might try to construe someone's "acceptance" of my value judgment as his way of indicating a willingness to express the same attitude in the same sort of way. But such attempts to "reinterpret" what look like perfectly natural uses of the expressions "true" and "false" are obviously strained and would require considerable justification. A philosopher certainly does not have to take what is said at face value, but if a philosopher, to save a view, must construe people as meaning something other than what they appear to mean, he owes us a strong philosophical justification for engaging in these machinations. I shall try in this book to develop a positive account of value judgments which accommodates what is of value in the non-cognitivist's insights while preserving value judgments as unproblematic descriptive judgments to which the notions of truth and falsehood apply.

THE IS/OUGHT GAP

The is/ought controversy is closely linked to the cognitivism/non-cognitivism controversy. Indeed, I would argue that, on many natural ways of understanding it, the question of whether there is an is/ought gap just *is* the question of whether cognitivism (descriptism) is true. Philosophers have at least implicitly argued over the conceptual connections between various "is" statements and "ought" statements for thousands of years, but the controversy in its present form was raised by David Hume in a famous passage from the *Treatise:*

> I cannot forbear adding to these reasonings an observation, which may, perhaps, be found of some importance. In every system of morality, which I have hitherto met with, I have always remark'd, that the author proceeds for some time in the ordinary way of reasoning, and establishes the being of a God, or makes observations concerning human affairs; when of a sudden I am surpriz'd to find, that instead of the usual copulations of propositions *is,* and *is not,* I meet with no proposition that is not connected with an *ought,* or an *ought not.* This change is imperceptible; but is, however, of the last consequence. For as this *ought,* or *ought not,* expresses some new relation or affirmation, 'tis necessary that it shou'd be observ'd and explain'd; and at the same time that a reason should be given, for what seems altogether inconceivable, how this new relation can be a deduction from others, which are entirely different from it. (p. 409)

It is more than a little ironic that Hume is credited by so many with "discovering" the is/ought gap, for given the way in which most *contemporary* philosophers understand the claim that there is a gap, I think it is fairly clear that Hume never thought there was one (I'll explain this later).

How do contemporary philosophers understand the claim that there is an is/ought gap? As the expression implies, the thesis involves the view that in some sense of "derives" one cannot derive "ought" statements from "is" statements. But before we can proceed, this claim must be made much more precise by clarifying the relevant notion of deriving and by indicating more clearly what is meant by "ought" statements and "is" statements. It is fairly obvious that the expression "'ought' statement" is intended to refer to a much broader class of statements than the class of statements containing the expression "ought". And it is equally clear that "'is' statement" refers to a much narrower class of statements than the class of statements containing the expression "is".

The expression "'ought' statement' in the context of discussing the is/ought gap refers to value statements in general. But how should we define a value statement? We might begin by saying that a value statement is any statement containing a paradigm value term (e.g., "good", "right", "ought") or containing a term whose philosophical analysis would involve the use of one of these paradigm value terms. Thus if "murder" does mean "wrongful killing", we will include as a value statement (an "ought" statement) "Jones murdered Smith."

What is meant by an "is" statement? At least the following two possibilities suggest themselves:

(1) Any statement of fact, i.e., any *descriptive* statement.
(2) Any nonmoral or value-neutral statement (where "value" is understood as above).

There is no sense in trying to decide which of (1) or (2) is the "correct" interpretation of "'is' statement". Let us simply consider the claim that there is an is/ought gap on each way of understanding "is" statements.

The last concept we need to clarify in order to make precise the is/ought controversy is the relevant logical connection whose presence or absence is at issue. The three most obvious candidates are:

(1) Formal entailment
(2) Analytic entailment
(3) Synthetic entailment

For our present purposes let us say that P formally entails Q if it is a formal tautology that P materially implies Q. P analytically entails Q if the statement that P materially implies Q can be reduced to a formal tautology through the substitution of synonymous expressions. P synthetically entails Q if the statement that P materially implies Q is a necessary truth in the strongest sense (employing the familiar metaphor, is true in all possible worlds) but cannot be reduced to a formal tautology through the substitution of synonymous expressions. Thus, to take a standard example, the statement that X is red might synthetically entail the statement that X is colored. It is notoriously difficult to plausibly define being colored as a disjunctive property containing being red as a disjunct, and without such a definition, it is correspondingly difficult to construe the statement that if X is red it is colored as an analytic truth.

Assuming that these problematic categories of entailment are clear enough for present purposes, we can understand the claim that there is an is/ought gap in any of the following ways:

(1) No descriptive (factual) statement formally entails a value statement.

(2) No nonmoral statement formally entails a value statement.

(3) No descriptive statement analytically entails a value statement.

(4) No nonmoral statement analytically entails a value statement.

(5) No descriptive statement synthetically entails a value statement.

(6) No nonmoral statement synthetically entails a value statement.

Statements (1) and (3) above are true if and only if descriptivism is false. Obviously, if moral statements are themselves descriptive, they will be formally entailed by themselves and thus will be formally entailed by descriptive statements. And formal entailment is a species of analytic entailment. On the other hand, if moral statements are not descriptive and lack a truth value, and if P formally, analytically, or synthetically entails Q only if the truth of P guarantees the *truth* of Q, then a noncognitivist (antidescriptivist) metaethics entails the acceptance of (1) through (6).[10] I conclude, then, that on interpretations (1) and (3) of the claim that there is an is/ought gap the controversy reduces to the cognitivism/noncognitivism issue discussed above.

10. The issue is complicated by the fact that at least one noncognitivist, Hare, wants to allow that utterances lacking a truth value can nevertheless be entailed by other "things" we accept. Even Hare, however, is quite adamant in claiming that value judgments never follow from descriptive statements alone. See Hare 1952, chap. 2.

At first glance, it might seem that (2) and (4) are trivially true whether descriptivism is true or not. If we accept the Kantian metaphor of analytic entailment holding only when the proposition entailed is "contained" in the proposition that entails it, then a nonmoral statement P will entail a moral statement Q only if the latter is at least implicitly contained in the former. But if Q is a part of what P means and Q contains value terms, then P is a value statement (given the conception of value statement sketched above). There is, of course, a formal "hitch" in this argument. Given contemporary concepts of formal and analytic entailment, the Kantian metaphor of containment is at best highly misleading. Suppose that value statements have a truth value. Then the proposition that it is snowing (P) entails:

(Q) That it is not snowing materially implies that X is wrong.

(R) That either it is snowing or X is wrong.

(S) That either X is wrong or it is not the case that X is wrong.

P's entailing Q, R, and S, however, is obviously not what anyone had in mind by bridging the is/ought gap. Should we say that Q, R, and S are not moral statements? If we do, then the nonmoral statements Q and not-P will entail the moral statement that X is wrong, and again *that* won't count as bridging the is/ought gap. It is perhaps better to try to distinguish *relevant* from irrelevant entailment and claim that P only trivially entails the "value" statements Q, R, and S. What makes the entailment trivial? Presumably, it is the fact that the crucial value predicate could be replaced by any other well-formed predicate without affecting the entailment.

With the distinction between relevant (nontrivial) and trivial entailment in hand, we can repeat the charge that (2) and (4) understood as claims about significant entailment are obviously and, indeed, trivially true. I cannot think of *any* philosopher who would have any interest in denying the existence of this sort of is/ought gap.[11]

That leaves only (5) and (6) as a way of defining the is/ought controversy in a manner that would make it both interesting and different from the cognitivist/noncognitivist controversy. Ironically, however, I don't think that many contemporary philosophers discussing the con-

11. Certainly when a philosopher like Searle tries to bridge the is/ought gap (in Searle 1964), he thinks of himself as showing that certain "nonmoral" facts are not really nonmoral at all.

troversy have either (5) or (6) in mind. Indeed, I should think that Moore is usually thought of as someone who holds that there is an is/ought gap, and he clearly thought that some nonmoral statements synthetically entail moral statements. (We examine Moore's views in more detail in the next chapter.)

Since I have already indicated my intention of rejecting noncognitivism, it should be clear that in this book I reject the claim that there is an is/ought gap in the sense defined by (1) and (3). One would have to be crazy to deny (2) and (4) (understood with the significant sense of entailment), and so I won't.

Where does Hume fit into all of this? He doesn't. This is an issue we shall return to in far more detail, but let me simply indicate here that the gap Hume asserted was a gap between a certain *kind* of descriptive statement and a value judgment. More specifically, in the passage quoted above Hume intended only to assert the existence of a gap between *objective* "is" statements and value statements.

OBJECTIVISM VS. SUBJECTIVISM

The debate over whether moral judgments (and, more generally, value judgments) are objective or subjective finds its expression even in the conversations and clichés of people who are not philosophers and who have no technical philosophical interests. In arguments over religion, the quality of life, the origin of the universe, the future of the economy, and so on, one party to the dispute will often characterize the other's view as *subjective*. Disagreement over the aesthetic value of some work of art often ends with the sage remark that beauty is, after all, in the eye of the beholder. There are, however, a wide range of things a person might mean by characterizing a belief or an opinion as subjective, many of them of little interest to the philosopher concerned with analyzing the *content* of value judgments. We should begin, then, by trying to define an objectivist/subjectivist controversy, or perhaps a set of such controversies, that does get to the heart of interesting and significant metavalue disagreements.

One of the most common uses of the term "subjective" involves epistemic assessment. If Jones says that there is a God and Smith characterizes Jones's belief as subjective, I suspect that Smith typically means to be saying something about the nature of the evidence Jones has for his belief. More specifically, in *this* sense of subjective, subjective judgments involve conclusions that are not well supported by evidence. One could just as well believe that there is no God, Smith might be saying, given the nature of the available evidence. Of course, if the available evidence really is neutral between two conflicting hypotheses, neither should be believed (we should simply withhold belief), and in this sense a charge of subjectivity is tantamount to a polite charge of epistemic irrationality. In the epistemic sense of "subjective", it seems to me that the charge of subjectivity leveled at a particular moral judgment is compatible with *any* plausible metaethical view.[12]

For the philosopher concerned with metaethical and metavalue issues, the more interesting concept of subjectivity of judgment is the metaphysical thesis implicit in that cliché that beauty is in the eye of the beholder. It is this conception of value as something that exists only "within" conscious beings which lies at the heart of Hume's rejection of *traditional* descriptivist metaethics:

> Take any action allow'd to be vicious: Wilful murder, for instance. Examine it in all lights, and see if you can find that matter of fact, or real existence, which you call *vice*. In which-ever way to take it, you find only certain passions, motives, volitions and thoughts. There is no other matter of fact in the case. The vice entirely escapes you, as long as you consider the object. You never can find it, till you turn reflexion into your own breast, and find a sentiment of disapprobation, which arises in you, towards this action. Here is a matter of fact; but 'tis the object of feeling, not of reason. It lies in yourself, not in the object. So that when you pronounce any action or character to be vicious, you mean nothing, but that from the constitution of your nature you have a feeling or sentiment of blame from the contemplation of it. (p. 469)

Note that in this passage Hume has apparently *found* a matter of fact with which to identify the subject matter of moral judgment and is consequently committed to denying the existence of an is/ought gap in the sense of (1) and (3) above. Unfortunately, the passage is ambiguous as between two interpretations of the otherwise innocent locution "your nature". In using that expression, Hume may have intended to refer to the nature of his fellow human beings taken as a collective, or he

---

12. A possible exception might be certain extreme forms of intuitionism with respect to questions of right and wrong action, but I think such views are so extreme as to lack any serious plausibility.

may have intended to refer to the nature of the particular *individual* reading the passage. The analogy of secondary properties suggests the former. When I say that something is red, I hardly mean to be characterizing only the way in which it affects me.[13] But for reasons I discuss in the next chapter, I am convinced that Hume intended the latter. In any event, the ambiguity suggests two quite different versions of descriptivist subjectivism. On the one view, value is "in the eye" of the average or normal observer. On the other, value is "in the eye" of the particular individual and may vary even among normal individuals under normal conditions. We might then define two concepts of objectivity with which subjectivity is to be contrasted.

> (D1) A belief or judgment is objective (1) if it is either true or false and its truth or falsehood is logically independent of the psychological states of people.

> (D2) A belief or judgment is objective (2) if it is either true or false and its truth or falsehood is logically independent of the psychological states of the person making the judgment.

For ease of presentation, it is convenient to construe subjectivist metaethical views as the contradictories of objectivist metaethical views, and for that reason I propose to include in the class of subjectivist views all versions of noncognitivism. We then have two versions of subjectivism corresponding to the negations of (D1) and (D2):

> (D3) A belief or judgment is subjective (1) if it is either neither true nor false OR if its truth (falsity) is logically dependent on the psychological states of people.

> (D4) A belief or judgment is subjective (2) if it is either neither true nor false OR if its truth (falsity) is logically dependent on the psychological states of the person making the judgment.

These characterizations of objectivist/subjectivist positions are, however, seriously defective as they stand and, in fact, invite a very poor argument for subjectivism which is all too often proposed. The objectivist is sometimes charged with holding the view that one could remove

13. A color-blind person can truthfully characterize an object as red even accepting the idea behind the empiricist's analysis of secondary properties. Such a person is presumably saying something about the way in which the object affects most *normal* perceivers under *normal* conditions.

from the universe all conscious beings and still be left with things that have value. And this thesis strikes many critics of objectivism as absurd. But though some objectivists, Moore in particular,[14] are prepared to defend the view that positive and negative value could be exemplified in a world without conscious beings, an objectivist, qua objectivist, *need* not defend such a view. An objectivist might hold the view that the only things that in fact have value, positive or negative, are conscious states and things or events that cause or produce certain conscious states. Within the framework of his objectivist metaethics, Moore *could* have held the view that the only things that have intrinsic goodness are mental states, and the only things that have instrumental goodness, therefore, are things that lead to the mental states that have intrinsic goodness. Indeed, Moore's favorite examples of things that are intrinsically good *are* conscious mental states—knowledge, personal affection, and aesthetic enjoyment. And as I say, Moore could have held (he didn't) that these *exhaust* the list of things that have intrinsic value. Were Moore to hold such a view, and were he to hold that it is a synthetic necessary truth that only conscious states have intrinsic value, he would fail to satisfy our characterization of an objectivist in either sense (1) or sense (2). The proposition that I am in a state of knowledge, a proposition describing my psychological state, would be a synthetically sufficient condition for the truth of my judgment that my knowledge is intrinsically good. My judgment that my knowledge is intrinsically good would not be logically independent of my psychological state. Yet clearly an objectivist should be able to hold even the thesis that it is a necessary truth that certain psychological states have intrinsic value and that *only* these states have intrinsic value. We must therefore revise our analyses of objectivism as follows:

(D1a) *S*'s judgment that *X* has value (is good, right, such that it ought to be done, etc.) is objective (1) if it is either true or false and, in describing *X* as having value, *S* is not describing *X* in whole or in part as being the intentional object of some psychological state, i.e., its having (lacking) value is not identical in whole or in part with its being (not being) the object of some attitude.

(D1b) *S*'s judgment that *X* has value is objective (2) if it is either true or false and, in describing *X* as having value, *S* is not describ-

14. See Moore 1903, chap. 6.

ing it as the intentional object of his psychological state, i.e., its having (lacking) value is not identical with its being (not being) the object of some attitude of S.

The negations of (D1a) and (D1b) give us the corresponding analyses of our two versions of subjectivism.

Even if Moore thought, for example, that pleasure was the only thing that had intrinsic value, he would be an objectivist in both our senses because within the context of his metaethical view pleasure's being intrinsically good would not be identical, in whole or in part, with pleasure's being the object of some psychological state. The fact that pleasure is intrinsically good would not be, for Moore, a fact about whether I or anyone else had certain beliefs about pleasure, certain desires toward pleasure, or any other intentional state directed at pleasure.

We might illustrate each of our two versions of *descriptivist* subjectivism (leaving aside for now noncognitivist versions of subjectivism) with a crude metaethical view, and in so doing we may consider and reject at least some of the standard objections to subjectivism. The following would be a crude version of subjectivism (1):

To say that something is good is to say that most people value (approve of) it.

And this would be one of the crudest versions of subjectivism (2):

"X is good" said by S means the same as "I value (approve of) X" said by S.

Moore and others[15] have criticized such analyses as being potentially circular. In at least one common use of such expressions as "value" and "approve", to say of someone that he values or approves of X just is a way of saying that that person *judges* X to be good! And it would be a sorry joke to try to use this sense of "value" or "approve" in an attempt to analyze value judgments. Our example of subjectivism(1) would become:

X is good iff most people think that X is good.

15. See Moore 1912, chap. 3, p. 75.

Our example of subjectivism (2) would become:

"*X* is good" said by *S* means the same as "I believe that *X* is good" said by *S*.

The analyses are viciously circular because they presuppose an understanding of the proposition believed (that *X* is good), the very proposition whose meaning we are trying to analyze.

Fortunately for the subjectivist, the way to avoid this objection is simple. Don't use the terms "value" and "approve" this way. Don't even worry about how these expressions are typically used. If Moore is right in characterizing their standard use, make them into technical philosophical expressions describing the relevant fundamental relation that on your subjectivist view is the underlying concept implicit in all value judgments. You will, of course, need to convince your opponent that you are not simply *inventing* a relation to avoid an objection, and the argument may eventually come down to a phenomenological appeal, but one must not be embarrassed (I shall certainly not be) about making such appeals at the appropriate crucial points. I make much use of what I take to be the fundamental concept of valuing later in the book, and I shall try to be as clear as I can be about the nature of this concept so important to understanding value judgments and rational action.

Even if the initial objection to subjectivism is avoided, there are obviously many other powerful arguments against both versions of the view. As they stand, both views are extremely counterintuitive, in part because they fail to make crucial distinctions between intrinsic and instrumental value. The version of subjectivism (2) we considered, for example, would be much more plausible if it made the more restrictive claim that a person's judgment of intrinsic value was a report of what that person intrinsically valued. Failing to make that distinction makes it look (implausibly) as though reaching conclusions about goodness and badness is *always* for the subjectivist (2) merely a matter of introspection. And as I have noted before, I take it to be a datum that it is extremely difficult to arrive at many moral conclusions. As we shall see, however, one can analyze intrinsic goodness in terms of intrinsic valuing and allow all kinds of room for error both with respect to judgments about intrinsic goodness and more obviously with respect to judgments about instrumental goodness and right and wrong action.

As Moore has pointed out in his famous attacks on subjectivism (2) (in its descriptivist versions), such views also face severe difficulties in trying to avoid counterintuitive consequences concerning the nature of ethical disagreement.[16] As long as value judgments are construed as descriptions of the present attitudes of the person making them, you and I will never be able to contradict each other using value statements, and I will not even be able to contradict my former self. In his excellent reply to Moore,[17] Stevenson does a great deal to diminish the force of Moore's arguments even against the form of descriptive subjectivism(2) that Stevenson is not ultimately interested in defending. Indeed, I don't think Stevenson does justice to the extent to which his conception of disagreement in attitude allows for genuine disagreement to be expressed by people who are merely describing their respective but opposite attitudes. Certainly, when one film critic says that he liked a film and another says that he didn't, we will not hesitate to report that they disagreed in their evaluation of the film. Yet neither contradicted the other, nor did they resort to nondescriptive utterances of the sort Stevenson sometimes seems to suggest would be needed to express genuine disagreement.

Nonetheless, however much recognition of the importantly different senses of disagreement will help the subjectivist (2), it is difficult to eliminate entirely the force of Moore's arguments against the view. It will still be a consequence of the view that if Adolf Hitler correctly described his relevant attitudes in saying "We ought to persecute the Jews," I would have to regard his utterance as true. Stevenson is, of course, right in suggesting that I would not be committed to saying myself "We ought to persecute the Jews," for according to the subjectivist (2), *my* utterance will express my attitudes. A defender of subjectivism (2) might even argue that *I* couldn't correctly say "What Hitler said was true" because (he might continue to argue) it is a convention of moral discourse that my endorsement of another's value judgment (as in "That's true") is a shorthand way of indicating my willingness to make the same statement (type) myself. But all of these sophisticated verbal machinations will not alter the fact that a subjectivist (2) will have to *believe* that Hitler's ethical statement expressed a truth provided that it correctly described his relevant attitudes, and that is, indeed, a bitter pill to swallow. The view I shall defend will not force us to recognize Hitler's statement as true, but it may force us to recognize that his more restricted statement that he, Hitler (as opposed to we, in general), ought to take steps to persecute the Jews *is* true, and this will no doubt strike most as just as bitter a pill. In what follows I shall try to eliminate at least some of the medicinal taste by making clear the unwelcome consequences of alternative views and by making a crucial distinction between the concepts of a moral judgment and a judgment of conventional morality.

For all of its counterintuitive consequences, descriptive subjectivism (2) is a far more plausible and interesting view than descriptive subjectivism (1). The latter makes the correctness of value judgments a matter of majority rule, and one is obviously under no logical constraints to conform one's ethical views to the attitudes that prevail among the majority.[18]

In addition to its inherent implausibility, subjectivism (1) will fail most miserably the crucial test we shall shortly develop for evaluating the plausibility of metaethical views, a test involving the implications of a metaethical view concerning the relationship between morality and rational action. With that in mind, let us leave for the moment our brief examination of subjectivism (1).

METAETHICAL RELATIVISM

The view that value judgments are subjective is closely related to, but importantly distinct from, the thesis of metaethical relativism. And the thesis of *metaethical* relativism is itself fundamentally distinct from other assertions concerning the relativity of value judgments, assertions that turn out to be compatible with a wide range of radically different metaethical views. Let me begin our discussion of relativism, then, by making clear the distinction between what I call metaethical relativism and other less fundamental theses and observations about the relativity of value judgments.

Anthropological Relativism

In examining one argument for noncognitivism, we discussed the seemingly uncontroversial fact that the value judgments people accept

18. It is a distressing feature of Hare's more recent views that he seems to be moving in the direction of a kind of "majority rule" metaethics in his final attempt to deal with the problem of the "fanatic". See Hare 1981 and 1982.

are likely to be heavily influenced by the culture in which they are raised and that value judgments vary significantly from culture to culture. Thus, to take a straightforward example, in our culture polygamy is generally frowned on. In other cultures it is the norm. In some cultures premarital sex is thought to be wrong. In others it is viewed as something one ought to engage in as preparation for marriage. In some cultures it is considered morally wrong to eat the flesh of certain animals. In others this same behavior is construed as completely innocent. By anthropological relativism, I simply mean the descriptive claim that there are differences among cultures concerning the acceptance of certain value judgments. This observation, of course, obviously *entails* no particular metaethical view concerning the *content* of value judgments, nor does it provide *by itself* particularly good reason for accepting some version of noncognitivism, subjectivism, or even some version of the metaethical relativism we shall define shortly. As I pointed out earlier, before drawing any inferences from the familiar facts of cultural relativity with respect to ethical *beliefs,* one would do well to remember that there exists the same relativity with respect to religious beliefs in Gods and afterlives. And it seems utterly clear to me that such relativity here does not support noncognitivist, subjectivist, or relativist interpretations of the meaning of such hypotheses as that there exists one God who will arrange a conscious life after physical death.

I said that it seems uncontroversial that there does exist dramatic cultural relativity with respect to ethical beliefs, and I think that when all is said and done there is. The interpretation of what goes on among cultures is complicated, however, by the truth of another innocuous and *almost* uncontroversial form of relativism that we might call *situation relativism* (after the "pop" philosophical conception of "situation ethics" that was in vogue in some circles not too long ago).[19]

Situation Relativism

The thesis of situation relativism simply maintains that a *kind* of action (say, keeping a promise) which is wrong for one person to perform in one set of circumstances (or culture) might be right for another person to perform in a different set of circumstances (or culture). This view is sometimes unfortunately offered as a description of

19. See Fletcher 1966.

the thesis that is supposed to be of fundamental philosophical interest to the philosopher concerned with the question of whether values are relative where the relativity of value judgments is contrasted with some form of objective moral realism. But in fact, given certain natural interpretations of "kind of action", it is surely an almost trivial claim compatible with almost any metaethical theory. More specifically, as long as action *kinds* are individuated without reference to *all* of their consequences, then *any* consequentialist in ethics will accept the thesis of situation relativism. If the rightness or wrongness of actions is even in part a function of what happens, might happen, or can be expected to happen as a result of that action, then obviously a kind of action which is right in one set of circumstances might be wrong in another set of circumstances. The *consequences* (actual, probable, possible) of a kind of action (e.g., keeping a promise) in one set of circumstances might be radically different from the consequences of that same action in a different set of circumstances. Even if one accepts some version of rule consequentialism (the different versions of which we shall discuss later) and one takes the rightness or wrongness of an action to be a function of the correct rules of morality, one can (and presumably will) still endorse the thesis of situation relativism. At least one will as long as the relevant rule can be sophisticated enough to take into account the circumstances in which a kind of action is performed. Thus if the rule consequential-ist's rule for promising is "Always keep a promise unless you can save a life by breaking it," this rule consequentialist will admit that a kind of action, promise keeping, will be right in one set of circumstances, wrong in another. The *only* metaethical position that might conceivably warrant a rejection of situation relativism is an extreme and wildly implausible version of intuitionism which takes the rightness or wrong-ness of actions (not the intrinsic goodness or badness—more about this later) to be simple properties of action *kinds*, where these kinds are specified independently of their causal consequences. I am not sure that anyone has ever held such a view, but I am sure that no one sensible has ever held such a view.[20]

20. Intuitionists like Ross (1930) and Prichard (1912) might seem to be proponents of the view that rightness or wrongness is always independent of circumstances. But in Ross's case it seems clear that the only "rightness" that is independent of circumstances is a prima facie rightness that is a far cry from the concept of an action being right all things being considered. The issue is more complicated in Prichard's case, but even here it seems to me that Prichard must allow that there is an important normative concept involved in

Because I take situation relativism of the sort discussed above to be uncontroversially true, I would concede that one must at least consider the possibility that some apparent cases of cultural relativity with respect to ethical *beliefs* are illusory. To be more precise, it is not obvious that the *contents* of what look like opposing ethical beliefs really are in opposition. If a group of islanders facing significant imbalances in the populations of males and females embrace the moral legitimacy of polygamy, it is always *possible* that a more complete description of their view would be that polygamous relationships are morally permissible for people like them in circumstances like these. This view, of course, does not even appear to conflict with the restricted view of the North American who holds that only monogamous relationships are right for people like us in circumstances like ours. And it would be plausible to suppose that, even if the above paraphrases captured the content of their respective value judgments, people in these respective cultures would continue to express their views using the more truncated and potentially misleading statement "Polygamy is (not) wrong." One should be aware of this possible complication in interpreting the familiar "facts" of cultural differences with respect to values, but as I said, I think that there is, indeed, the more dramatic sort of genuine cultural disagreement. When the European missionaries came to Hawaii, it became painfully evident that they intended their views concerning the wrongness of polygamy to extend to all cultures in all circumstances. The important thing for us to remember is that sensible people need not and should not embrace such sweeping claims concerning the rightness or wrongness of action *kinds* across a wide range of dramatically different circumstances—circumstances that will ensure dramatically different outcomes of these actions.

Metaethical Relativism

As I use the term, *metaethical relativism* is a thesis about the meaning or content of value judgments. One might try to clarify the view by identifying its consequences. Keeping firmly in mind the distinction between kinds of actions and particular actions, we might say that the

---

choosing between conflicting "right" actions which depends on circumstances. It is not clear to me that a view like Ross's is significantly different from the generic utilitarianism I discuss later which allows actions to be intrinsically good.

metaethical relativist is committed to the view that the truth or falsity of a value judgment made about some particular act is relative to or dependent on the person who makes that judgment or the circumstances in which the judgment is made. A view we might call *metaethical cultural relativism* would take the critically important circumstances to be the rule-governed culture of which the person making the judgment is a part and might construe ethical assertions as descriptions of the rules and regulations of that culture. One can obviously use the term *metaethical relativism* in perfectly useful ways consistent with at least some traditional meanings, but I do not believe that this is the best way for me to proceed, given the distinctions I want to stress. For one thing, the above characterization of metaethical relativism makes subjectivism (2) a species of metaethical relativism, and I am concerned with defining the latter so as to make it interestingly different from subjectivism. My suggestion is to model a relativistic understanding of value on the relative frequency conception of probability discussed earlier.

The heart of the relative frequency conception of probability, you recall, is that in at least one important sense of probability one cannot meaningfully talk about the probability of some individual a having some characteristic F, simpliciter. Rather, the logically perspicuous way to express such judgments always involves relativizing the probability of a's being F to a's being a member of some class, that is, to its having some other set of characteristics. On the classic view, the probability judgment is then construed as describing the frequency with which members of that class have the characteristic F.

Notice that a proponent of the view need not deny that we make probability judgments that do not *appear* to be relativized. In fact, most often people say such things as that Jones will probably catch his wife's cold, the stockmarket will probably turn downward, I probably won't live past one hundred, and the Congress probably won't eliminate the deficit. The relative frequency theorist, however, can plausibly take such claims to be enthymematic *presupposing* some reference class that could be made explicit on demand. Sometimes the context will make fairly clear the reference class presupposed, and there may be some rather vague "rules" we rely on governing the interpretation of the relevant reference class presupposed in various contexts. On the other hand, in at least some contexts there may be no clear way of telling what reference class is presupposed by the probability assertion, and indeed, the person making the assertion may not even be able to supply on demand the reference class he "had in mind." In this event (according to the theory I am describing), we are simply unable to evaluate the assertion of probability until we do specify a reference class.

Relying on this analogy, we can define metaethical relativism as the view that value is always value for, or relative to, some individual or group of individuals (such as a culture). More precisely, sentences of the form "X is good (right, such that it ought to be chosen)" disguise their underlying logical structure, which is "X is good (right) for ————", where one gets different versions of metaethical relativism depending on how one construes the "meaning rules" for filling in the blanks and depending on how one analyzes the truth conditions of the logically perspicuous representation of the assertion.

The view we might call *metaethical cultural relativism* could be construed as holding that when I say "X is good or right" my judgment should always be construed as elliptical for "X is good or right for (most of? all of?) the members of some culture". A proponent of this view might go on to suggest that the culture implicitly referred to in one's ethical statements is always or usually that of the speaker, the listener, or both.[21] This sort of relativist might also allow, however, that one can make value judgments about the rightness or wrongness of actions taken by members of some other group or culture intending to construe that rightness or wrongness as rightness or wrongness for members of *that* group.[22]

The metaethical relativist as I have characterized her is not committed to the view that ethical statements always involve implicit reference to groups or cultures. One can very plausibly hold within the framework of that view that the logically perspicuous representation of some value judgments will describe the value as relative to some individual (we might call this *metaethical individual relativism*). And indeed, even if one (mistakenly, I believe) thinks that our ordinary ethical judgments should always be construed as relativizing the relevant values to groups or societies, I think one will still have to take the most fundamental concept of value to be the concept of something being good for an

---

21. Harman (1977) seems to argue that value judgments always presuppose that the speaker, the listener, and even the person about whom the value judgment is made share certain common conventions of morality. See chap. 9.

22. This might correspond to Hare's characterization of secondary value judgments— see our earlier discussion of Hare's distinction in connection with the cognitivism/noncognitivism controversy.

individual. I say this because I assume that, in analyzing the truth conditions for statements of the form "*X* is good for *S*" where *S* refers to all or most of the members of some culture, the metaethical relativist, just like the subjectivist, will need to rely on the concept of people *valuing X* where valuing is a relation not to be understood in terms of the acceptance of ethical judgments. And I assume that we are all reductionists enough to realize that one cannot understand the concept of something having value for a group in terms of that group valuing it without understanding the more fundamental concept of something having value for an individual in terms of that individual valuing it. Groups, after all, are collections of individuals, and talk about "their" wants, desires, approvals, and values can be understood only in terms of talk about the wants, desires, approvals, and values of the individuals who make up those groups. The metaethical cultural relativist who does not ultimately rely on some concept such as valuing is obviously in danger of encountering circularity of the sort that haunts incautious statements of subjectivism. The metaethical cultural relativist, for example, who construes ethical statements as descriptions of the ethical norms of some society is going to be hard pressed to define ethical norms without recourse to the concept of ethical judgment, which concept is precisely the one to be analyzed.

The version of metaethical relativism in which I am primarily interested, then, takes the most fundamental concept of value to be the concept of something being good *for S* where *S* can be either an individual or a group. On this view, whenever anyone meaningfully asserts that something is good, that person must always have "in mind" a reference class, that is, an individual or group *for whom* the thing in question is being described as good. And if the fundamental ethical concept is the concept of intrinsic goodness and other ethical concepts are definable at least in part by reference to intrinsic goodness, it would follow that all ethical evaluations are implicitly relativized in the way just discussed.

By far the most natural and plausible view would hold that, unless otherwise specified, evaluations about what someone or some group *S ought* to do (or what it would be right for *S* to do) are always to be understood (in part) by reference to the relativistic concept of what is intrinsically good *for that individual or for that group.* If we adopted such a view, the main source of ambiguity would be those statements describing things or states of affairs simply as good where it may be unclear *for whom* the things in question are supposed to be good. Just as in probability theory the context in which a probability judgment is made may suggest a plausible reference class presupposed, so too the context in which a value judgment is made may suggest the individual or group to whom the good is relativized. But as also seems true of probability judgments, some contexts may simply leave open the question of how to construe the implicit reference class presupposed by the value judgment.

If we suppose for the moment that the most fundamental ethical concept is intrinsic goodness and we endorse the relativistic thesis that intrinsic goodness is an incomplete concept always to be understood in terms of intrinsic goodness for S, we must, as I suggested above, seek an analysis of such statements in their logically perspicuous form. And as I suggested above, it seems to me that here the similarities between subjectivism and relativism emerge, for just as paradigm subjectivists turn to the concept of valuing (or approving) in order to describe the content of value judgments subjectively understood, so the relativist will naturally turn to the concept of valuing (approving) to explicate the meaning of her relativized value judgments. More specifically, one very natural and, I believe, ultimately defensible view *identifies* X's being intrinsically good for S with S's valuing X intrinsically. (As we shall eventually see, all kinds of complications arise when we try to generalize the view beyond intrinsic goodness.) One can still get importantly different versions of this kind of metaethical relativism, depending on how the critical notion of valuing gets fleshed out and on how the concept of intrinsic value is conceptually linked to the other crucial ethical concepts of right and wrong action.

Given the obvious similarities, what is supposed to be the difference between, for example, descriptive subjectivism (2) and the kind of metaethical relativism we have sketched above? The main difference is simply this. The descriptive subjectivist (2), you recall, holds that all value judgments describe the attitudes (values, approvals) *of the person making the judgment*. Thus, according to this view, if I say that *you* ought to do X, or even that X would be good for you, I am still describing *my* attitude toward your doing X. The metaethical relativism sketched above, however, holds that it is far more natural to take my judgments about what you ought to do (or what would be good for you to do) as being dependent for their truth (in part) on what *you* value intrinsically, on what would be intrinsically good *for you*. If we do understand second- and third-person value judgments as the relativist I am imagining suggests, then second- and third-person value judgments would *not* be subjective (2), given our understanding of that term. Interestingly, though, my first-person value judgments, the judgments I make about what is good for me or what I ought to do, would be subjective (2), given the metaethical relativism sketched above. Both the subjectivist (2) and the metaethical relativist, in other words, might well agree in their account of what these judgments assert. Both may agree that my first-person value judgments describe (in part) my values and are thus dependent (in part) for their truth on the attitudes of the person making the judgment. For this reason, it is very easy to confuse what are really two quite distinct metaethical views.

Notice that metaethical relativism is logically independent of the existence of ethical disagreement and even of differences in values between people. Metaethical relativism is neither entailed by nor entails cultural relativism. Nor does metaethical relativism entail that there actually are differences between what is good for one person and what is good for another. It entails only that there *could* be such differences. Metaethical relativism is a thesis about the *meaning* of value judgments and as such it involves no normative or cultural claims at all.[23]

In general, I am highly sympathetic with the underlying intuition behind metaethical relativism and am even more strongly convinced of the analogous view with respect to rational action. It is essentially the

23. The danger of confusing metaethical issues with anthropological facts is made evident by Harman's discussion of emotivism and its presuppositions. Harman (1977, pp. 29–31) seems to suggest that the controversy over whether values are relative depends on certain questions concerning the uniformity of human nature. Such questions are utterly irrelevant to the plausibility of *metaethical* relativism.

In discussing metaethical relativism, I have ignored an argument made popular by Harman in the work referred to above. Harman argues that we should decide the question of whether there are objective nonrelative moral properties by asking whether we need to postulate the existence of such properties in order to explain the value judgments people make. Given my metaphilosophical presuppositions, it should be clear that I would be completely unsympathetic to the attempt to construe metaethical inquiry as analogous to reasoning to the best explanation. It seems patently obvious to me that we do not decide metaethical disputes the way we evaluate a physicist's postulation of a theoretical entity. A metaethical dispute is a dispute about the meaning of value judgments. I can easily imagine an objectivist in ethics arguing that it is possible that everyone is deceived with respect to the truth of moral judgments even though such judgments *assert* the existence of objective moral facts. We may not need to postulate objective moral properties to explain value judgments, but then we do not need to postulate a physical world in order to explain our belief in a physical world (perhaps a Humean explanation is correct). But what has this to do with the question of whether people are asserting the existence of objective moral facts in making moral judgments?

view I defend in this book as part of an effort to identify morality with rationality, but as will become apparent I shall add to the view a great many qualifications.

CONSEQUENTIALISM

I have already suggested my commitment to the view that the conceptual building block of all ethical concepts is the concept of intrinsic goodness. If metaethical relativism is correct, that concept will be more perspicuously expressed as intrinsic goodness for some person. A wide range of radically different metaethical theories can *agree* on the premise that the concept of intrinsic goodness is fundamental. Objectivists, subjectivists, and metaethical relativists, for example, can take this position within the framework of their quite different analyses of intrinsic goodness. One pleasant consequence of this is that philosophers with radically different metaethical accounts of intrinsic goodness can set such disagreements aside and work to discover the conceptual connections between intrinsic goodness and other ethical concepts.

One of the most ancient and most plausible metaethical views maintains that one can *define* other ethical concepts, like the concept of right action, in part by reference to intrinsic goodness. And the most obvious way to proceed is through some version of a teleological or consequentialist analysis of what one morally ought to do. My purpose in these few preliminary remarks is not to argue for any particular version of consequentialism, nor is it to reply to the many serious objections raised against various versions of consequentialism. This I will do after a detailed discussion of rational action and the possibility of interdefining rational action and morality. Rather, I am primarily interested in making clear some fairly straightforward terminological decisions that should facilitate subsequent discussion.

Despite the longstanding controversy between deontological and teleological, or consequentialist, ethics, it is notoriously difficult to define the distinction clearly. As we shall see, even the claim that a consequentialist believes that consequences of an action are relevant to its rightness or wrongness is highly misleading, given the sort of philosophers who are viewed as paradigmatic consequentialists. Let us briefly distinguish at least some of the views that might be called consequentialist ethical theories.

Hedonistic Utilitarianism

Perhaps the best-known consequentialist view is hedonistic utilitarianism, and perhaps the best-known representative of the view is still John Stuart Mill. As we know, however, it is not east to find two philosophers who will agree on precisely what Mill's view was in his classic work *Utilitarianism*. In that book Mill describes the principle of hedonistic utilitarianism this way:

> The creed which accepts as the foundation of morals 'utility' or the 'greatest happiness principle' holds that actions are right in proportion as they tend to promote happiness; wrong as they tend to produce the reverse of happiness. By happiness is intended pleasure and the absence of pain; by unhappiness, pain and the privation of pleasure. (p. 10)

From this description some would infer that Mill held the view that one ought to do whatever would produce the most happiness (least unhappiness).[24] We might call such a view *actual consequence hedonistic utilitarianism*. The term "hedonistic" reminds us that the relevant consequences determining rightness and wrongness are human pleasure and pain. The term "actual consequence" indicates that the consequences we are to consider in evaluating alternative actions are the consequences that would *actually* occur were the action taken. Notice that even in the statement of this most straightforward version of consequentialism we must use the subjunctive conditional to describe the factors determining rightness and wrongness. What Jones ought to have done is, trivially, not a function of what actually happens as a result of what he did— he might not have done what he ought to have done, in which case the action he ought to have taken will have no consequences. This, of course, presents no problem for the actual consequence utilitarian, for it should be clear from the outset that the consequences referred to are the hypothetical consequences that would result from certain actions.[25]

Although Mill does sometimes seem to express his hedonistic utilitar-

24. It might be misleading to say that an action is right on such a view only if it maximizes happiness. Presumably, we might want to allow that, even though the *best* action is the one that maximizes happiness, our ordinary standards for right action are flexible enough to allow that a person can be acting in a way that is "all right" when it is among the top "contenders" for being the best action.

25. There is an unfortunate confusion of this point by Marcus Singer in his attack on the intelligibility of actual consequence utilitarianism in Singer 1977. For an effective reply, see Temkin 1978.

ianism as an actual consequence utilitarianism, he also occasionally provides hints that he would insist on the relevance of *probabilities*. Even in the passage quoted above, reference to the *tendency* of actions to produce certain effects suggests that he had in mind something other than consequences that would actually occur. More specifically, I suspect he would have endorsed the view that we might call *probable consequence hedonistic utilitarianism*. The probable consequence hedonistic utilitarian says that the right action is the one that of the alternatives would probably result in the most happiness (least unhappiness). And anyone who thinks that probable consequence utilitarianism is more plausible than actual consequence utilitarianism can usually be brought to realize that improbable but *possible* consequences should also be considered in calculating the rightness or wrongness of actions. A hedonistic utilitarian will undoubtedly wish to view an act of drunken driving, for example, as wrong, even if statistics indicate that most acts of driving while drunk do not lead to accidents (unhappiness). The conclusion many would draw is that one needs to model one's utilitarianism on the well-known theory of maximizing *expected utility*. On one version of this view, what one ought to do is a function of the possible consequences of one's action compared to the possible consequences of alternative actions, where the value of these possible consequences is adjusted for the probability of their occurring. The units of value for the hedonistic utilitarian are, of course, units of human happiness. To emphasize the structural similarities between this view and actual and probable consequence hedonistic utilitarianism, and to underscore the fact that on the view I am interested in the possibilities and likelihoods involved are *epistemic* possibilities and likelihoods (as opposed to so-called subjective probabilities), I prefer to label the above view *value adjusted possible consequence hedonistic utilitarianism*. As will become evident, I am most interested in exploring and defending value adjusted possible consequence accounts of morality and rationality, and I shall have much more to say about the key concepts involved in setting forth such a veiw later in the book. I am not interested in defending *hedonistic utilitarianism*.

In discussing hedonistic utilitarianism in general, and in evaluating some particular version of hedonistic utilitarianism like Mill's, one must try to determine whether the view is offered as a normative ethical theory or a metaethical theory. I have already indicated my intention to focus on metaethical issues, and for that reason I am not primarily concerned with discussing hedonistic utilitarianism as a normative theory (though I make comments that bear on the normative theory later). In fact, I think most philosophers who embrace any of the hedonistic utilitarianisms sketched above do so as normative theories of morality. Mill, for example, *probably* didn't regard the principle of hedonistic utility as an analytic truth (although there is a complication that is noted below). But Mill and most other hedonistic utilitarians in all likelihood accepted their view only because they accepted *generic* or *ideal* utilitarianism as an analytic truth.

Generic or Ideal Utilitarianism

Generic (ideal) utilitarianism[26] is the consequentialist view that takes the consequences relevant to evaluating the morality of an action to be those that are intrinsically good and intrinsically bad. Essentially, generic utilitarianism is the same view as hedonistic utilitarianism without the hedonism, that is, without the view that happiness and only happiness is intrinsically good, unhappiness and only unhappiness, intrinsically bad. Put another way, a hedonistic utilitarian is virtually always a generic utilitarian with the additional view that happiness is the only thing intrinsically good. One can obviously distinguish three different versions of generic utilitarianism corresponding to our three different versions of hedonistic utilitarianism. One can define right actions in terms of the sum of intrinsic goodness (badness) that would actually be produced by an action compared to alternatives (actual consequence generic utilitarianism); in terms of the sum of intrinsic goodness (badness) that would probably be produced by an action compared to alternatives (probable consequence generic utilitarianism); or in terms of the sum of intrinsic goodness (badness) that might result from an action compared to what might result from alternatives where the amount of goodness (badness) is adjusted for the probability of its occurring (value adjusted possible consequence generic utilitarianism). This last view obviously presupposes that intrinsic goodness can come in degrees—X and Y can both be intrinsically good while X is nevertheless better than Y.

I should also make clear that, as I am using the term, *generic utilitari-*

---

26. Prichard (1912) used the term *generic* to refer to this sort of utilitarianism. Ross (1930) referred to the same view as *ideal utilitarianism.*

anism does not presuppose a concept of nonrelativized objective goodness. One can be a generic utilitarian with a *relativized* conception of intrinsic goodness.[27] If one is a generic utilitarian who is a relativist, one will obviously have to define a relativized concept of right action in terms of that relativized concept of goodness.

I have been referring to the different versions of generic utilitarianism as consequentialist views even though no consequences that actually do occur are necessary or sufficient for the truth of a moral judgment on any of the views. There is a further complication in locating generic utilitarianism within the teleological/deontological controversy, and that involves the relevant interpretation of *consequences*. I shall be defending a version of value adjusted possible consequence generic utilitarianism,[28] but I would emphasize at the outset that I number among the consequences of an action its logical consequences, including, for example, the fact that it logically precludes the possibility of doing certain other things.[29] I would also argue that there is no a priori reason to suppose that an action cannot itself be intrinsically good or bad. And since an action will be a logical consequence of itself, its intrinsic

27. Thus, for example, one could define X's being intrinsically good *for* S in terms of S valuing X as an end. Korsgaard (1983) points out that one can define intrinsic goodness in such a way that something's being intrinsically good presupposes a nonrelativized conception of goodness. One *can* say that X is intrinsically good only if its goodness does not depend ontologically on anything but X's nonrelational properties. It should be obvious that I do not use the locution "intrinsically good" in this way.

28. More precisely, I shall be defending this view as an analysis of the primary or "first-level" content of moral deliberation. As we shall see, we must introduce some rather sophisticated ambiguities to capture different "levels" at which one can evaluate the morality/rationality of action.

29. In a very interesting paper, "Ultimate Ends in Practical Reasoning," Scott Mac-Donald argues that one should make some important distinctions among the senses in which one performs an action *in order to* achieve some result where the result is not to be understood straightforwardly as either effect or deductive consequence. He suggests, for example, that a person can run a race in order to compete in the triathlon where the race is neither a cause nor a logically sufficient condition for the goal of competing in the triathlon (he labels this means "constitutive subordinate" to its end). I would say that the race is a logically necessary condition for achieving the end, and I assume that the fact that my *not* performing an action will frustrate a perceived good will be construed by a generic consequentialist as a reason for performing the action.

MacDonald also wants to recognize a sense in which a particular action can be undertaken in order to bring about the occurrence of some more generally characterized state of affairs (he calls such a means "specification subordinate" to its end). Thus, as a consequentialist, if I think that my being famous is good, I might become a famous painter *in order to* achieve the good of being famous. We can clearly view this means/end relationship as a species of noncausal necessary connection.

goodness or badness, if it has any, will need to be included in the calculations that determine the rightness or wrongness of the action. Once we allow that an action like telling the truth might have intrinsic goodness, it is not easy to see that there is any difference between this version of consequentialism (generic utilitarianism) and those views sometimes represented as deontological which emphasize the prima facie rightness of certain acts, where this prima facie rightness is something independent of consequences. Indeed, one might suspect that there is only a terminological difference between the two views. I don't really care whether one views a generic utilitarianism that allows actions to be intrinsically good as a consequentialist or a deontological view. The label doesn't matter as long as we understand what the view is.

Rule Utilitarianism

The six versions of utilitarianism distinguished above are all versions of *act* utilitarianism, and many philosophers would argue that there are persuasive objections to act utilitarianism in any of its guises. These objections are of utmost concern to us and are treated at length later in the book. The issue is critical because, if they are effective against act consequentialist accounts of morality, they will probably be effective against act consequentialist accounts of practical rationality, and my strategy is to defend an act consequentialist account of rationality which I then try to employ in an analysis of moral concepts. The most common attacks on act consequentialist accounts of morality and rationality involve the charge that these theories have wildly implausible consequences. Actions will turn out to be morally right and rational which "no one" would want to be morally right and rational. Act consequentialists are supposed to be committed to the view that it will be right to lie, steal, cheat, and forgo civil obligations far more often than anyone with an ounce of moral sensitivity would allow. Again, I consider these objections thoroughly later, after I have developed a specific, detailed account of rational and moral action which I am prepared to defend. For now I am only interested in distinguishing some of the different versions of rule utilitarianism which I shall later discuss.

The idea behind rule utilitarianisms is, of course, that the rightness or wrongness of an action is logically determined by the correct *rules* of morality. These rules might be either prescriptive (telling us what we ought to do) or permissive (telling us what we are morally free to do).

Having made these preliminary remarks, one should always hasten to add that the act consequentialist can certainly allow for the importance of rules (rules of thumb) in calculating the rightness and wrongness of actions. In response to the charge that his utilitarianism makes it difficult to decide questions of right and wrong when time is short, Mill replies:

> there has been ample time, namely, the whole past duration of the human species. During all that time mankind have been learning by experience the tendencies of actions; on which experience all the prudence as well as all the morality of life are dependent . . . mankind must by this time have acquired positive beliefs as to the effects of some actions on their happiness; and the beliefs which have thus come down are the rules of morality for the multitude, and for the philosopher until he has succeeded in finding better. . . . It is a strange notion that the acknowledgement of a first principle is inconsistent with the admission of secondary ones. (pp. 30–31)

These remarks, however, do not make Mill a rule utilitarian.[30] They merely suggest that he was aware that one can learn from the accumulated wisdom of generations the tendencies of certain kinds of actions to have certain kinds of results and thus inductively predict that in the present circumstances that same kind of action will likely have that same kind of result. If you asked Mill the crucial question of whether his "secondary principles" (even, for example, his beloved harm principle)[31] were *in principle* eliminable in favor of a direct application of an act utilitarian principle, I am confident that he would say yes; however, it is probably not useful to pursue an exegetical question concerning what Mill would have said concerning a distinction that simply hadn't been made at the time he was writing.

One gets different versions of rule utilitarianism depending on how one understands the correctness of the rules that determine right and wrong action. And it is in defining the notion of a correct rule that the rule utilitarian finally ends up talking about consequences, thus making

---

30. For arguments that Mill was a rule utilitarian, see, for example, Urmson 1953 and Singer 1961, pp. 204–6.

31. The cornerstone of *On Liberty*. Much debate has focused on the question of how to reconcile Mill's harm principle with his utilitarian principle. Those who think Mill was implicitly committed to rule utilitarianism argue that Mill thought of the harm principle as one of the rules that define morality. It seems to me much more likely that the harm principle was a convenient rule of thumb strongly supported by our experience in dealing with other people.

the view at least a candidate for a consequentialist moral theory. Although one can distinguish many more variations than these,[32] I am primarily interested in the six versions of rule utilitarianism which correspond to our six versions of act utilitarianism. The fundamental distinction between hedonistic utilitarianism and generic utilitarianism applies again when we are talking about rule utilitarianism, and so does the distinction between actual consequence, probable consequence, and value adjusted possible consequence utilitarianism. The difference is that this time we are not talking about the actual, probable, or possible consequences of particular acts in particular circumstances. Rather we are talking about the hypothetical actual, probable, or possible consequences of people (in general) following a rule.[33]

Thus the actual consequence generic rule utilitarian might define the correct rule of morality covering a certain kind of action as the rule that would actually have better consequences if everyone were to follow it than if they were to follow some alternative rule. The probable consequence generic rule utilitarian might define the correct rules of morality in terms of the rules that would *probably* have better consequences were they followed than if alternative rules were followed. And the value adjusted possible consequence rule utilitarian will have to compare rules in terms of the possible consequences of people following them, where the value attached to these possible consequences is adjusted for the probability of their occurring. The correct rules will be those such that the accumulated adjusted possible value of following them outweighs the accumulated adjusted possible value of following alternative rules. Each of these versions of generic rule utilitarianism taken with the view that happiness and only happiness is intrinsically good yields one of the corresponding three versions of rule hedonistic utilitarianism. Obviously, as with act utilitarianism, much more would need to be said by way of fleshing out the details of the above views, and this will be done when we treat them more carefully.

Are rule utilitarianisms consequentialist views? In a way they are. Consequences eventually get talked about. But even in actual consequence rule utilitarianism, the relevant "actual" consequences are the

---

32. The most comprehensive treatment of variations of rule utilitarianism (and its "generalized" counterparts) is still probably David Lyons's *Forms and Limits of Utilitarianism.*

33. We shall see later that the notion of following a rule which one must understand in understanding rule utilitarianism admits of some subtly different interpretations.

consequences that *would* actually occur if people *were* to follow certain rules. What actually happens in the real world as a result of what people actually do is logically independent of the rightness or wrongness of actions. But as I argued earlier, if we take *this* feature of the view to entail that it is not a consequentialist view, then even actual consequence *act* utilitarianism won't fall under the concept of a consequentialist morality, for the rightness of a particular action is a function of its *hypothetical* consequences compared to the hypothetical consequences of alternatives. Again, the labels don't matter as long as we understand clearly the implications of the different views.

Generalizability

Another thesis we might briefly discuss in this introduction to consequentialist conceptions of right and wrong action is the thesis that rightness and wrongness are determined at least in part by the *generalizability* test. There is a *very* close similarity between this view and rule utilitarianism. Both views insist that in calculating which action one morally ought to take one must consider a *hypothetical* question concerning the consequences of people in general acting in a certain way. Before concluding that one ought to act in a certain way, the proponent of generalizability argues, one must ask what the consequences would be of everyone acting in that way. On the simplest version of the view, if the consequences of everyone acting that way would be bad, then the action would be at least prima facie wrong. One can also (more plausibly) hold the view in a comparative form, maintaining that if the consequences of everyone acting that way would be worse than the consequences of everyone acting in some alternative way, then the action would be at least prima facie wrong. Following our earlier terminological conventions for utilitarianisms, we might call the comparative and noncomparative versions of the above thesis *actual consequence generic generalizability theories*. And one can easily define probable consequence and value adjusted possible consequence generic generalizability tests in both comparative and noncomparative forms as well. Just as with rule utilitarianism, adding to the generic view the proposition that only happiness is intrinsically good will give us hedonistic versions of the generalizability test. It is formally possible to hold the correctness of the generalizability test as either a normative or a metaethical theory, but it seems to me that it is best construed as a test intended to be *definitive* of moral reasoning.[34]

If we count rule utilitarianism as a consequentialist ethical theory, then it seems as though we should count the generalizability theory as a consequentialist view as well. Both theories do eventually get around to talking about consequences, albeit hypothetical consequences of a hypothetical situation, in evaluating questions of right and wrong. Indeed, the similarity between the two views raises the question of whether there really is any significant difference between them. Proponents of the generalizability test don't talk about rules, but they do talk about kinds of actions and the consequences of people generally acting in a certain way. And to ask what would happen if people were to act in a certain way seems to me no different than to ask what would happen if people followed a rule prescribing a certain kind of action. In fact, it seems to me that the generalizability theory in its *comparative* form is different from rule utilitarianism as we defined it only if the generalizability test is thought of as an *additional* test that an action must pass after having qualified as the right action on other criteria. The rule utilitarian takes rules themselves to define the rightness and wrongness of actions. Proponents of the generalizability test might think of the hypothetical question as just one additional necessary condition an action must meet in order to be considered right. I shall not be overly concerned with the fine details concerning differences between rule utilitarians and proponents of the generalizability test. It will become evident that, if my reasons for rejecting rule utilitarianism are good, they apply equally well to the generalizability test.

METARATIONALITY CONTROVERSIES

I have in this chapter tried to sketch my understanding of some of the most important metaethical controversies. In doing so, I have tried in some cases to suggest the position I am interested in defending and even to sketch in very general terms my reason for taking certain metaethical

---

34. Perhaps its most famous proponent, Singer (see 1961, chap. 1) probably isn't all that comfortable with the metaethical/normative distinction as I have drawn it. Those of us who are, however, are almost certain to evaluate the generalizability test in the context of a metaethical theory.

positions to be prima facie implausible. I have discussed these controversies in the context of *metaethics* because it is with metaethics that we shall begin and because, historically, it is in the context of metaethical debate that these controversies have most explicitly surfaced. I have, however, made clear my intention of eventually tying our metaethical discussion to the question of practical rationality, and I have indicated my desire at least to seriously consider the possibility of interdefining the key concepts of morality and practical rationality. It should come as no surprise, then, to find that I take all of the above controversies to apply equally well to questions concerning the nature of practical rationality. Thus one can be a cognitivist or a noncognitivist, a subjectivist or an objectivist, a relativist or a nonrelativist, with respect to the question of what constitutes a rational goal or end. And one can endorse any of the consequentialist views discussed above concerning the conceptual connections between rational action (corresponding to morally right action) and rational goals or ends (corresponding to intrinsic goodness).

My identification of morality with practical rationality will be in some respects qualified, but I shall be defending later in this book a relativistic, value adjusted possible consequence act consequentialist conception of rational action. More precisely, I shall defend this as an account of *one* analysis of rational action on which others are derivative. Before I do, however, we must consider again, more carefully, some of the fundamental ethical debates left hanging in this chapter, beginning with the crucial subjectivist/objectivist and relativist/nonrelativist controversies. And to proceed, I think it best that we leave the generalities of this chapter and turn to an examination of these issues in the context of evaluating detailed proposals concerning the analyses of ethical concepts. As so many others do, I begin with Moore's *Principia Ethica,* not because I take his position to be a straw man, but became Moore most clearly presents the sort of objectivist, nonrelativist position I want to reject. The Humean rejection of Moore's view will apply equally well to a host of other ethical theories and will provide, in effect, a new open question test concerning the plausibility, or at least the relevance, of a metaethical theory. It is a test, however, that we can use only if we turn our attention to the analysis of rational action.

CHAPTER 3

Moore, Hume, and a New Open Question Argument

In the preceding chapter I tried to develop a conceptual framework within which to locate the fundamental metaethical controversies that shall concern us. Although we reached some tentative conclusions regarding the prima facie plausibility of certain positions, we left unanswered the most critical questions concerning objectivism, subjectivism, and relativism. We turn to these questions now, through an examination of the fundamentals of Moore's metaethical theory.

Moore's theory provides a logical starting point for two reasons. First, Moore's open question argument was an attack on the very possibility of providing an analysis, with a special emphasis on a naturalistic analysis, of fundamental ethical concepts. And since I intend to defend a version of naturalism, I must reply to Moore's arguments. Second, because of its stark and unequivocal defense of a nonrelativistic objectivism, Moore's theory enables me to present most clearly the dilemma I believe all nonrelativistic objectivist metaethical theories face, a dilemma most eloquently articulated by Hume in Book III of *A Treatise of Human Nature*. Although I do not accept without considerable revision Hume's argument, I do think that of the two philosophers it was really Hume who developed the most plausible "open question" test of the adequacy of a metaethical theory, a test that Moore's theory in particular, but all objectivist metaethical theories in general, fails. The conclusions one reaches with respect to Hume's argument constitute a crucial crossroads in the philosophical search for an understanding of the nature of morality and its relation to rational action.

MOORE'S OBJECTIVISM

As I have already had occasion to note, Moore clearly took the most fundamental ethical concepts to be those of intrinsic goodness and its counterpart, intrinsic badness. The view is at least as old as Plato, and it has always seemed to me to border on the self-evident. Most of the things we take to be good we do so only because we view them as a *means* to something else we take to be good. We think it good that we take the medicine the doctor orders, that we exercise, that we turn down the fourth glass of wine, because we think these things will either produce good effects or avoid bad effects. But what makes these effects good or bad? If it is because they in turn have good and bad effects, and if *all* things good or bad are so only in virtue of their effects, we would seem to encounter a never-ending search for the source of goodness. Although formally the problem looks like a vicious regress, it might be more accurately characterized as a problem of circularity. We cannot *understand* the concept of instrumental goodness without understanding a concept of goodness that is not defined instrumentally.[1]

That the concept of something being good as a means presupposes the concept of something being intrinsically good is, perhaps, obvious. It is, of course, more controversial to suppose, as did the Moore of *Principia Ethica,* that the concept of right action, the concept of what one morally ought to do, also presupposes an understanding of intrinsic goodness. The most natural defense of such a view involves a defense of generic utilitarianism in one of its act or rule forms. Again, I confess that

---

1. I have argued elsewhere (Fumerton 1988) that there is an analogy between the conceptual role of intrinsic goodness and the conceptual role of noninferential justification for a foundationalist. Just as the concept of intrinsic goodness is essential to an understanding of instrumental goodness, so the concept of noninferential justification is essential to an understanding of inferential justification. The regress argument for foundationalism is usually thought of as an epistemological regress argument, but it could just as plausibly be offered as a conceptual regress argument. Of course, not all philosophers would agree that the concept of intrinsic goodness is essential to an understanding of goodness. See Beardsley 1965.

it has always seemed obvious to me that one must *somehow* bring the concept of intrinsic goodness into the analysis of what one morally ought to do. Once we disarm (as we shall presently do) the open question argument as a weapon against proposed analyses of ethical concepts, it is difficult for me to think of a plausible way of understanding ethical concepts which is not parasitic on an understanding of intrinsic goodness. But the final defense of this position involves the working out of a plausible version of generic utilitarianism.

After deciding that the key to an understanding of all ethical concepts is the understanding of intrinsic goodness, Moore, of course, reaches the anticlimactic conclusion that one cannot philosophically analyze the property of intrinsic goodness. According to Moore, philosophical analysis of a concept or property is possible only when the concept or property is complex and can be broken down into its constitutive parts (p. 7), and of goodness he says:

> It is one of those innumerable objects of thought which are themselves incapable of definition, because they are the ultimate terms by reference to which whatever *is* capable of definition must be defined. (pp. 9–10)

We can hold the property of intrinsic goodness before our consciousness. Indeed, we inevitably do every time we consider ethical questions:

> Whenever [a person] thinks of 'intrinsic value,' or 'intrinsic worth,' or says that a thing 'ought to exist,' he has before his mind the unique object—the unique property of things—which I mean by 'good.' Everybody is constantly aware of this notion, although he may never become aware at all that it is different from other notions of which he is also aware. (p. 17)

The mistake of trying to define goodness in terms of *natural* properties Moore calls the *naturalistic fallacy*. The mistake of trying to define goodness at all, we might call, following Frankena (1939), the *definist fallacy*.

Now the idea that there exist concepts that are fundamental and indefinable in Moore's sense is one with which I have no quarrel. Indeed, I agree entirely that one often takes the road to philosophical error by trying to analyze that which does not admit of definition. I have argued, for example, that the basic error of contemporary externalist epistemologies lies in not recognizing the sui generis, indefinable character of fundamental epistemic concepts such as acquaintance and epistemic probability (Fumerton 1988). I have also argued that there is nothing else like the intentional feature of certain mental states which allows them to correspond to reality (Fumerton 1985). It would be no more surprising to find that the conceptual framework of morality rests on a simple unanalyzable moral concept than it would be to find that the theory of Euclidean geometry rests on primitive, unanalyzable geometrical concepts.

To argue that a concept is unanalyzable in Moore's sense is not, of course, to argue that one can say nothing informative about it. Simple properties have properties even if they are not composed of properties, and Moore is not reluctant to tell us about the properties of goodness. Negatively, he tell us that goodness is distinct from certain other properties, such as the property of being pleasing or the property of being desired. Positively, he tells us that goodness is *objective* and *nonrelative* in senses of these terms we have defined earlier. He also tells us that goodness is *nonnatural*.

Of the properties of being simple, being objective, and being nonnatural, the last is, in many respects, the most philosophically interesting. Of Moore's claims about goodness, however, his assertion that it is a nonnatural property is the one that concerns us least. To understand fully Moore's category of nonnatural property, one must delve into the intricacies of the metaphysics Moore accepted at the time of writing *Principia Ethica,* a task that would take us rather far afield. Although it is often described this way, the concept of a nonnatural property goes beyond the concept of a property whose presence is not discovered through the senses or, as a property of the mind, through introspection. Rather, the metaphysics of Moore's view seems to have involved a fundamental distinction between the spatiotemporal natural properties that are in some sense constituents of things, and abstract properties of these bundles of natural properties whose existence is entirely dependent on these natural properties.[2] Interesting as the concept of a nonnatural property is, a discussion of it would not be justified, given that my primary dialectical interests in Moore's view concern his claims about the unanalyzability and the objectivity of goodness, claims to which we now turn our attention.

2. See Moore 1903, p. 41. For a more extensive discussion of the metaphysical views he held around the time of writing *Principia,* see Moore 1899 and 1900–01.

Goodness as a Simple Property

As I read Moore, his defense of the view that goodness is a simple property rests on both a phenomenological appeal and what appears to be a dialectical argument. The phenomenological appeal, which *may* in the final analysis be Moore's fundamental reason for accepting his view, involves the simple request that his readers reflect on the question they ask when they wonder whether something is good. By carefully thinking of the various properties with which philosophers have tried to identify goodness, one is supposed simply to "see" that what one "has in mind" by goodness is something different. I have already admitted that the use of phenomenological appeal is indispensable in philosophy. But one must be equally candid in admitting that it is notoriously ineffective in persuading philosophers to accept a controversial view. Moore could obviously persuade himself that he was acquainted in thought with a simple *objective* property of goodness and was convinced that his readers would discover this same property were they to reflect on the matter with appropriate philosophical care. Hume, however, was equally convinced that he could *not* find moral properties as *objective* properties of the objects we take to be good and bad—he could not find value that was independent of the attitudes people held toward objects judged to have value. And like Moore, Hume was quite willing to take his case to the court of phenomenological appeal. Recall that passage to which we have already referred:

> Take any action allowed to be vicious: Wilful murder, for instance. Examine it in all lights, and see if you can find that matter of fact, or real existence, which you call vice. In whichever way you take it, you find only certain passions, motives, volitions and thoughts. (p. 468)

Frankly, it is Hume's phenomenological appeal that strikes me as the most persuasive. But I would no more expect a Moorean to be impressed by Hume's rhetorical appeal than I would expect a Humean to be moved by Moore's rhetorical flourishes.

Those who are convinced that Moore was essentially correct will no doubt find ways of explaining the Humean's inability to find in thought the problematic objective value. In a fascinating and ingenious defense of a Moorean position, for example, Panayot Butchvarov (1982) argues that Moore himself invited Humean complaints when he compared the simple property of goodness to the simple property of yellow. If objective goodness, like yellow, is supposed to be something *thrust* unproblematically on consciousness, it is small wonder that Hume and I complain that we just don't find it. But, Butchvarov argues, if we recognize and emphasize the abstract character of goodness, we will be in a position to explain how it has escaped so many philosophers. Goodness, Butchvarov would maintain, stands to the various natural properties in virtue of which things are good, as being colored stands to the various shades of color in virtue of which things are colored. Although it is notoriously difficult (impossible, Butchvarov and I would both argue) to define being colored as a complex disjunctive property (being red or yellow or . . .), the property of being colored is, in a sense, always ontologically determined by the presence of some particular color. If goodness were an indefinable abstract property determined by the presence of certain determinate natural properties, it would not be surprising if it escaped the attention of a philosopher like Hume, to whom abstract properties were anathema. Hume, after all, would be no more capable of finding the abstract property of goodness than he would be of finding the abstract property of being colored.

Now although Butchvarov's suggestion is highly original and dialectically ingenious, it both postpones and broadens the initial problem. Hume, as we know, will make the same kind of phenomenological appeal he made against objective goodness, against the existence of abstract properties. And those of us who think that such properties do exist must still find in thought that determinable property of objective goodness whose exemplification is ontologically determined by what appears to be such a *wide* range of natural properties. I am willing to wager that, even after Butchvarov does his best to illuminate the relation between these "good making" natural properties, one will still find a great many philosophers who, like Hume, complain on phenomenological grounds that they cannot find the abstract objective value whose existence is at issue. Again, I stress, this is not to argue that one cannot ultimately base even philosophically controversial conclusions on phenomenological considerations. As I indicated in dealing with other problems, I have paid no attention to those critics on whose deaf ears my phenomenological appeals fall. One must, however, be realistic when it comes to the efficacy of these appeals in getting philosophers to accept controversial philosophical views.

Of course, Moore's metaethical view became one of the most talked about in twentieth-century analytical philosophy, in part because it appeared to go beyond phenomenological appeal in arguing for the indefinability of goodness. This brings us to the open question argument.

The Open Question Argument

The impact of the open question argument is one of the strangest phenomena in metaethical inquiry. For one thing, I have never really been able to find in *Principia Ethica* a clear statement of the argument that has become *known* as the open question argument, although Moore himself appears to have accepted the standard interpretation of what he had in mind. Although this is undoubtedly an odd way to proceed, let us first look at that standard interpretation and then compare it with the text.

Moore makes clear that, though naturalistic analyses are most commonly guilty of the mistake exposed by the open question argument, the focus of his attack is any attempt to analyze goodness in a philosophically illuminating way. In fact, the focus of his attack is even broader than that of part/whole definitions of good. Rather, I think Moore would have viewed the argument as a way of attacking *mistaken* identifications of goodness even with *simple* natural properties or other different simple nonnatural properties. What is this argument?

Suppose that I argue that being intrinsically good is identical with being intrinsically valued (a view that, if properly relativized and qualified, I do in fact defend). On one standard interpretation of the open question argument, one would use it to attack this proposed analysis as follows (for simplicity I leave out the adverb *intrinsically*):

(OQ) (1) If being good is the same as being valued, then to ask whether what is valued is good is the same as to ask whether what is valued is valued (or whether what is good is good).

    (2) These two questions are not the same. (The proof is that one is significant or open; the other is a trivial question, the answer to which is a tautology.)

Therefore,

    (3) Being good is not the same as being valued.

The argument (like so many famous philosophical arguments) has the simple valid structure of modus tollens, and one can find ways of interpreting each premise so that it is true and provable. The question, as we shall see, is whether one can find interpretations of the premises which retain their plausibility without destroying the valid structure of the argument.

Before evaluating the argument, I return with some trepidation to Moore's text. Something like the above argument is supposed to be found in the following passages, each of which I shall briefly consider:

> The hypothesis that disagreement about the meaning of good is disagree-ment with regard to the correct analysis of a given whole, may be most plainly seen to be incorrect by consideration of the fact that, whatever definition be offered, it may be always asked, with significance, of the complex so defined, whether it is itself good. To take, for instance, one of the more plausible, because one of the more complicated, of such pro-posed definitions, it may easily be thought at first sight, that to be good may mean to be that which we desire to desire. Thus if we apply this definition to a particular instance and say 'When we think that A is good, we are thinking that A is one of the things which we desire to desire,' our proposition may seem quite plausible. But, if we carry the investigation further, and ask ourselves 'Is it good to desire to desire A?' it is apparent, on a little reflection, that this question is itself as intelligible, as the original question 'Is A good?'—that we are, in fact, now asking for exactly the same information about the desire to desire A, for which we formerly asked with regard to A itself. But it is also apparent that the meaning of this second question cannot be correctly analysed into 'Is the desire to desire A one of the things which we desire to desire?': we have not before our minds anything so complicated as the question 'Do we desire to desire to desire to desire A?'. (pp. 15–16)

To have the structure of the open question argument as it has come to be known, the questions that *should* have been compared are: "Are things which we desire to desire things which are good?" and "Are things which we desire to desire, things which we desire to desire?" The former is significant in that it requires reflection to answer. The latter is trivial—its answer is a tautology. The meaning equivalence of these two questions would follow from the meaning equivalence of "is good" and "is desired to be desired". But the assertion that the desire to desire X is one of the things that we desire to desire is *not* a trivial tautology. Given an identification of being good with being desired to be desired, it would be equivalent to the assertion that it is good to be good, an assertion about the goodness of the state of affairs of something's being good. In fact, Moore's complaint in the above passage is that the question "Is the desire to desire A one of the things which we desire to desire?" is *more* complicated than the question "Is it good to desire to desire A?" To fit the standard interpretation of the open question argument, the former question should have been less complicated than the latter.

The only other passage that seems to bear a significant resemblance to the open question argument is the following discussion of views that identify pleasure with goodness:

> But whoever will attentively consider with himself what is actually before his mind when he asks the question 'Is pleasure (or whatever it may be) after all good?' can easily satisfy himself that he is not merely wondering whether pleasure is pleasant. (p. 16)

Part of the difficulty here is that the focus of Moore's attack is a philosopher who has identified a *state*, pleasure, with a *property*, goodness. We don't need an open question argument to attack such a philosopher; we need a grammarian. The original assertion made by Moore's hypothetical opponent was that pleasure is *the* good, that is, is the one and only one *thing* that has the property of being good. I can't even understand the view that pleasure *has* the property of being good at the same time that it *is* that property. The question "Is pleasure pleasant?"—like the question "Is the desire to desire A, one of the things which we desire to desire?"—does not appear to be a question whose answer is a trivial tautology. Rather, it appears to be a very odd question about whether we are pleased by the state of being pleased. It may be true that we are pleased by the state of being pleased, but if it is true it is only contingently true.

Presumably, one gets the open question argument out of the above passage by reformulating Moore's discussion so that it makes more sense. Thus the philosopher at whom the argument is directed is construed by Moore's interpreter as holding not the ill-formed thesis that the state of pleasure is identical with the property of being good, but the more plausible thesis that being good is identical with being pleasing (or pleasant). The two questions that are then compared are the questions "Are things which are pleasing, good?" and "Are things which are pleasing, pleasing?" Although I honestly do not think that is what Moore's words say, he did, as I said, appear to accept something like this as his intention in the problematic passage.[3]

Does the open question argument as it is standardly interpreted establish the indefinability of goodness? Let us hope not. As critics have pointed out (Langford 1942), if an argument like this establishes the indefinability of goodness, the possibility of interesting philosophical analyses of *anything* is eliminated. Epistemologists could save themselves a great deal of energy wasted constructing ingenious counterexamples to the view that knowledge is justified true belief. They could simply rely on an open question argument:

(1) If knowing is the same as having a justified true belief, then to ask whether anyone who knows has a justified true belief is the same as to ask whether anyone who has a justified true belief, has a justified true belief.

(2) But these two questions are obviously not the same—one is significant; the other, trivial.

Therefore,

(3) Knowing is not the same as having a justified true belief.

To point out that there must be something wrong with the argument is not, of course, to say what the error is. To find the error we should first recognize that (OQ) is ambiguous as between the following valid arguments:[4]

(OQa) (1) If "is good" means the same as "is valued", then the questions "Is what is valued, good?" and "Is what is valued, valued?" ARE the same.

(2) These questions are not the same. (One is significant; the other, trivial.)

Therefore,

(3) "Is good" does not mean "is valued".

3. This seems clear to me in Moore's famous reply (1942) to Langford 1942.
4. Since writing this section, I have discovered that the ambiguity I discuss and the corresponding objections to each interpretation of the argument are treated in a similar form by Fred Feldman (1978, chap. 13) in a very nice introductory text.

(OQb) (1) If being good is identical with being valued, then the questions "Is what is valued good?" and "Is what is valued, valued?" ARE the same.

(2) These questions are not the same. (One is significant; the other, trivial.)

Therefore,

(3) Being good is not identical with being valued.

(OQc) (1) If "is good" means "is valued", then the question "Is what is valued good?" MEANS the same as the question "Is what is valued, valued?"

(2) These two questions do not have the same meaning. (One is significant; the other, trivial.)

Therefore,

(3) "Is good" does not mean "is valued".

(OQd) (1) If being good is identical with being valued, then the question "Is what is valued good?" MEANS the same as the question "Is what is valued, valued?"

(2) These questions do not have the same meaning. (One is significant; the other, trivial.)

Therefore,

(3) Being good is not identical with being valued.

Each version of the argument has either an obviously false or an obviously problematic (unproved) premise. In (OQa) and (b) the second premise of the argument is uncontroversially true. The linguistic items "Is what is valued good?" and "Is what is valued, valued?" *are* obviously distinct linguistic items, and one can, I suppose, prove that they are distinct by noting that one is more significant than the other. Leibniz's Law (unlike the principle so often confused with it, the principle allowing the substitutivity of co-referential expressions) admits of no exceptions, applies in all contexts. If a thing X has a property that a thing Y lacks, then X is not identical with Y. If a linguistic item X has a property, say being significant, that a linguistic item Y lacks, then X and Y are not the same linguistic items. Of course, one doesn't need to appeal to the property of being significant as the differentiating mark. The linguistic item "Is what is valued, valued?" has two adjective tokens of the same type, whereas the linguistic item "Is what is valued good?"

does not. And *this* is sufficient to conclude, by Leibniz's Law, that the linguistic items are distinct. But though (OQa) and (b) have *trivially* true second premises, they have trivially false first premises. One would be simply foolish to infer from the identity of being good and being valued, or the synonymy of "being good" and "being valued", that one could substitute the one linguistic item for the other without changing the identity of the linguistic complex in which the substitution takes place. More formally, one cannot substitute either co-referential or co-intentional expressions salva veritate in quote contexts.[5] Even if it were true that "is good" means the same as "is valued", one could not take the following true statement: The question "Is what is valued good?" is the same as the question "Is what is valued good?", and substitute for the last occurrence of "good" the expression "valued". (OQa) and (b), then, are hopelessly bad arguments.

(OQc) and (d) are probably, at least prima facie, more promising. The first premise of (OQc) is true provided only that we assume that the meaning of linguistic complexes is a function of the meaning of their constitutive parts. And even if one can find a counterexample to this thesis as a general principle, it is difficult to see how in this context the substitution of the synonymous expression "is valued" for "is good" could alter the meaning of the complex question in which the substitution takes place.

The first premise of (OQd) is more problematic. Given certain contemporary views in the philosophy of language, one cannot infer that two predicate expressions referring to the same property have the same meaning. Moore would have argued (and I actually think he is right) that if two *predicate* expressions refer to the same property they are synonymous. Moore believed this because he thought that the meaning of a predicate expression is exhausted by its referent. And I think that for this reason Moore would have felt comfortable moving back and forth from talk about the identity of properties, the identity of concepts, and the synonymy or analytic equivalence of predicate expressions.

One can, then, certainly defend the first premises of (OQc) and (d). The problematic premise is obviously (2). Can one infer that two questions have different *meanings* by pointing out that one of them is easier to answer than the other? The answer is obviously not. Some

---

5. It seems to me that Quine (1953, chap. 8) still has the best explanation of why this is so. " 'Cat' " strictly speaking does not contain the word "cat" even though it contains the letters "c", "a", and "t".

questions are easy to answer precisely *because* one can determine their answer without *reflecting* on the meaning of the constitutive terms. And the question "Is what is valued, valued?" is just such a question. When one recognizes the *syntactic* structure of the question, one knows that the answer to it is yes.

But surely Moore can reply that even after we take the time to reflect on the meaning of "Is what is valued good?" it will never strike us as a question as trivial as the question "Is what is valued, valued?" That is no doubt true, but one perfectly natural explanation for this fact is that we realize full well that even after reflection we might be *mistaken* in thinking that "Is what is valued good?" has the same meaning as "Is what is valued, valued?".

But how can people who *understand* two expressions fail to realize that they are synonymous? This is a good question that needs an answer. Philosophers who engage in the task of providing philosophical analyses of concepts must resolve the paradox of analysis. They must find a philosophical explanation of how they, as philosophers, can quite comfortably use and understand such expressions as "good", "cause", "know", "self", and "mind" and yet fail so miserably when it comes to saying philosophically what they mean. I have tried to dissolve the paradox of analysis elsewhere.[6] But for our present purposes it is perhaps sufficient to observe that the sense in which we understand philosophically problematic concepts is analogous to the sense in which linguistically unsophisticated people can still know how to follow the enormously complex syntactical rules governing the structure of well-formed sentences. To *follow* a syntactical rule is, of course, not the same thing as to know what that rule is. In one sense, to follow a syntactical rule is to exemplify a (perhaps very complex) disposition to behave linguistically in certain ways. We understand expressions whose meaning is enormously difficult to discover in the sense that we follow certain semantic rules relating language to the world. We follow these semantic rules, I have argued, by exemplifying dispositions to regard certain descriptions as correct descriptions of the world as thought of in a certain way. To follow these rules (to exemplify these dispositions) is not the same thing as to know what these rules are (to know what these dispositions are). It is the latter sort of knowledge that the philosopher wants when he wants to know the correct analyses of philosophically

6. Fumerton 1983.

fundamental and problematic concepts. The philosopher wants not only to follow the rules. He wants to know what rules he follows.[7] And this knowledge is hard to come by. One can think, for example, that one uses the term "know" in such a way that one would regard "knowledge" as the correct description of all and only those states of justified true belief and then run across a Gettier thought experiment that convinces one otherwise.

The work of discovering the adequacy of a philosophical analysis is long and hard, and it certainly cannot be accomplished simply by introspecting the meaning of a given term. Realizing this, we can dismiss the mechanical test of sameness of meaning that the open question argument seems to propose.

The phenomenological appeal for the unanalyzability of the primitive, objective property of goodness will be rejected by those of us who reach precisely the opposite conclusion on the same phenomenological grounds. The dialectical open question argument is a bad argument. But we have yet to present an argument against the view that the idea of intrinsic goodness is the idea of a simple objective quality that attaches to things intrinsically good. One can, of course, argue once again from cultural relativity that the idea of a value property whose presence is self-evident is contradicted by the widespread disagreement over what is good. There are, however, two obvious difficulties with this argument. First, it is not at all clear that there *is* widespread disagreement over what things are *intrinsically* good. There are cultures, our own included, that sometimes stress that suffering is good for one. But who in his right mind thinks that suffering is intrinsically good? There are cultures that think that certain sorts of pleasure are bad for you. But who thinks that these pleasures are intrinsically bad? Second, one can surely allow that a proposition can be self-evident to one person while it is unknown to another. The philosophical account of this possibility will vary, depending on one's philosophical conception of self-evidence. But Moore himself certainly allowed for the possibility of confusing goodness with some other different property, a confusion that he felt often led to ethical error.

To find a more effective, albeit a highly controversial, argument against the existence of objective goodness, we might profitably turn again to Hume.

---

7. Because I don't think the philosopher is primarily interested in what other people mean, I deliberately put the question in terms of the individual's search for the rules he follows.

HUME'S METAETHICS

We have already noted that, like Moore, Hume is willing to stake much on phenomenological appeal. Again, the irony is that, unlike Moore, Hume counts on his reader to be unable to find any objective property of value. *Some* would argue that Hume would go a step further and deny the existence of *any* moral properties, objective or otherwise.[8] And indeed, in his most serious metaethical discussion, Book III, Sections I and II of the *Treatise,* one can find passages in which Hume certainly seems intent on arguing that moral judgments do not concern matters of fact. On p. 458 Hume tells us that "Reason is the discovery of truth or falsehood," and that truths or falsehoods are of two kinds: "Truth or falsehood consists in an agreement or disagreement either to the *real* relations of ideas, or to *real* existence and matter of fact." The two kinds of truths he is talking about are, of course, conceptual necessary truths and contingent truths. And I will not deny that in some passages Hume seems to be moving toward a version of noncognitivism. Following an argument we shall eventually examine more closely, Hume says straight out (p. 457) that "the rules of morality, therefore, are not conclusions of our reason." If we identify the conclusions of reason with truth and falsehood, it would seem to follow that Hume believes that moral judgments are neither true nor false. Furthermore, as we have earlier had occasion to note, the famous is/ought passage *can* be read as denying that moral statements have a descriptive use. In another passage (already quoted in the context of our discussion of the is/ought gap), however, Hume does *finally* appear to identify a plausible matter of fact to serve as the subject matter of moral statements:

> The vice entirely escapes you, as long as you consider the object. You never can find it, till you turn your reflection into your own breast, and find a sentiment of disapprobation which arises in you towards this action. Here is a matter of fact; but it is the object of feeling, not of reason. It lies in yourself, not in the object. So that when you pronounce any action or character to be vicious, you mean nothing but that from the constitution of your nature you have a feeling or sentiment of blame from the contemplation of it. (pp. 468–69)

If we take the passage literally, Hume was a subjective descriptivist who

8. For an interpretation of Hume as an early noncognitivist (emotivist), see Flew 1963.

took our moral statements to be descriptions of our dispositions to react psychologically in certain ways to the contemplation of states of affairs.

All in all, it seems to me most likely that Hume never really *meant* to assert that moral conclusions are not conclusions with respect to some matter of fact. Rather, I suspect that Hume only meant to be arguing that moral conclusions are not conclusions with respect to some *objective* matter of fact, where "objective" is understood in either of the two senses distinguished in Chapter 2. I simply think that Hume became confused in asserting his thesis and in drawing some hasty inferences from it. Convinced that our moral judgments have *something* to do with the *passions,* he then argued, correctly, of course, that passions do not have a truth value. Truth, you recall, consists in an agreement that our thoughts have to real relations of ideas or real matters of fact. Hume then argues that:

> Whatever, therefore, is not susceptible of this agreement or disagreement is incapable of being true or false and can never be an object of our reason. Now it is evident our passions, volitions, and actions, are not susceptible of any such agreement or disagreement, being original facts and realities, complete in themselves, and implying no reference to other passions, volitions, and actions. It is impossible, therefore, they can be pronounced either true or false, and be either contrary or conformable to reason. (p. 458)

Again, Hume is obviously correct in concluding that *passions* lack truth value. Wants, desires, sentiments of approbation can no more be true or false than can tables and chairs. But one is obviously messing things up if one tries to infer from (1) moral judgments "involve" in some sense the passions and (2) the passions lack truth value to (3) moral judgments lack truth value. The issue is *how* moral judgments involve the passions. If Hume believed, à la Stevenson, that moral judgments *express* the passions, then he was a proto-emotivist, and we can comfortably accommodate those passages in which he seems to declare that moral judgments lack truth value, but at the cost of having to assume that he misspoke in that passage I quoted earlier in which he characterizes what we *mean* when we say that an action is vicious. If Hume held that moral judgments *describe* the passions, then we can take at face value his own apparently unequivocal statement describing the meaning of ethical terms, but at the cost of concluding that he confused things rather badly in some earlier passages.

Like disputes over whether Mill was an act or a rule utilitarian, the question of whether Hume was a cognitivist subjectivist or a noncognitivist subjectivist is, perhaps, academic. I am convinced that Hume was struggling to assert either some version of emotivism or some version of descriptive subjectivism in our sense (2), that is to say, a version of descriptive subjectivism according to which moral judgments describe the psychological properties of the person making the judgment. As I read the text, it seems to me that everything fell into place for Hume around the "So that when you pronounce" passage I emphasize so much, and for that reason I would guess that he would prefer the descriptivist view, but I will not discuss the issue any further here.

If we conclude that Hume was advocating the view that ethical judgments describe passions, however, why should we conclude that the passions in question are those of the person making the judgment? As I noted earlier, because Hume compared vice and virtue to secondary qualities, one might suppose he held that moral statements are descriptions of the way people in general typically respond on considering certain states of affairs.[9] After all, the most defensible analysis of redness as a property of physical objects construes it as a disposition that the object has to produce in *normal* people under normal conditions certain sensations. To understand why we should construe Hume as holding that moral judgments are tied to the passions of the person making the judgment, we must look beyond his phenomenological objections to objectivism and turn to his dialectical argument against objectivism. Our discussion of this argument will lead us to consider a new kind of open question test for the adequacy of a metaethical theory, an open question test that Moore's theory, and all objectivist analyses, fails.

HUME'S DIALECTICAL ARGUMENT AGAINST OBJECTIVISM

As I interpret Hume, he rejects any analysis of moral judgments which makes their truth or falsehood dependent on *objective* matters of fact, where "objective" is understood in the second sense distinguished

9. Hume seems to have been interpreted this way, for example, by Stevenson 1963, p. 13, and MacIntyre 1959.

in Chapter 2. When he complains about those authors in "every system of morality to which I have hiterto met with" who move from "is" statements to "ought" statements, his complaint, on my view, would be more perspicuously stated in terms of their inexplicable move from *objective* claims to moral advice. I have argued that Hume is willing to rely heavily on phenomenological appeal in rejecting the existence of objective value. But like Moore, Hume seems prepared to bolster his phenomenological appeal with a dialectical argument. The importance Hume places on this argument is underscored by its prominent place in the early stages of his metaethical inquiry. This dialectical argument proceeds from the observation that the very concept of morality is intimately connected to *action*. Our concept of morality requires that there be some sort of connection between reaching moral conclusions and being moved to act in certain ways. All versions of metaethical objectivism pay the unacceptable price of severing this conceptual connection. The very concept of an objective fact is the concept of a fact that is logically independent of attitudes, desires, wants—what Hume called the "passions". But on Hume's view, the only thing that can move one to action is a passion. Since metaethical objectivism denies the logical connection between recognition of value and the exemplification of "passions", metaethical objectivism denies the logical connection between recognition of value and inclination to action. The basic thrust of Hume's argument is summarized in the following passage:

> Philosophy is commonly divided into *speculative* and *practical;* and as morality is always comprehended under the latter division, it is supposed to influence our passions and actions, and to go beyond the calm and indolent judgments of the understanding. . . .
> Since morals, therefore, have an influence on the actions and affections, it follows that they cannot be derived from reason; and that because reason alone, as we have already proved, can never have any such influence. Morals excite passions, and produce or prevent actions. Reason of itself is utterly impotent in this particular. The rules of morality, therefore, are not conclusions of our reason. (p. 457)

Now to argue against *metaethical* objectivism, one must maintain a thesis that is really stronger than the one Hume sometimes seems to support. One must maintain that there is an *analytic* or *conceptual* connection between recognition of value, the having of passions, and being influenced to act in a certain way. An objectivist can, for example, maintain that value is objective but that, when we recognize its presence, all or most of us are caused to want that which has value and are correspondingly causally influenced to act so as to bring about that which has recognized value. The critical question is whether there is a connection stronger than a nomological connection between the recognition of value, the having of passions, and the inclination to act. It is because I think Hume intended to assert a conceptual connection between my recognition of value and my being moved to act that I earlier argued we should construe Hume as the kind of subjectivist who takes moral judgments to be descriptions of the attitudes (passions) of the person making the judgment. If we define a thing's having value in terms of what *most* people want or would approve of, then there would be no conceptual connection between *my* recognizing that X has value and *my* being disposed to pursue X. After all, I might be different from most people in terms of what I take an interest in.

Hume may have been the first philosopher to *clearly* assert a conceptual connection between recognition of value and inclination to act, but he is, of course, not the only philosopher to make this sort of claim. In his now-classic paper "The Emotive Meaning of Ethical Terms," Stevenson puts forward criteria for evaluating proposed metaethical views. And one of the most important of these criteria is the requirement that an adequate metaethical theory capture the "magnetism" of ethical terms. Stevenson defines magnetism in terms of the basic Humean thesis:

> A person who recognizes X to be "good" must *ipso facto* acquire a stronger tendency to act in its favour than he otherwise would have had.[10]

Hare takes Stevenson a step further and argues that sincere acceptance of the moral judgment that one ought to do X entails that one does X. Moral judgments, for Hare, are imperatives, and the only way to accept an imperative is to act in the way commanded, provided that it is possible for one to do so.

I think there is a great deal of force behind Hume's dialectical argument and its contemporary variations, but one must search very carefully for the most plausible way of describing the crucial conceptual connection. One must be particularly cautious about defending too strong a connection between accepting a moral conclusion and acting in

10. Stevenson 1963, p. 13.

a certain way.[11] Hare's view, for example, is a paradigm of a view that requires too strong a tie. Despite his noble efforts to accommodate "weakness of the will,"[12] it still seems obvious that one can realize that one ought to do something and yet decide not to do it. To take a familiar example, the world is full of smokers who have quite sincerely decided that they really ought to quit smoking and who could, after some short-term suffering, succeed in quitting. Yet many of these people will not quit, and *not* because they are convinced that the short-term benefits (the pleasures of nicotine) outweigh the possible disvalue of premature, slow, and painful death. There are still people who know full well that they ought to go to the dentist and who will not bring themselves to hurdle that initial needle pushed into their gums followed by the high-pitched whirring of the drill. Again, it is not that they do not believe that the initial pain will be more than compensated by future freedom from pain. And it is not that they are causally unable to see a dentist (although they are no doubt *caused* by their fear of short-term pain not to act as they ought).[13] Rather, they are simply acting in a way that they realize full well is irrational—they may even be quite ashamed of the way in which they are behaving.

Some might not view the above situations as involving *moral* choice. But one can describe even more obvious situations involving moral deliberation in which people act contrary to what they believe they morally ought to do. There are, for example, a great many people, and some prominent philosophers, who *say* that they regard the happiness and well-being of other people as being just as great a good as their own happiness. These same philosophers, particularly the more prominent, often have rather comfortable salaries and live in what would pass for luxury in most parts of the world. They also know full well that they could sell their stereos, their record collections, their second cars, and use the proceeds to, quite literally, save lives. To avoid sophistical skeptical concerns about whether money donated to charities actually makes a difference, we can imagine such a person, for example, hopping a plane for the nearest depressed country, grabbing an orphaned child, and adopting it as her own. Now what *shall* we say about wealthy

11. For useful discussions of this point, see Falk's "'Ought' and Motivation" and "Action-Guiding Reasons" in Falk 1986.

12. See Hare 1963, chap. 5.

13. I assume without argument that determinism is compatible with being able to act in ways other than one does.

altruists who *know* that they are not doing what their altruism[14] demands? We could, of course, maintain Hare's position and argue that their altruism is insincere—they do not really view the well-being of others as being as important as their own. And in fact it wouldn't surprise me if this was usually the case. But *must* we reach this conclusion? Can we not allow that there are all sorts of perfectly sincere altruists who have simply decided (perhaps with guilty consciences) that they will no more part with their expensive stereos than will the cigarette smoker part with his cigarettes?

Stevenson's requirement of magnetism might seem to fare better than Hare's insistence that sincere acceptance of moral conclusions entails action. After all, on Stevenson's view, when you sincerely decide that you ought to do *X,* all that follows is that you "feel a pull" toward doing *X.* Any number of factors, like the fear of short-term pain, might prevent you from doing *X.* The concept of feeling a pull is, however, extremely vague. There is a sense, for example, in which it might be true that our sincere altruist who, with her guilty conscience, turns her back on her fellow human beings, has long since learned to live with that morally reprehensible decision. Having made the decision, having put the plight of others "out of mind," she may no longer feel any pull toward doing anything else. Similarly, that cigarette smoker who sincerely recognizes that he ought to stop smoking might be so reconciled to his weakness of will that he no longer even hesitates when it comes to taking his next cigarette.

I suspect that Stevenson's conception of magnetism comes close to what Hume had in mind, certainly close to what he should have had in mind. For one thing, though Hume's own metaethical view (as I interpret it) does tie value judgments to the "passions" of the person making the judgment, the passions in question are of a very particular sort:

> Nor is every sentiment of pleasure or pain which arises from characters and actions, of that *peculiar* kind which makes us praise or condemn. The good qualities of an enemy are hurtful to us, but may still command our esteem and respect. It is only when a character is considered in general, without reference to our particular interest, that it causes such a feeling or sentiment as denominates it morally good or evil. (p. 472)

14. I am using "altruist" in such a way that it characterizes someone who does not ignore his own happiness but who is neutral as between his own happiness and the happiness of others.

Hume goes on to distinguish these moral sentiments from sentiments of self-interest. From this, it would seem to follow that one can be moved in one direction by one's *moral* sentiments while one is moved in another direction by one's nonmoral sentiments. And interestingly enough, Hume gives us no guidance as to how these respective forces will act on a well-ordered, rational person. The critic can certainly point out that for all Hume's concern with the action-guiding character of morality, on his own view, a person who is so constituted as to be moved primarily by nonmoral sentiments might find conclusions of morality a matter of relative indifference when it comes to decision making. Hume is praised by some for the subtlety of his view concerning what counts as a moral sentiment.[15] But if one remembers the structure of Hume's dialectical argument against metaethical objectivism, one might well conclude that Hume's characterization of moral sentiments was too subtle for his own good.

ANOTHER OPEN QUESTION TEST

Hume, Stevenson, and Hare would have been in a stronger position, I think, if they had described the problematic conceptual connection as holding not between the reaching of a moral conclusion and action, but, rather, in terms of reaching a moral conclusion and regarding oneself as having a *reason* to act. The concept of reason to act is ambiguous in ways we shall explore in the next chapter. For now, let us simply understand the relevant concept of reason as the one critical to rational deliberation. Reasons for acting, in this sense, are the prudential analogues of the epistemic reasons we must consider in deciding what it would be epistemically rational to believe. The Humean objection to metaethical objectivism could be paraphrased as follows. According to the objectivist, objective value is something about which one could be completely indifferent. Indeed, one could have a decided distaste for objective goodness. But if one is indifferent to objective value, one has no reason to pursue it. It follows that if one defines morality in terms of the pursuit of (actual, probable, possible) objective value, one might have no reason to do what one morally ought to do. Given metaethical objectivism, moral conclusions will no longer occupy the conceptual center stage for

15. See Darwall 1983, chap. 5.

the rational person deciding what to do. It is a tautology to assert that a rational person will do what he has the most reason to do. If morality is conceptually divorced from rationality, if questions about what we morally ought to do are divorced from questions about what we have the most reason to do, then so much the worse for morality. The most fundamental question for a person deciding what to do will *not* be a question concerning the morality of action.

I am making the charge, then, that metaethical objectivism faces a dilemma. Either there is or there is not a conceptual connection between deciding what one morally ought to do and deciding what one has the most reason to do. If there is a conceptual connection, and *if* what one has a reason to do is at least in part a function of one's subjective values or interests, then metaethical objectivism is false. If there is no conceptual connection between deciding what one morally ought to do and deciding what one has the most reason to do, then questions of morality are not the fundamental questions for rational people concerned with making rational choices. As is obvious from the way in which I presented the argument, one way for an objectivist to escape the dilemma is to deny that what one has reason to do is even in part a function of one's psychological make-up. Let us illustrate the nature of the dilemma with reference to Moore's view of goodness and at the same time cast prima facie doubt on the plausibility of the above attempt to escape the dilemma.

Intrinsic goodness is, according to Moore, a simple objective property that some things have and that some things lack. Because it is an *objective* property, I assume that one can adopt any attitude toward it whatsoever. One can take an interest in things that have objective goodness, one can be indifferent to the exemplification of intrinsic goodness, or one can loathe those things that are intrinsically good. *Formally,* the situation is precisely the same as with any other *objective* property, say, purple. Some people like the color purple and take an interest in things that are purple. Some people neither like nor dislike purple things. And some people positively loathe the color purple.

Moore appears to define what one morally ought to do in terms of what (among the alternatives) will bring about the most good—he appears to be an actual consequence generic act utilitarian. But it should be obvious that the point I am about to make would apply equally well to any of the other act or rule utilitarianisms distinguished in Chapter 2. Why would a rational person do what Moore says he ought to do given

Moore's understanding of what makes an action right? Again, let us pursue our analogy. Suppose that I introduce the concept of an action that one *shmought* to take. I define the action one shmought to take in terms of the action that, of the alternatives open to one, will actually result in the largest number of things being purple. (I could, of course, define *probable* and *possible* and rule variations of what one shmought to do.) Let us suppose that, to humor me, you allow into our language this newly defined concept. What would be the conceptual connection between deciding what one shmought to do and deciding on a rational course of action? There would obviously be none. If you are trying to decide what to do one evening, I could point out that what you shmought to do is get your can of purple paint and walk around painting things purple. You might well agree. But obviously in convincing you that this is what you shmought to do, I haven't convinced you that you have any reason to do it. Indeed, if you are at all normal, you would be mad to do what you shmought to do. And why? The most obvious, almost trivial, answer is that you take no special interest in things being purple. *If* you were an exceedingly bizarre person who not only took an interest in the color purple, but who cared about nothing else other than the exemplification of this property, then one could understand why you would be preoccupied with questions about what you shmought to do. But your having a reason to do what you shmought to do would be entirely contingent on the having of this peculiar character trait.

Now *logically* the concept of what I ought to do on Moore's view, indeed on *any* version of metaethical objectivism, would seem to be exactly the same as the concept of what I shmought to do. I am trying to figure out what to do and Moore advises me that what I morally ought to do is X. Suppose, contrary to fact, I understand what Moore's objective intrinsic value is, and thus I understand the concept of moral obligation defined in terms of producing things that have objective value. I agree that what I morally ought to do tonight is X, whereas what I shmought to do is Y. Which of either X or Y would I have the most reason to do? It is possible that my attitude toward Moore's objective value would be the same as my attitude toward objective purple, in which case, I would argue, questions of what I morally ought to do are no more relevant to my rational decision making than are questions about what I shmought to do. What I morally ought to do might be more important to me than what I shmought to do. But then what I shmought to do might be more important to me than what I morally ought to do. Does one want questions about what we morally ought to do to be on the same conceptual footing as questions about what we shmought to do? If it is an open question as to whether we have any reason to do what we morally ought to do, just as it is an open question as to whether we have any reason to do what we shmought to do, then why would we concern ourselves with questions of morality at all? Why wouldn't we figure out what we have the most reason to do and do it? It might turn out that we have the most reason to act morally. It might turn out that we have the most reason to act shmorally. Or it might turn out that we have the most reason to act in some other way entirely.

If the most fundamental question for me as a rational person deciding between alternative actions is "Which alternative ought I to choose?", then this "ought" must be conceptually linked to the question of what I have the most reason to do. In Chapter 1 I said that I would leave open the question of whether one should distinguish an "ought" of morality from an "ought" of rationality. But if there is a moral "ought" that leaves open the question of whether one rationally ought to do what one morally ought to do, then the "ought" of morality must take a back seat to the "ought" of rationality. The crucial question for me as a rational person making a choice must always be which of the alternatives I have the most reason to choose, for until I have decided *that,* it is tautologous to say that I cannot make a rational choice.

One might object to the above view by arguing that, if one distinguishes the "ought" of rationality from the "ought" of morality, one will need a more fundamental use of "ought" still, for it is an open question as to whether I ought to do that which I have the most reason to do. Because we are so used to responding to questions of the form "Why ought I to do so and so?" we might initially be tempted to think that this question is as intelligible as any other having the same form. But surely on reflection we would be puzzled. One cannot respond to the question "Why ought I to do that which I have the most reason to do?" once one realizes that given the question no *reason* would be relevant, that is, once one realizes that to offer a reason would be to beg the question. The sheer inability even to know what would count as an answer to the question indicates that there is no concept of "ought" more fundamental than the one defined in terms of what one has the most reason to do.

I have presented the metaethical objectivist with a dilemma. In fact, I think that the concept of "ought" is univocal and that deciding what one ought to do is conceptually linked to deciding what one has the most reason to do. Contrary to Hare, we can, it seems, sincerely decide that we ought to do something and yet not do it. And contrary to Stevenson, we can make that decision so emphatically that we no longer feel any "pull" toward doing that which we know we ought to do. But it would surely be more than just "odd" if a cigarette smoker told us that he knows he ought to quit while maintaining that he has no reason at all to do so. Our bad-faith altruist may have reconciled herself to a life that is at odds with her moral principles, but she will surely admit that she is acting contrary to what she has the most reason to do. It does seem to me obvious that in the standard use of "ought", whether we are talking in a moral context or a nonmoral context, one cannot consistently conclude that one ought to do X at the same time one concludes that one has no reason to do X.

Like Moore, then, I am inclined to propose an open question test for the adequacy of a metaethical view. I want to evaluate a proposed analysis by determining whether, given the analysis, a certain question is open or closed. I shall ask whether, given the proposed analysis, someone can decide that he ought to choose X rather than its alternatives without deciding that he has more reason to choose X than any of its alternatives. If, given a proposed analysis, the question of whether there is reason for me to do that which I ought to do remains open, the analysis must be rejected. I am claiming that in the action-guiding sense of "ought" (and I assume this includes "ought" as it is used in moral deliberation) there is a logical impropriety involved in someone deciding both that of the available alternatives (all things being considered) he ought to do X and that at the same time (all things being considered) there is more reason for him to choose one of its alternatives over X. If someone told us that he had finally decided that he ought to do X instead of Y but was going to do Y rather than X because he had also decided that he had more reason to do Y than X, I think his statement would strike us as contradictory. We would wonder what on earth he meant by telling us that he had decided that he ought to do X.

In endorsing this test for the adequacy of a metaethical view, I am, then, suggesting that the metaethical objectivist would be ill-advised to try to escape the dilemma by divorcing morality from rationality. I nevertheless have presented the other horn of the dilemma because, dialectically, I want to make clear that in the final analysis it will not matter to me if my opponent insists on a concept of morality which conceptually divorces it from rationality. The day my opponent convinces me that questions of morality are distinct from questions of rationality is the day my opponent also convinces me not to worry anymore about questions of morality. It is the day my opponent convinces me that morality does not, after all, go beyond the "calm and indolent judgments of the understanding."

In advancing the above open question test for what we might call a *relevant* analysis of "ought", I have been arguing only that the crucial conceptual connection obtains between someone S deciding that she ought to do X and S deciding that X is what she has the most reason to do. The issue concerning conceptual connections between value judgments and reasons for acting becomes much more complicated when we try to understand second- and third-person value judgments. Specifically, one who is convinced of Humean, Stevensonean, Harean, or Fumertonean criteria for evaluating metaethical theories must decide what the connection is between *my* judging that Jones ought to do X and my acting, or being moved to act, or thinking of myself as having reason to act, so as to aid Jones in doing X. I think Hare, Stevenson, and probably Hume all failed to mark what seems to be a crucial distinction between the judgments I make about what I ought to do and the judgments I make about what other people ought to do. I think all three, but certainly Hare and Stevenson, mistakenly thought that when I judge that Jones ought to do X, it follows, in Hare's case, that I help Jones to do X (when it is in my power to do so) and, in Stevenson's case, that I am moved toward helping Jones do X.

I have argued in Chapter 2, relying on the example of "ought" judgments made in the context of competition, that it is absurd to suppose in general that, when one thinks to oneself that one's opponent ought to do something, that commits one to, or moves one toward, aiding that opponent. And of course, I would say the same thing about the connection between "ought" judgments and judgments about the rationality of action. In thinking that my opponent ought to hit to my backhand, I am surely not thinking to myself that I have any reason to aid my opponent in achieving this goal. In thinking to myself that I, all things being considered, ought to hit to my opponent's backhand, I *am* (I would argue) committed to thinking of this as the most rational course of action for me to follow.

The most natural view to take concerning second- and third-person value judgments is to argue that, when I think that someone else ought to do X, that commits me to thinking that X is what that other person has the most reason to do. If what one has a reason to do is, in part, a function of one's psychological make-up (one's values, interests, wants), then it would follow that we should *not* attempt to tie second- and third-person "ought" judgments to the "passions" of the person making those second- and third-person value judgments. Rather, we should attempt to tie second- and third-person "ought" judgments to the "passions" of the persons about whom the judgments are made.

The open question test I proposed for the adequacy of "ought" judgments does *not* support a subjectivist (2) interpretation of *all* "ought" judgments, even on the assumption that what one has a reason to do is in part a function of one's attitudes. Rather, the open question test supports only a subjectivist (2) interpretation of first-person "ought" judgments. If second- and third-person "ought" judgments are conceptually linked to the reasons the people have for acting about whom the judgments are made, then the metaethical view implied would seem to be that metaethical *relativism* I distinguished from metaethical subjectivism (2) in Chapter 2. The issue of how to understand second- and third-person value judgments is complicated, however, by the fact that there are standards one can use in evaluating the goals and ends of others which one cannot use in evaluating one's own goals or ends. Put crudely, one can evaluate the goals or ends of others by reference to one's own goals or ends. One has, I shall argue, no goals or ends other than one's own in evaluating one's own goals or ends. This crucial difference introduces a complication in how to understand second- and third-person value judgments, a complication that we shall address in due course (Chapter 7).

To accept the claim that one's first-person "ought" judgments are conceptually linked to what one has the most reason to do is not, by itself, to abandon metaethical objectivism. One needs the further controversial premise that the concept of a reason to act is inextricably bound to the concept of a goal or end, where the concept of a goal or end is itself inextricably bound to the concept of human valuing or interest. One could try to turn the tables on the Humean. One could try to argue that it is only recognition that a thing has objective value which could give us a reason for having it as a goal or an end, a reason that would exist *regardless* of what interest one contingently has in the property of objective value.[16] Our demented follower of shmorality, of

16. This is essentially the view defended by Audi (1983). One could also argue that *recognition* of objective value is itself a kind of desire. The objective property of being

course, could also claim that knowledge that an action leads to another purple thing in the universe gives us a reason to take that action regardless of what contingent attitude one has toward the color purple. "Yes," the Moorean might reply, "one could." But one would be wrong. That is just the difference between intrinsic goodness and purple. Knowing that an action leads to something intrinsically good does give one a reason for taking that action regardless of what attitude one has toward objective goodness. Knowing that an action leads to something purple does not give one a reason for taking that action regardless of what attitude one has toward purple.

At this point we may have come to one of those rock-bottom issues in philosophy where it is difficult to see how argument will resolve the disagreement. It seems obvious to me that the concept of having a reason to do something is inextricably bound to the concept of goals or ends, and that if there were objective goodness, it would be on precisely the same footing as objective purple. But perhaps the best way to try to convince others that this is so is to develop a concept of practical rationality resting on a radically relativistic concept of reason, an account that can effectively deflect criticism.

I have argued that there is a conceptual connection between my first-person "ought" judgments and judgments about what I have the most reason to do. I want to infer from this that a version of metaethical relativism is true. But to do that, I must present and defend a conception of practical rationality. After I do so, I shall discuss again the implications of what will then be a fully analyzed open question test for the adequacy of ethical judgments. The analysis of practical rationality will be offered without the mention of value terms like "good", "right", and "ought", but afterward I shall show how one could most simply "hook up" the concepts of practical rationality to the concepts of morality. Despite my preliminary indication that I take the meaning of "ought" to be fundamentally univocal, I have not forgotten that I owe the reader an account of why it *seems* to make perfectly good sense to ask whether one ought to act morally. I address some objections to the account of practical rationality/morality as I develop it, but I save my replies to certain objections until Chapters 6 and 7.

Let us now explore the concept of rational action.

---

good could be exemplified without anyone recognizing it, but to be recognized is to be desired. I have more to say about this view in Chapter 5.

CHAPTER 4

The Concept of
Rational Action

The general conception of rational action I defend is not new. Indeed, versions of it have existed for well over two thousand years. Some would even claim that it is the received view particularly in fields outside philosophy such as economics. But one must be careful to distinguish explanatory theories from conceptual analyses. In fact, I suspect that the concept of maximizing expected utility is most often appealed to in economics, for example, in the context of explaining and predicting how people behave, and it will become clear that I have no interest in arguing that people always, or even usually, act so as to maximize expected utility. More generally, I have no interest in defending the view that people always or usually act *rationally*. My interest is solely with the *concept* of rational action. Given any plausible analysis of rational action, it seems evident to me that people are often deplorably irrational in their behavior, and I shall certainly not take it to be a defect of my view if it implies that people often act irrationally. Indeed, I shall later argue that some standard objections to the act consequentialist account of rational action I defend lose their force once one really appreciates how odd people can be.

In the last chapter I cautioned against trying to secure too close a tie between accepting ethical judgments and action. Since I am ultimately interested in identifying what one morally ought to do with what one has the most reason to do, it should come as no surprise that I would also caution against attempting to secure too close a tie between a person's accepting the conclusion that he would be rational to do X and his doing X. People often do know what they rationally ought to do without doing it, and this is one source of irrational behavior. A far more common source of irrational behavior, however, has its roots in mistaken belief about what one has the most reason to do. All sorts of people try to behave rationally but are notoriously unsuccessful in their endeavors.

Despite its long history, I am interested in articulating and defending the conception of rational action presented below for several reasons. The radically relativistic act consequentialist view of rational action I defend has come under repeated philosophical attack, especially in the twentieth century, and I am not convinced that it has yet received the most careful statement and defense. On the one hand, there are extraordinarily complex and subtle ambiguities in the concept of rational action which must be carefully distinguished. Some of these ambiguities have their source in the way in which consequences enter into concepts of rationality. Others center on alternative conceptions of an agent's goals or ends. Still others involve important differences between first-person perspective and second- and third-person perspective. Finally, there are ambiguities of "level" which must be recognized. But although many views within the same general framework I defend do not do full justice to some of the intricacies of our concepts of rational action, these same views also too often stray from the fundamental insight of an act consequentialist analysis of practical rationality. In particular, it seems to me that too often act consequentialism is "softened" or "modified" to accommodate criticisms instead of meeting them head on.

Though it may seem an odd ambition, it will become evident that I am interested in defending an extreme, polemical version of a relativistic act consequentialist conception of rational behavior. My sympathies lie with the views of Glaucon, playing devil's advocate for Thrasymachus, and Hobbes in *Leviathan,* views that are, in my opinion, too often dismissed on the way to a discussion of more "sophisticated" but ultimately less defensible positions. Philosophers are by and large less sympathetic than nonphilosophers to the conception of rational action which I present below, in part because they realize that the view does have extreme—many would argue, counterintuitive—consequences. The key to defending the view is not to run away from these consequences, but to argue that we have been conditioned by a variety of circumstances to embrace mistaken beliefs about what is rational behavior. With these few provocative promissory notes, let us begin our search for the most plausible analysis of the concept of rational action.

REASONS FOR ACTING

Causal Reasons

I briefly noted in the last chapter that talk of a person's reasons for acting is ambiguous at least between the concept of reason as *cause* and the concept of reason as something relevant to the *justification* of an action.[1] As a confirmed Humean on these matters, I would argue that it is conceivable for any two logically independent events or states to stand in causal connection. It is, therefore, a priori possible that any antecedent state of a person or her environment could constitute a causal explanation of her behavior. It is certainly true that we often cite a person's reasons for acting, or more accurately a person's beliefs about what she has reason to do, in a causal explanation of her behavior, but we might also cite evolutionary "programming," posthypnotic suggestion, sublimated fears, and any number of other factors as the (causal) reasons why that person behaved as she did.

In what follows we shall not be primarily concerned with the causes of human behavior. Rather, we shall be concerned with the justificatory concept of what a person had reason to do whether or not that person acted as a result of having those reasons. The distinction between justificatory reasons and causal reasons for acting can become blurred, however, for as we shall see in a moment there *is* a concept of acting rationally which is conceptually tied to the causes of the agent's action.

Justificatory Reasons

The concept of reason we are interested in first is the one relevant to a determination of what it would be *rational* to do. It seems almost self-

---

1. There is a useful discussion of the contrast between justificatory reasons and other sorts of reasons in Darwall 1983, chap. 2.

evident that one can define rational action in terms of the concept of reasons for acting. More specifically, we might begin by suggesting that a person S is acting rationally in doing X only when S has more reason to choose X than any of its alternatives. It might be appropriate, however, immediately to qualify this suggestion by noting that it is intended to capture only an "ideal" concept of acting rationally. In ordinary discourse, our standards for rational action are probably much looser. We might allow that a person has acted rationally even if there were things that he had even more reason to do, provided that the action he took was among the "leading contenders" for the most rational action. The concept of "leading contender" is, of course, irremediably vague. But if we can successfully define what one has the most reason to do, we will have surely understood the continuum along which actions can be viewed as more or less rational. In what follows I continue to make the simplifying assumption that an action is rational only if it is what the agent had the most reason to do.

Again, S's having more reason to do X than anything else may not be *sufficient* for S's acting rationally, that is S's acting *with* or *for* those reasons.[2] My primary goal here is to understand what it is for there to *be* justificatory reasons for S to do X. I am not initially trying to say what it is for S to be acting with or for those reasons. One can have reasons for acting without acting on those reasons, just as one can have reasons for believing something without having the relevant belief. Furthermore, one can do what one has the most reason to do even though the action is caused by factors that have nothing to do with those reasons, just as one can believe what one has the most reason to believe even though the belief is caused by factors having nothing to do with those reasons. As a result, certain ambiguities arise concerning the terms "rational action" and "rational belief". In what follows I shall try to reserve the term "acting rationally" for actions that are caused in the appropriate way— I'll say more about what the appropriate way is later. I shall use the terms "action for which the agent has reasons" or simply "rational action" to describe an agent's action when there exist reasons for that agent to act whether or not he acted because of those reasons. It should be obvious that if we do define acting rationally in terms of how the

2. In "Acting for Reasons," Audi makes this distinction clearly. As the title of the article implies, he is concerned with analyzing what it is to act for reasons and convincingly argues that an action must be guided by relevant desires and beliefs if the agent is to be acting for reasons. I shall develop my own understanding of acting for reasons shortly.

agent's reasons for acting causally affect his action, then the concept of acting rationally is parasitic on the concept of rational action.

Our first task, then, is to analyze what it means to say of someone S that he has more reason to do X than any of its alternatives. And we might begin this task with the still more modest task of analyzing the concept of having *a* reason for doing X. Just as one can have reasons for believing P at the same time one has reasons for believing not-P, so one can obviously have reasons for doing X at the same time one has reasons for not doing X. Deciding what one would be epistemically justified in believing and what one would be rational in doing involves *weighing* the reasons for and against the belief and action, respectively.

For those of us sympathetic to the Humean idea that only the subjective states of a person can ultimately give that person a reason to act, the following might seem like a natural analysis of the concept of having a reason for acting:

(D1) S has a reason for doing   = Df   Either X is an end for S or
      X. X has as either a logical or
               a nomological conse-
               quence some Y which is
               an end for S.

The above analysis obviously relies on the critical concept of an *end* or a *goal*. Eventually, we must say what it is for something to be an end for someone and we must answer objections to building our conception of rational action on the foundation of goals or ends. As must already be clear from previous remarks, I want to defend the relativistic view that the concept of a goal or end must always be relativized to a given individual. An end is always an end *for* someone or some group. And it should be equally apparent that I want to analyze X's being an end for S in terms of X's being something that S *wants* or *values* for its own sake.

On the approach we are pursuing, it is ends that partially define reasons *for* acting, where these ends are defined in terms of what one values intrinsically. Reasons against acting would presumably be partially defined in terms of what we *disvalue* intrinsically. Unfortunately, there is no convenient antonym for "end" or "goal", and though we talk about an action's satisfying an agent's ends or goals, there is no parallel locution to describe an action's producing that which one intrinsically disvalues. In what follows I sometimes refer to an action's (actually, probably, possibly) frustrating some end. On its most natural interpretation, to say that an action frustrates an agent's end is to say that the action prevents the occurrence of some Y that the agent values intrinsically. However, let us use the locution in a broader technical sense and allow that an action can frustrate an agent's end by producing that which the agent intrinsically disvalues.[3]

In what follows I usually focus, for simplicity, on the positive concept of reasons for acting, but the reader should assume that everything I say about what one values intrinsically and its relation to having reasons for acting applies mutatis mutandis to what one disvalues intrinsically and its relation to having reasons against acting. In *weighing* reasons for acting, one will obviously have to consider both consequences that one intrinsically values and consequences that one intrinsically disvalues.

Because I want to define what a person has reason to do by reference to what that person values intrinsically, I believe it is essentially unintelligible to raise questions about the *intrinsic* rationality of a person's goals or ends. Ends or intrinsic valuings are the ultimate appeals on all questions of rational behavior. *There is no higher court to which one can appeal in judging the rationality of the fact that one intrinsically values something.* This is obviously one of the most controversial moves in the view I am developing. We must eventually analyze this concept of intrinsic value in much more detail, and we must respond to the claim that one can and must introduce the concept of irrational wants or values. But for dialectical reasons I want to postpone that discussion. For now, I ask the reader to presuppose the concept of an end sketched above so that I may introduce some ambiguities in the concept of having a reason for acting. These ambiguities are in turn reflected in alternative possible conceptions of rational action. Once we attempt to resolve a number of controversies that arise *within* the framework I am presupposing, we shall return to some of the more controversial assumptions that define that framework.

Definition (D1) allows that we can value an action for its own sake and asserts that S has a reason to do X when either X is an end for S (is intrinsically valued by S) or has as either a logical or a causal consequence some other state of affairs Y which is an end for S. Given this

---

3. It *may* be that whenever we say that Y is disvalued intrinsically we can also say that the nonoccurrence of Y is intrinsically valued, but these do not seem to be analytically equivalent. Consequently, it is not clear to me that one can *translate* X producing something Y that is intrinsically disvalued into some alternative to X producing not-Y that is intrinsically valued. In other words, it is not clear to me that one can translate talk about the reasons against doing X into talk about reasons for taking some alternative to X.

concept of having a reason to act, there may be reasons for me to do X even though I would have no reason at all to believe that these reasons exist. Indeed, it might be that I could take some action X that would accomplish one of my goals despite the fact that I have every reason to believe that X would frustrate that goal. It could, for example, turn out that the medical researchers miscalculated and that the surest way to avoid high blood pressure is to maintain high salt intake. All experiments to date failed to take account of a hidden variable, and the researchers and everyone who trusted them had justified false beliefs about the consequences of high-salt diets. Now though I believe there is a concept of reason that is perfectly compatible with our characterizing the above situation as being one in which there were reasons no one knew about to maintain a high-salt diet, it seems equally obvious to me that our *justified* false beliefs about the detrimental effects of too much salt in one's diet also give us a reason to avoid high-salt diets. And if we want to analyze a concept of reason for acting which is compatible with that intuition, still within the framework of reasons defined by goals, we might consider the following analysis of having a reason to act:

> (D2) S has a reason for doing $=$Df S is justified in believing
> X.   that either X is an end for
> S or that X has as either a
> logical or nomological
> consequence some Y
> which is an end for S.

If we assume that avoiding pain is one of my ends, in this sense of reason we may say that my justified belief that high salt intake will lead to serious disease and subsequent suffering gives me a reason to avoid high salt intake.

One might plausibly argue that (D2) is too restrictive in characterizing what we might call the concept of reason constrained by epistemic considerations. Specifically, one might argue that there is surely a sense in which I can have a reason for doing something X even when I have rather good evidence indicating that X will frustrate all of my goals (and even when it is *true* that X will frustrate all of my goals). We often take the fact that an action *might* accomplish some end to be a perfectly salient reason to consider in calculating whether or not to pursue that action. The standard lottery examples are perhaps the clearest way to make the point. Suppose, for the argument, that I know that the more money I have the happier I will be and that my happiness is one of my ends. If I have the opportunity of entering a lottery for the cost of a dollar with a prize of one million dollars and odds of only ten to one against winning, I surely have a rather powerful reason to enter the lottery. And I have this reason even if it is true and I am justified in believing that it is true that I will be poorer for my participation. To capture this obvious sense in which I can have reasons that depend not only on probabilities but also on possibilities, we might broaden (D2):

(D3) S has a reason for doing   =Df   Relative to S's evidence, it
     X.   might be the case that X is
                                        an end for S or has as ei-
                                        ther a logical or causal
                                        consequence some Y
                                        which is and end for S.

Although it is the concepts of having a reason to act defined by (D1), (D2), and (D3) which form the most plausible candidates for the building blocks of an analysis of rational action, there is another less interesting concept of having a reason to act which finds expression in ordinary discourse and which works its way into some philosophers' conceptions of rational action. Sometimes when we characterize a person's reasons for acting we intend merely to call attention to the goals that person was *trying* to accomplish through his action. And we do this without intending to comment on whether it was true that the action would accomplish these goals or whether the person had any reason to believe that it would or might accomplish these goals. On the assumption that one can try to bring about Y by doing X only if one believes that X will or might bring about Y,[4] we might try to capture this sense of reason as follows:

(D4) S has a reason for doing   =Df S believes that it either is
     X.   or might be the case that
                                        X is an end for S or that X
                                        has as either a logical or
                                        nomological consequence
                                        some Y which is an end
                                        for S.

4. Searle (1983, p. 104) argues that intentions to do X presuppose at least a belief in the possibility of success.

Notice that all of these concepts of having a reason for acting leave open the possibility that one might not know what one's ends are, that is, one might not know what one values intrinsically. Although this is a somewhat unusual view within the tradition I represent, I argue later that, given certain plausible conceptions of intrinsic value, one can indeed be hard pressed to know what one values intrinsically.

We have four possible ways of understanding the concept of having a reason to act. We have tentatively decided that we might understand rational action as that action the agent had the most reason to choose (from among the available alternatives). Since there can be reasons for and against taking a given course of action, the concept of rational action will involve the concept of *weighing* reasons. Because I am interested in eventually uniting the concepts of rationality and morality, it should come as no surprise that the way in which the different concepts of weighted reasons determine the rationality of action will parallel the actual, probable, and value adjusted possible consequence act generic utilitarian conceptions of what one morally ought to do (see Chapter 2). Just as the generic utilitarian relied on the idea that intrinsic goodness admits of degrees, so too we will suppose that a person's ends can vary in strength—in some sense, ends may be ranked. S may value some state of affairs X for itself, and some state of affairs Y for itself, and yet value X more than Y. What this amounts to must again await our more detailed discussion of what it is for something to be valued intrinsically.

Let us also suppose that when an action (actually, probably, possibly) satisfies or frustrates more than one end, it makes sense to talk of "adding" the positive and negative reasons a person has for taking that action to get the collective weight of reasons. Each of (D1) through (D4) represents a conception of reasons for acting which in turn suggests a corresponding account of how to calculate the collective weight of the relevant reasons for and against taking a given course of action. All of the concepts of having a reason to act which we distinguished take into account the satisfaction and frustration of ends, but they do so in different ways. And these different ways force a different understanding of how to "add" positive and negative reasons. Thus if we understand a reason to act as in (D1) and analyze the rational action as that action the agent has more reason to choose than any of its alternatives, we get the following actual consequence act consequentialist analysis of rational action:

(R1) S has more reason to   =Df   The collective weight of

| choose X than any of its alternatives. | S's ends that would be satisfied or frustrated by X is greater than the collective weight of his ends that would be satisfied or frustrated by any of the alternatives to X. |

Let us say that an end is satisfied by X when that end is either a logical[5] or a causal consequence of X so that if X is valued intrinsically, X will, as a logical consequence of itself, satisfy at least one end.

Given (R1), then, the rationality of an agent's action is a function of the number and strength of the goals that agent has which would actually be satisfied or frustrated by the action. If we think of positive and negative numbers as representing satisfied and frustrated goals, respectively, where the size of the number represents the importance of the goal (the degree to which it is valued intrinsically), then the collective weight of reasons for doing X would be metaphorically represented by the addition of these positive and negative numbers. The sum would be compared to the collective weight of ends satisfied and frustrated by alternative actions, and the action that would yield the greatest net "gain" wins the contest of rationality. In cases of ties, more than one alternative will presumably be equally rational. Although useful, the idea of representing the strength of a goal by numbers, the process of calculating collective weight as addition, obviously lends a highly misleading air of precision to what is an inherently vague idea. I have more to say about this when we finally get around to that promised discussion of goals or ends.

The concept of reason defined by (D2) suggests, of course, a probable consequence act consequentialist account of rational action:

| (R2) S has more reason to choose X than any of its alternatives. | =Df | S is justified in believing that the collective weight of S's ends that would be satisfied (frustrated) by X is greater than the collective weight of the ends that would be satisfied (frustrated) by any of the alternatives to X. |

5. I attach a broad sense to "logical consequence". It includes tautological, analytic, and even synthetic entailment.

The addition of satisfied and frustrated ends would be understood just as in (R1), but this time the relevant consequences are those that are *probable* relative to the agent's evidence.

The analogous account of rational action implied by the concept of reason defined by (D4) takes into account ends *believed* to be satisfied or frustrated by an action, ignoring the question of whether those beliefs are true or justified:

> (R4) *S* has more reason to choose *X* than any of its alternatives.   =Df   *S* believes that the collective weight of *S*'s ends satisfied (frustrated) by *X* is greater than the collective weight of the ends that would be satisfied (frustrated) by any of its alternatives.

Because it is the most complicated, I save to last the analysis of rational action suggested by the concept of reason defined by (D3). Obviously, in weighing the reasons defined by (D3) for and against taking a given course of action, one must "add" the value of the ends that *might* (relative to the agent's evidence) be satisfied or frustrated by the action. But if both actions *X* and *Y* might satisfy some end *E*, it would be absurd to assign the same value to *E* in our calculations if *E* was much more likely to occur as a result of *X* than as a result of *Y*. We clearly need the familiar notion of weighting the value of possible outcomes for the probability or improbability of their occurring. Intuitively, if *E* is an end that might be satisfied by *X*, we not only must calculate how much we value *E* (we must rank *E* on our scale of value), but must subsequently adjust the value downward for the probability of its occurring. The less likely it is that *X* will produce *E*, the less of its value we take into account in calculating the reasons we have for choosing *X*. Again, it is highly misleading to employ a mathematical model for what is an inherently vague idea, but the widely accepted concept of multiplying value by probability seems a useful way to indicate how we must "downgrade" the possible satisfaction of an end for the probability of its occurring. We get, then, the following analysis of rational action:

(R3) *S* has more reason to   =Df   The collective weight of
     choose *X* over any of its   *S*'s ends that might (rela-
     alternatives.   tive to *S*'s evidence) be sat-
                                     isfied (frustrated) by *X*,
                                     when the value of each end
                                     is adjusted for the proba-
                                     bility (relative to *S*'s evi-
                                     dence) of its occurring, is
                                     greater than the collective
                                     weight of the ends calcu-
                                     lated in a similar fashion
                                     that might (relative to *S*'s
                                     evidence) be satisfied by
                                     any of the alternatives
                                     to *X*.

The conception of rational action sketched by (R4) obviously admits of a similar treatment. Rather than treat equally all of the ends believed to be satisfied by *X*, it might be more plausible to assign these ends a value whose strength depends at least partly on the strength of the belief concerning its satisfaction. Indeed, the reason I avoid using the familiar locution "maximizing expected utility" to refer to the conception of rational action captured by (R3) is that more often than not people have in mind something more like the modified version of (R4), where even when one believes that an end will likely not be satisfied, one still assigns that outcome *believed* to be possible a value that depends on how strongly one believes that it will not occur. Let us call this more sophisticated version of (R4), (R4*).

Which of (R1) through (R4*) offers the most plausible analysis of rational action? In answering the question, we might do well to remember that, even if one rejects the identification of moral action with rational action, one must surely admit that there is a remarkable parallel between the different act consequentialist conceptions of rational action sketched above and the different generic act utilitarian conceptions of morally right action outlined in Chapter 2. The parallel strikes me as a powerful reason for trying to conceptually link these two frameworks, but whether one agrees with this or not, I think the arguments we shall consider below in choosing between (R1) through (R4*) apply mutatis mutandis to actual, probable, and value adjusted possible generic act utilitarian conceptions of right action. It will be useful, then, to consider these questions concerning consequentialist analyses of rational action and morally right action together.

The most striking feature of actual consequence act consequentialist conceptions of rational and right action is that the rational or right action for an individual to take might well be one which he had every reason to believe would be disastrous. (In discussing the following examples, presuppose conventional views about which things are intrinsically good and suppose that these goods are also ends for the agents in question.) Given actual consequence act consequentialist conceptions of rational and right action, it might turn out that the rational and morally right action for Jones, my bored neighbor, is to visit the local shopping mall, point his shotgun at the first person he sees, and pull the trigger. It might be that the person he kills is a deranged terrorist about to detonate a nuclear device that would destroy millions of innocent lives, in which case Jones's action might well produce more of value than any of the alternatives open to him. But obviously, most of us would characterize Jones's action as neither rational nor morally right unless we thought that Jones had some reason to believe that his action would have these effects. Given the intuitive force of this objection, it is surprising to me that so many philosophers take seriously actual consequence analyses of reasons for action and of rational and moral action. John Rawls, for example, seems to identify a rational plan of life for a person as one "which would be chosen by him with full deliberative rationality" (Rawls 1971:408). And he later suggests that the calculations that define the hypothetical state of full deliberative rationality involve "no errors of calculation or reasoning . . . the facts are correctly assessed" (p. 417). In *Impartial Reason,* Stephen Darwall appears to defend an initial account of reasons for acting according to which "any consideration that would move an agent to act were she to 'bring it to mind with full belief and maximal vividness' is a reason for her to act" (p. 99). Because the counterfactual conditionals that define rationality or reasons to act, on these views, ignore the actual epistemic situation of the agent, it would seem to follow that it is possible for conduct to be rational despite the fact that the agent had no reason to believe that its consequences would be better (valued more) than those of its alternatives—indeed, despite the fact that the agent had every reason to believe that the consequences would be far worse. If I were to know all of the information that bears on some decision, I might well act in ways that in fact I have every reason to believe would be disastrous. But surely we want to make the rational/right course of action for me to take a function of my epistemic situation.

Now I am not arguing that there is *no* ambiguity in the concept of having a reason to act and the corresponding concept of what one rationally ought to do. It is certainly the case that such judgments often *appear* to reflect a concern with *actual* consequences, ignoring the epistemic perspective of the agent. Suppose, for example, I am in a high-stakes poker game and, following conventional poker wisdom, I fold rather than draw hoping to fill an inside straight. When I discover that, if only I had not folded, the card I would have drawn would not only fill my straight but win the biggest pot of the evening, observers might well comment that I should not have folded. *I* will no doubt think to myself, "Oh, my God, I should have drawn the card!" On the other hand, if people start to chide me for my "irrational" decision, I will eventually point out that only a fool gambles good money in an effort to fill inside straights. I will, in other words, defend my action as being rational, as being precisely the action one ought to take in situations like the one I was in. I am not sure whether the above considerations point to a genuine ambiguity in the concept of rationality or simply indicate the confused, (epistemically) irrational way in which a great many people make their value judgments.

In the context of moral judgments, this same "schizophrenia" in the common person's evaluation of right and wrong is even more evident. Parents think that children shouldn't throw footballs near the picture window in the living room. But we all know that parents tend to raise rather drastically their evaluation of the moral impropriety of this behavior after the window gets shattered into a thousand pieces. Even if the unfortunate children had the philosophical sophistication to point out that the only difference between today's heinous behavior and yesterday's mischievous behavior is a matter of bad luck, it probably wouldn't do them any good. It is notoriously difficult for people to ignore what actually happens and consider instead what was *likely* to have happened relative to the agent's epistemic situation. When the president of the United States supports a policy that actually has disastrous consequences, far worse than would have occurred had he taken alternatives open to him, the majority of people will conclude that these policies were wrong. Had the president acted in that same way with that same body of evidence and produced good results instead, these same people would proclaim the policy worthy of their support. Had Carter's rescue attempt of the hostages in Iran succeeded (whether through sheer luck or not), he probably would have been reelected president. If the bomb truck that killed the marines in Lebanon had not detonated, Reagan's Lebanon policy might have been hailed as a success, a clear example of a president doing what he ought to have done. Even our laws, which one would assume are formulated by people more reflective and sophisticated than the majority of those questioned in national polls, seem to reflect a curious emphasis on actual, as opposed to rationally foreseen, consequences. The would-be assassin who has the misfortune to have his bullet deflected in midflight by a wayward seagull is punished less severely than the successful assassin. And one presumes that the rationale involves the judgment that the latter is guilty of a more seriously wrong action than the former. The drunk driver who makes it home safely is punished *much* less severely than a similar driver who through bad luck hits and kills someone on the way home. Again, if we suppose that views on appropriate punishment reflect views about the seriousness of the wrongdoing, it is difficult to escape the conclusion that people are evaluating at least some actions on the basis of what actually happens as a result of those actions, ignoring the evidential perspective of the agent.

Do the above observations suggest that we sometimes think of moral and rational action defined in terms of actual consequences? Perhaps, but I think it much more likely that it reflects only the fact that ordinary people, and even intellectuals who should know better, are simply not very (epistemically) rational in trying to reach retrospective conclusions about what people rationally or morally ought to have done. I am relatively confident that careful and patient argument will usually suc-ceed in getting people to realize that their own concepts of rationality and morality require that they should pay less attention to what actually happens, more attention to what was likely (relative to the agent's evidence) to have happened.

Of course, retrospective epistemic judgments about what an agent was justified in believing are often harder to make than retrospective judgments about what actually happened as a result of an agent's action. Moreover, one might argue that in some contexts it is reasonable to take what actually happens as one of the best indicators of what was likely to have happened. But when one realizes that the likelihood we should be concerned with is likelihood relative to the agent's (almost always tiny) body of evidence, it should be obvious that the principle that usually what happens was likely to have happened is simply false.

Those moral philosophers who support an actual consequence act conception of right action nearly always try to "soften" the view and make it more palatable by distinguishing sharply the concept of a good person from the concept of a person who (usually) does the right thing.[6] The good person, it will be argued, should be understood in terms of her *intentions*. The good person is the person who tries to do the right thing, who acts believing that she is doing the right thing. Praise and criticism, reward and punishment, the argument continues, is much more appropriately tied to evaluation of a person's motives in acting rather than the rightness or wrongness of her action.

This distinction between good people and people who do the right thing is one that should be made even given conceptions of right action which insist on taking into account the agent's epistemic perspective. I certainly wouldn't want to view a person as a morally bad person just because that person is too stupid to understand what was probable or possible relative to his evidence, for example. And making a distinction between evaluation of the moral character of an agent and evaluation of his action *might* deflect some of the force behind the obvious counterexamples to actual consequence views discussed earlier. We criticize *Jones* for acting as he did in the mall, we are morally outraged at *him* for doing what he did, because we cannot reconcile his behavior with that of a *well-intentioned* person. But we shouldn't confuse our evaluation of Jones through our evaluation of his intentions with the question of what makes an action right. A good person tries to do the right thing. And what does this amount to? Well, surely a good person tries to bring about the most possible good. But this implies that the right action, the action the good person tries to perform, is, after all, the action that would bring about the most good.

Of course, if we *do* define right action in terms of what would actually produce the best consequences, and rational action in terms of what would actually maximize satisfaction of ends, it is going to be extremely difficult for a person ever to figure out what he morally or rationally should do. Since the consequences of our actions go on and on (far beyond any point we can foresee), one can certainly sympathize with the actual consequence generic utilitarian, Moore, when he despaired of ever knowing what we ought to do.[7] Now at a certain level, I am actually highly sympathetic with philosophical skepticism concerning

6. On this obvious distinction, see Mill 1957, pp. 23–26, and Moore 1912, chap. 5.
7. See Moore 1903, chap. 5.

the possibility of making rational nondeductive inferences, but I do think that a plausible analysis of ordinary concepts should at least try to accommodate people's *beliefs* concerning judgments that employ these concepts. As I pointed out in Chapter 1, people at least think that there is such a thing as justified belief and have at least dispositional beliefs about nondeductive evidential connections. Furthermore, most people seem to think that on occasion they have enough evidence from which to rationally conclude that they (rationally/morally) ought to take a given course of action. These same people know full well that they cannot possibly know what all of the consequences of their actions will be. They know that the consequences of having a child, for example, might extend, literally, into an infinite future. It would seem, then, that actual consequence act conceptions of rational or moral action will have a difficult time explaining why people believe what they do with respect to the possibility of reaching justified conclusions about what they rationally/morally ought to do.

The actual consequence act consequentialist might try to deflect at least some of the force of the above argument by making a distinction between being able to rationally conclude that we (rationally/morally) ought to do X and being able to conclude that it is more likely that we (rationally/morally) ought to do X than that we ought to take any particular alternative to X. Put another way, one may rationally conclude that of the alternatives to X, A_1 through A_n, it is likely that either A_1, or A_2, or . . . A_n will be a better alternative than X, and at the same time insist that X is more likely (given the available evidence) to be a better alternative than A_1, than A_2, and than A_n. One might further argue that, for a conception of rational/right action to be *useful* in guiding action, this is all that is required. An analogy might be helpful. Suppose that A, B, C, and D are in a coin-tossing contest. Each will toss his coin a thousand times, and the winner will be the one who gets the most heads. After observing the first three tosses of each participant, I am *forced* to bet on who will win (just as in life we are *forced* to make choices—even inaction is a de facto decision with consequences). Now suppose that on the first three tosses A got two heads and the others got two tails. As a rational person, on whom should I bet? The answer seems obvious. A is ever so slightly more likely to win than B, than C, and than D. Of course, it is also true that it is even more likely that either B or C or D will beat A, but knowing this does not affect the rationality of my bet on A.

Now this example parallels, one might argue, our epistemic situation vis-à-vis placing "bets" on rational/right action. Although we cannot know all, or even very many, of the consequences of our actions, we can see into relatively near possible futures and compare the hypothetical consequences of alternative actions as far as we *can* see. One of these alternatives may well have better foreseeable consequences than the others, and we can, on that basis, conclude that since we *must* do something (again, inaction counts as doing something in this context) the action with the best foreseeable consequences is the most promising candidate for being the rational/right thing to do. The actual consequence act consequentialist can argue, then, that we do think of the rational/right action as being a function of what would actually happen as a result of doing it compared to doing something else. Our "commonsense" beliefs that we can reach justifiable conclusions concerning what is rational/right to do simply reflect in a somewhat misleading way our belief that we can rationally believe that (of the alternatives) an action has the best (not very good, but the best) chance of being the rational/right action to take.

This is, I think, the best that an actual consequence act consequentialist can do as far as reconciling his analysis of rational/right action with our prephilosophical beliefs about what we can rationally believe concerning rational/right action. Still, it is not very good. As should be obvious from the above discussion, we must still conclude that the view entails skepticism with respect to what we (rationally/morally) ought to do. Given our beliefs about what makes likely what, one will rarely be in a position to rationally conclude that the most promising candidate for being the rational/right action is the rational/right action. It is so tempting to embrace the obvious and admit that in any event one surely *ought* to choose the most promising candidate for having the best consequences. But if one makes this admission, one in effect abandons the actual consequence view, for the "ought" employed in the judgment that one ought to back the alternative with the best chance of having the best consequences clearly reflects something more like a probable consequence act consequentialist view.

If the choice were between actual consequence and probable consequence act consequentialist analyses of rational and right conduct, it might be worth pursuing further this debate. But the reasons we have for preferring value adjusted possible consequence views to probable consequence views themselves provide decisive reasons for rejecting actual consequence conceptions of rational/right action, at least when conceptions of rational or right action are intended to be relevant to rational people concerned with making choices.

Consider again that lottery that we have a reason to enter only if reasons can include unlikely but possible valued outcomes. The lottery costs a dollar to enter, the odds against winning are ten to one, and the prize is a million dollars. (In thinking about the example, altruistic readers can imagine spending the money on noble causes; egoistic readers can imagine spending it on themselves.) Obviously, we can hypothesize a similar sort of choice in a more paradigmatic moral setting. We can send ten good people on a mission to assassinate one very bad leader. There is a ninety percent probability that all ten will die for nothing, but a ten percent chance that the mission will succeed and will, by overturning the tyranny, save millions of innocent lives.

Now concepts of rational/right action are important for the rational/moral person because that person is going to try to guide his life by the conclusions he reaches concerning what is most likely to be the rational/right action. Since I know that the probability is that entering the lottery will cost me a dollar for nothing, I would not enter the lottery if I were trying my best to act rationally in the senses defined by either (R1) or (R2). If I were trying my hardest to choose the action with the best consequences, the most likely way to succeed is to choose the action that will probably have the best consequences. Conversely, if I decide that an action will have the best consequences, I am surely committed, as a rational person, to the belief that, relative to my evidence, it will probably have the best consequences. From the perspective of an agent trying to make a decision and committed to the rational/right choice of action, it shouldn't make the slightest difference whether that agent is an actual or a probable consequence consequentialist. It is only in second- and third-person value judgments, and in retrospective first-person value judgments (judgments about what I ought to have done), that the conceptual distinction between actual and probable consequence consequentialist views makes a practical difference to the value judgments one makes. So again, both actual and probable consequence consequentialist views of rational/right action would force us to conclude that we (rationally) should not enter the lottery and (morally) should not send in the assassination squad. But we agreed earlier that it would be manifestly *irrational* not to enter that lottery with the tiny cost, the relatively good odds, and the huge payoff.

Only an idiot would turn down such an opportunity. And it would surely be just as outrageous not to risk the ten good soldiers for the one-in-ten probability of saving millions of other good people. The latter might seem more controversial but only because the hypothetical situation is so far-fetched. We know full well one can rarely overturn tyrannies by killing tyrants and that, consequently, the one-in-ten probability is grossly unrealistic.[8]

If you are an act consequentialist and want to act in the way you judge to be (probably) rational, then the conception of rationality required would seem to be the value adjusted possible consequence view defined by (R3). If you are an act consequentialist and want to act in the way you judge to be (probably) right, then the conception of moral rightness required would seem to be value adjusted possible consequence generic act utilitarianism. It is these conceptions of rational/right conduct which allow you to conclude that it is rational to enter the lottery, right to risk the ten lives.

Again, I would not assert categorically that we never employ a concept of rational/right action defined in terms of actual consequences. As I indicated earlier, we sometimes seem to emphasize the importance of what actually happens as a result of an agent's action. It is, however, an open question as to whether this appearance reflects the genuine use of an actual consequence conception of rationality/morality. It is just as likely, I argue, that one could correctly describe the situation as one in which people are confused about what they mean by "ought" and fail rather miserably in their efforts to reach epistemically rational retrospective conclusions about what people ought to have done. Careful, patient argument might convince them that there is only one plausible conception of rational action and that they often reach mistaken conclusions in their attempts to employ that concept. In any event, careful argument should convince them that the concept of rational action *relevant to first-person choice* is that defined by (R3). (I'll explain the reason for emphasizing first-person choice when I discuss ambiguities of perspective.)

The only act consequentialist analysis of rationality we have not discussed is that defined by (R4) and (R4*). These views about what makes action rational obviously suggest parallel metaethical analyses of

8. In "Ethical Theory and Utilitarianism," Hare stresses the importance of taking with a grain of salt one's immediate "intuitive" responses to these sorts of unrealistic hypothetical situations. See pp. 31–33.

morally right action which we might call subjective consequence act generic utilitarianism and value adjusted subjective possible consequence act utilitarianism. On the former (the metaethical analogue of [R4]), the morally right thing for an agent to do is that action he *believes* will have the best consequences. On the latter (the more sophisticated analogue of [R4*]), the right thing to do will be a function of what is believed by the agent to be possible good and bad consequences of that action where the amount of goodness or badness is adjusted downward for the agent's subjective conception of the odds.

The former view is, of course, subject to the same problem facing actual and probable consequence consequentialist views. In lotteries with reasonable odds, we surely want it to be possible for rational people to take gambles even when they believe that they will not succeed. We can concentrate, then, on (R4*) and its metaethical equivalent.

The most striking feature of these views is, of course, the fact that it makes reaching conclusions about what one rationally/morally ought to do a matter of reaching conclusions about what one *believes*. Now I take it that the judgments we make about what we ourselves rationally/morally ought to do have at least the following related features:

(1) Such judgments are often not trivial, not the sort of thing we can settle merely through an introspective check of our attitudes and beliefs.

(2) In trying to decide what we ought to do, we often feel we need to consider all of the empirical evidence at our disposal concerning the consequences of alternative actions, and insofar as we are not sure we have carefully considered all of the evidence we possess, we feel corresponding uncertainty as to the truth of the judgment about what ought to be done.

(3) After reaching the tentative conclusion that we ought to do X rather than Y, we are often prepared to admit that we might be mistaken and at some later time may even decide that we were. And this fear of error is consistent with our being quite certain about the nature of our *beliefs* concerning the outcomes of alternative actions.

These features of our first-person value judgments argue strongly against making what we have reason to do a function of what we believe, rightly or wrongly, justifiably or unjustifiably, about the means to achieve our ends. Given (R4) and (R4*), discovering what is rational or right to do is no more problematic than finding out what one believes about the consequences of our actions and performing the relevant "mathematical" computations. The rationality/morality of our action will not be affected no matter how much evidence we ignore, no matter how careless we are in the evaluation of that evidence, no matter how *irrational* our beliefs are.

Now I am not arguing that the conceptions of rational/right action understood as a function of subjective probabilities do not allow any possibility of error with respect to first-person value judgments. Although some philosophers seem to presuppose a privileged epistemic status for our beliefs about our beliefs, it doesn't follow that whenever we believe something we believe that we believe it. Certainly, if the concept of belief is construed broadly enough to include dispositional belief, we may well be ignorant of many of the things we believe. If, for example, we try to define dispositional belief in terms of subjunctive conditionals (one dispositionally believes *P* if one would occurrently believe *P* were one to consider it),[9] knowing what one dispositionally believes would involve knowing the truth of these subjunctive conditionals. But I would still argue that (R4) and (R4*) clearly ignore some sources of error in the making of value judgments. More specifically, they ignore the extent to which epistemic irrationality infects practical rationality.

The concepts of rational and moral action are *normative concepts*. When we judge that someone is making decisions rationally, we are giving our seal of approval to the decision-making mechanism, so to speak. But surely a part of the decision-making mechanism involves a careful, *epistemically rational* evaluation of the evidence we possess concerning the possible outcomes of our actions. And if that part of the mechanism is defective, the whole decision-making procedure is defective and the individual is unlikely to be able to act rationally. One can, of course, try to bolster this conclusion by giving examples of paradigmatic irrational behavior where the apparent source of irrationality is epistemically irrational belief. The fanatic who beats his child in an effort to exorcise the devil acts irrationally even if, given his *beliefs*, this

9. There are obviously difficulties with such an analysis. Can we not make a distinction between dispositional beliefs that we already have and beliefs we would have were we to consider certain propositions for the first time? It is also true given the subjunctive analysis that one *always* dispositionally believes that one is entertaining a proposition.

would turn out to be a perfectly rational (and, indeed, moral) action as defined by subjective conceptions of rational (moral) action. For all I know, it might follow from the subjective conceptions of rational and moral action that Adolf Hitler was acting rationally and morally in trying to exterminate a whole race. Who knows what a person that crazy believes and who cares? The manifest irrationality of Hitler's apparent beliefs is a sufficient reason to conclude that actions based on those beliefs are irrational.

As I indicated in another context, one should not confuse the issue discussed above with issues concerning the blameworthiness or praise-worthiness of the *person* who behaves rationally (irrationally) or morally (immorally). And as I also indicated earlier, there may be many good reasons to tie punishment more closely to the character of a person than to the character of his acts. I was arguing above that a person too stupid to reach epistemically rational conclusions will have a very difficult time acting rationally. But one certainly doesn't need to blame people for being stupid and for acting irrationally. To criticize an *action* as being irrational or to criticize a *belief* as being irrational is not necessarily to blame the person who acts and believes irrationally. If we think such a person is too stupid to be affected by stimulus/response behavior modi-fication, we may pity rather than punish the person. But none of this gives us a reason for turning to subjective conceptions of consequences in the analysis of rational/right action, unless we perversely insist on tying our evaluation of actions to evaluation of an agent's character.

Of the different act consequentialist analyses of rational and right action, then, the value adjusted possible consequence view would seem to be the most promising.

Let us leave again the theory of morality and questions concerning its relation to the theory of rational action until later and focus on the value adjusted possible consequence account of practical rationality. Ques-tions have yet to be raised concerning some of the fundamental features of that account. In the next chapter we must reply to those who object to the *arational* character of goals or ends presupposed by the view. And in Chapter 6 we must consider a host of objections focusing on the *act* consequentialist features of not only the value adjusted possible conse-quence analysis of rational action but its metaethical counterpart as well. Doing this requires us to become clearer as to the concept of *alternative* actions, which we have hitherto taken for granted. But in the remainder of this chapter I want to explore some other very important ambiguities that should be noted and distinctions that can be made, all within the spirit of the general account suggested.

Ambiguities and Important Derivative Concepts of Rationality

Ambiguities of Perspective

Earlier I argued that (R3) is the most plausible concept of rational action relevant to understanding first-person choice. As promised, I want to explain that emphasis on the first-person perspective. Although I am confident that (R3) captures the most fundamental concept of rational action, one must be cautious in translating that account into the ordinary use of "ought". It does seem to me that when I ask myself what I (rationally) ought to do, I am asking myself what I have the most reason to do in the sense defined by (R3). But others sometimes ask me for advice concerning what *they* (rationally) ought to do. In such contexts, I sometimes have evidence that is more comprehensive than that of the person seeking advice, and consequently, what is probable relative to my evidence might be quite different from what is probable relative to the evidence of the agent whom I am about to advise. Now obviously, I *could* imaginatively consider the epistemic perspective of this agent, reach conclusions about what it would be rational for her to do (from that epistemic perspective), and advise her of these conclusions using the "ought" of reason. I might decide that relative to her epistemic perspective she (rationally) ought to do X. But if I have reason to believe that my evidence concerning possible outcomes is better than my friend's, and I care at all for her well-being, I am unlikely to tell her that she ought to do X when I believe that another course of action Υ is more likely to maximize satisfaction of my friend's ends when their value is suitably adjusted for probabilities relative to *my* evidence. Rather, I will probably tell her that she (rationally) ought to do Υ. Time permitting, I will probably give her the evidence I have that she lacks, evidence that will presumably give her reason to do what she previously had no reason to do.[10]

10. Richard Foley claims that similar ambiguities of perspective arise even in connection with assessments of epistemic rationality (1987, pp. 123–24). I think he is probably right, although I also think that the ambiguities are more pronounced when it comes to evaluations of practical rationality.

The point is a subtle one and invites confusion. Failure to be clear about it may be another source of misguided support for actual consequence consequentialist conceptions of rational/right action. One might be inclined to infer that, since in giving others advice about what they ought to do I often ignore what was likely relative to *their* evidence, I must be implicitly accepting the view that rational action is a function of what actually happens. But this conclusion would be doubly flawed. First, our lottery example still illustrates the necessity of construing rationality as a function not just of actual but of possible consequences. If my friend has failed to realize that the million-dollar lottery has extraordinarily good odds, I might tell him that he ought to enter the lottery even knowing that it is not the best thing for him to do from his epistemic perspective. But in giving my friend this advice, I adopt my own epistemic perspective vis-à-vis the possible outcomes of my friend's action concerning the satisfaction of my friend's goals or ends. I still do not concern myself only with what is likely to happen as I should if I am only concerned with reaching the best guess about actual consequences.

Furthermore, despite the fact that in offering advice to a friend I sometimes use my evidence base instead of his, there is still a clear sense in which it is my friend's evidence base that I must presuppose in evaluating the rationality of my friend's actions. If my friend rationally believes that high salt intake causes high blood pressure, and for that reason avoids a high-salt diet, I should acknowledge the rationality of his behavior. And I should acknowledge that rationality even if *I* know that high salt intake *prevents* high blood pressure. If I have the opportunity of giving him advice, I might express that advice by telling my friend that he *ought* to abandon his low-salt diet, but if I don't get the opportunity of offering this advice I will still think to myself that my friend is doing what he (rationally) ought to do, given his epistemic situation. So though "*S* rationally ought to do *X*" can be defined in terms of *S*'s having more reason to choose *X* than any of its alternatives in the sense analyzed by (R3), and though such a definition is in one sense perfectly adequate, there is another sense in which it fails to capture the content of second- and third-person value *statements* as opposed to judgments. The verbal *advice* I give to another concerning how he ought to behave often reflects my calculations concerning the collective weight of that person's ends that might be satisfied relative to *my* evidence, where the value of those ends is adjusted for their probability (relative to *my* evidence).

Although I have made the point in connection with second- and third-person advice conerning rational action, it should be obvious that the distinction applies equally well to second- and third-person moral advice. As I shall argue later, there is yet another ambiguity of perspective which enters particularly into second- and third-person moral judgments, but which is also sometimes present in second- and third-person judgments of rationality, an ambiguity concerning whose *ends* we presuppose in giving advice. Just as when I reach conclusions about what Jones ought to do I can adopt either his epistemic perspective or my own, so too I can adopt either his system of ends or goals or my own. In questions concerning rationality, it seems to me obvious that the concept of rational action requires one to evaluate the rationality of an agent's action relative to that agent's goals or ends. If my friend cannot stand the taste of liver, I am hardly going to advise him that he rationally ought to order Liver Supreme at the local restaurant even though that is my favorite dish. The issue is more complicated with respect to paradigm moral contexts in which I am expressing my evaluation of another person's behavior when it becomes evident that that person has a radically different and, to me, highly distasteful set of goals or ends. This is a question we shall pursue in much more detail when we discuss the conceptual links between rationality and morality in the last chapter.

Ambiguities Involving Available Evidence

(R3) understands the rationality of an action as being relative to the agent's goals and epistemic perspective. The consequences that determine the rationality of an action compared to alternatives are those epistemically possible relative to the agent's evidence. And the amount a possible consequence's value is adjusted is a function of its probability relative to the agent's evidence. I have already outlined in a very general way my views about epistemic probability in Chapter 1. But there are ambiguities I have not discussed inherent in talk about what is possible or probable relative to an agent's evidence.

Suppose that my total body of evidence is E. E consists of all of the propositions I justifiably believe, where these beliefs can, of course, be occurrent or dispositional. And suppose, further, that my evidence base E contains information from which I *could* infer that action X will probably lead to Y, but I fail to realize that my evidence would allow me to infer that if X then probably Y. The situation I am imagining is not one in which I lack the wherewithal to realize that X makes probable Υ. I have the ability to recognize this evidential connection, but I simply haven't put two and two together. In the sense relevant to (R3), is Υ a probable (for me) consequence of my doing X? Although there *is* justification for me to believe that X will lead to Υ, there is also a sense in which the existence of that justification does not give me a justified belief that X will lead to Υ even if I believe (spontaneously, for example) that X will lead to Υ. There is one clear sense in which, even if there is an evidential connection between the things I know and some proposition P, P is not probable *for me* relative to that evidence unless I am aware of that evidential connection. Yet there is another clear sense in which I can realize later on, for example, that there was evidence available to me all along for believing P.

What sense of agent-relativized possibility and probability should be assumed in (R3)'s analysis of rational action (and its metaethical counterpart)? Because the question involves a relatively sophisticated philosophical distinction, it is probably foolish to suppose that there is any clear answer suggested by our ordinary way of evaluating the rationality of behavior. However, in the spirit of our objections to (R4) and the idea that normative evaluation of an action involves evaluation of the agent's decision-making procedure, I would suggest that agents who fail to realize the implications of the evidence they in fact have are clearly guilty of a kind of epistemic irrationality (at least exemplify a kind of epistemic defect) that infects the rationality of the decision-making procedure.

I should make clear that this point applies only to evidence the agent actually has in his possession. We could also broaden the concept of an agent's epistemic perspective to make the relevant probabilities and possibilities relative to all *available* evidence, where available evidence includes all the propositions the agent could come to know or justifiably believe.[11] But this would surely be a mistake. There is literally no end to the evidence we could accumulate which would bear on the probability of various outcomes of actions we contemplate. And it is obvious that rational people do not (could not) postpone decision making until they acquire all of the potentially relevant evidence they could get their hands on. But if this is true, then one cannot criticize the rationality of an

---

11. You recall that Rawls and Darwall seem to endorse the very strong thesis that the perspective that defines rational action includes knowledge of *all* the relevant facts.

agent's action by referring to the implications of evidence he does not possess and had no reason to acquire. At the same time, I would stress that we can evaluate the rationality of our decisions to forgo the accumulation of further evidence before acting. Failing to acquire more evidence about the outcomes of some action X itself has possible and probable consequences, and it may well be that, particularly in life-and-death situations, rational behavior requires painstakingly researching information that bears on the causal consequences of our actions. We might then be in the position of acknowledging that an agent acted rationally in choosing X over its alternatives but acted irrationally in not acquiring more evidence before he made his decision to do X. And again, in nonphilosophical contexts, this distinction might be blurred. We might well criticize the rationality of an agent's doing X because we realize that he was irrational in not being more diligent in the process leading up to the making of his decision.

Level Distinctions and Derivative Concepts of Rationality

There is another troubling, nearly always overlooked, question that arises concerning an attempt to understand the concept of rational action. The answer to that question will force us to recognize a Byzantine framework of derivative concepts of rational action. Suppose that we accept the conception of rational action sketched by (R3). Initially, it would seem that an agent can have a justified *false* belief that she has more reason to do X than anything else. To take a rather far-fetched example, suppose that she actually tries to mathematize her calculations, succeeds in calculating all of the relevant possible and probable consequences of all of the relevant alternatives, succeeds in adjusting the value of the possible consequences in the relevant ways, but even after double-checking her arithmetic makes a mechanical error in addition that leads her to the false conclusion that the accumulated adjusted value produced by X is greater than any of its alternatives. Assuming that one can have justified false beliefs about the correct sum of a set of numbers added together, what shall we say about the rationality of this agent's action X? It seems to me that we can at least feel a pull toward the conclusion that if an agent has an epistemically justified belief that she is doing the rational thing by doing X, then she *is* doing the rational thing by doing X. But if we reach this conclusion and allow that on (R3) one

can have justified *false* beliefs that one is acting rationally, then we have
an argument against (R3). More generally, we must accept as problematic *any* analysis of rational action which allows the possibility of a
person's acting with a justified false belief that she is acting rationally.

Notice that, if one thinks this is a problem, it is not obvious that one
can solve it by modifying (R3) to characterize rational action as action
undertaken by an agent with the justified belief that it satisfies the
conditions stated by (R3). The difficulty is that it may be possible in
general to have a justified but false belief that one has a justified belief,
and specifically, it may be possible to have a justified but false belief that
one justifiably believes that the conditions of (R3) are satisfied. Such a
person could again be acting irrationally despite the fact that he had a
justified belief that he was acting rationally.

Of course, one could argue that the contemplated revision of (R3)
does not give rise to the problem we are discussing. One could argue
that it is *not* possible to have a justified but false belief that one has a
justified belief that P.[12] Such a claim could not be made by most
philosophers today, who deny the existence of infallible justification.
And even those who think that one can be infallibly justified in believing
some propositions might find it difficult to suppose that one could be
infallibly justified in believing a proposition as complicated as the proposition that one is justified in believing some other proposition. Still, it
is not that easy to describe uncontroversial examples of situations in
which one has a justified but false belief that one has a justified belief. To
be sure, I can easily imagine a situation in which I have a body of
evidence E that gives me a justified but false belief that another body of
evidence E_1 justifies me in believing P, but one could argue that in such a
situation E by itself not only justifies me in believing that E_1 justifies me
in believing P but also justifies me in believing P. Thus so long as I am
justified in believing that something justifies me in believing P, I am
after all justified in believing P.

Even if one finds this controversial argument initially plausible, however, one must reflect on the fact that the conclusion of a series of
inferences often has less strength than each of the intermediate conclusions. For simplicity, suppose that it makes sense to quantify over
epistemic probability. Suppose further that E makes probable for me to
degree .7 that E_1 makes probable for me to degree .7 that P. If these

12. This suggestion was made to me by Richard Feldman.

probabilities are independent, it seems clear that E might not justify me in believing P even though it does justify me in believing that E_1 makes probable P. If this is so, then one can again conclude that it is possible to have a justified but false belief that one has a justified belief that P, and the problem we are worrying about cannot be dissolved by revising (R3) to describe the condition of someone justifiably believing that the conditions of (R3) are satisfied.

The dilemma again is this. On the one hand, we feel the force of allowing that an action is rational provided that the agent justifiably believes that the action is rational. On the other hand, on *any* analysis of rational action it looks as if an agent can have a justified but *false* belief that his action is rational. Thus every possible analysis of rational action seems subject to counterexample.

There are at least four relatively straightforward responses to this alleged dilemma, none of which is very convincing. First, one can try to argue that contrary to initial appearances (R3) does not really allow the possibility of a person justifiably believing that his action is rational when it is not. The example I gave *seems* plausible enough, but only because I was presupposing too narrow a conception of justification. There may be a sense in which I can justifiably believe that the sum of a column of numbers is 180 when it is not, but there is another sense in which I possessed evidence that made probable some other answer. My error was a result of my not reflecting carefully enough on that available evidence. Before one continues this heroic effort, however, one would do well to realize that there are any number of ways in which one could reach a justified belief that X is the rational action for one to take. You might, for example, rely on some authority who is very good at calculating probabilities and who tells you that X is the rational action for you to take. The testimony of this authority will not bear on the specific probabilities of any of the possible outcomes of alternative actions, but it may be reasonable to rely on this testimony nevertheless in reaching the conclusion that X would be the rational course of action to take.

Second, if one cannot convince oneself that (R3) makes impossible an agent's having a justified false belief about the rationality of her action, one can, as I pointed out earlier, redefine an action as rational for an agent when the agent has a justified belief (true or false) that the action satisfies the conditions of (R3). (There is a complication we shall shortly discuss which would require a somewhat more sophisticated approach even if we adopt this general strategy.) As I indicated, however, such a move will help only if the problem doesn't rearise with the possibility of having a justified false belief that one has a justified belief. Some extreme internalists in epistemology argue that one can have a justified belief only if one has justification for believing that one has a justified belief. I have argued against this thesis elsewhere,[13] but in any event, what is needed to block the present problem is the different thesis that having a justified belief that one has a justified belief that P entails having a justified belief that P. I have argued above that this thesis is implausible.

Third, one could argue that the appearance of a dilemma disappears if we keep clearly in mind the distinction alluded to earlier between rational action and acting rationally. To be sure, we do want to say that an agent is acting rationally if that agent acts with the justified but false belief that his action is rational, but that doesn't mean that the action itself is rational. The problem, however, is that even having made this distinction one feels the force behind saying that a person's justified belief that his action satisfies the conditions of (R3) *gives* that person a reason to act even if the person does not act for that reason. In at least one sense, it is the *existence* of reasons that seems parasitic on a person's justified beliefs about what he has reason to do. And this is a matter that is independent of questions concerning the appropriate causes of a rational agent's actions.

Finally, one could simply reject the idea that an action is rational if the agent has a justified but false belief that it is rational. After all, by hypothesis, the belief is *false,* and if it is false and we have the correct analysis of rational action, then an agent's action is not rational even if that agent justifiably (but falsely) believes that it is rational. This, however, seems to me to ignore the undeniable force of the suggestion that there is at least *some* sense in which an agent's justified beliefs about what she has reason to do *give* her reasons to act.

In conclusion, there doesn't appear to be any *straightforward* solution to the problem. Rather, I think that the most promising way to handle the apparent dilemma caused by the possibility of having justified false beliefs about the rationality of action is simply to acknowledge that the possibility gives rise to fundamental and important ambiguities in the concept of rational action. It does seem to me that in evaluating an action I am asking myself about its possible and probable consequences. This is the kind of thing I think about in asking myself whether this is

13. Fumerton 1988.

the rational course of action for me to take. In thinking about the matter, I am, of course, trying to reach a rational conclusion about what I have the most reason to do. In this sense, (R3) seems to me to capture adequately the intentional object of my thought that X is the rational course of action for me to take. Furthermore, (R3) states conditions that we might appeal to in criticizing the rationality of an agent's action. If it is, however, possible to reach an epistemically justified false conclusion that an action satisfies the conditions stated by (R3), then there is surely *another* sense in which an agent can have reason to do something by virtue of his having a rational belief that his action is rational in the sense defined by (R3). We can then recognize the following derivative concept of rational action:

(R3d1a) *S* has more reason to   =Df *S* is justified in believing
           choose *X* over any of   that, in the sense defined
           its alternatives.   by (R3), he has more rea-
                                          son to do *X* than anything
                                          else.

Furthermore, if a person can rationally but falsely believe that he rationally believes that X satisfies the conditions of (R3), we might allow *again* that there is yet another sense in which the person who acts with *this* justified belief is doing what he has the most reason to do even if his actions fail to satisfy the conditions required by both (R3) and (R3d1a). We can then introduce one more derivative concept of rational action:

(R3d1b) *S* has more reason to   =Df *S* is justified in believing
           choose *X* over any of   that *X* is rational in the
           its alternatives.   sense defined by (R3d1a).

There is, of course, no reason to stop here. For still higher-level justified metabeliefs about the rationality of action defined at these lower levels, we can introduce higher-level senses in which an action can be rational. We will have, then, as many different derivative senses of rational action as we please—(R3d1c), (R3d1d, (R3d1e), and so on. In these derivative senses of rational action, we can let our criteria for rational action "float" to the highest-level relevant metabelief the agent had in acting. Notice that, in introducing these derivative senses in which an agent can have reason to act, we are not requiring that all of these derivative concepts of rational action be satisfied in order for an agent's action to be rational. To do so would probably make it impossible for an action to be rational for an agent. We are incapable of having infinitely complex metabeliefs. Rather, we are simply allowing that there are indefinitely many derivative concepts of rational action and that we can judge the rationality of an agent's action by any of them.

If we allow that an agent's action can be rational by virtue of her having the justified beliefs described by (R1d1a), b, c, . . . , n, we should probably also allow derivative senses in which an agent's action can be irrational by virtue of her having either reason to believe that her action fails to satisfy (R3) or no reason to believe that it does satisfy the conditions of (R3). And we can introduce indefinitely many derivative concepts of irrational action by defining these concepts in terms of the relevant higher-level metabeliefs. Again, there is no vicious regress. I may have no reason to do X in the sense defined by (R3d1b) even though I do have reason to do X in the sense defined by both (R3D1a) and (R3). In this situation, if I do X, am I doing what I have the most reason to do? The answer is, trivially, that I did what was rational in the senses defined by (R3) and (R3d1a). There is no *need* for philosophers to choose between these different concepts of rational action. Indeed, it seems to me that, by recognizing an extremely interesting and subtle continuum of related concepts, one can understand better the ways in which one can easily become confused in discussing issues of practical rationality.

If one accepts the legitimacy of recognizing the above derivative sense in which an agent's action is rational if he acts with the rational belief that his action satisfies the conditions of (R3) (that is, satisfies the primary concept of rational action), one should also find compelling an argument for broadening still further derivative concepts of rational action.

Suppose that I am contemplating three alternatives, X, Y, and Z, and though I do not justifiably believe that X is the rational course of action for me to take, I do justifiably believe that X is more likely to be rational than Y and more likely to be rational than Z. Put another way, I justifiably believe that X has the best chance of being rational (in the sense defined by [R3]) even though that chance is still less than 50/50. If I am forced to choose among X, Y, and Z, and I choose X while I justifiably believe that it has the best chance of being rational in the primary sense defined by (R3), then there is surely a derivative sense in which my action is rational. The same intuition that leads us to recognize as rational the actions of people who act with the justified belief that their actions are rational (in the primary sense) surely also leads us to recognize as rational the actions of people who justifiably believe that their actions have the best chance of being rational (in the primary sense). We then have the following derivative concept of rational action:

(R3d2a) *S* has more reason to   =Df   *S* is justified in believing
          choose *X* over any of   that, in the sense defined
          its alternatives.   by (R3), *X* is more likely
                                          than each alternative con-
                                          sidered by itself to be the
                                          rational course of action.

Our reasons for introducing the "higher-level" derivative concepts of rational action defined in terms of justified belief about rational action will apply again here, of course. We want to allow a sense in which an action can be rational for me by virtue of my having a justified (true or false) belief that it is rational in the sense defined by (R3d2a). Thus we have the following continuum of derivative concepts of rational action:

(R3d2b) *S* has more reason to   =Df   *S* is justified in believing
          choose *X* over its al-   that *X* is rational in the
          ternatives.   sense defined by (R3d2a).

(R3d2c) *S* has more reason to   =Df   *S* is justified in believing
          choose *X* over its al-   that *X* is rational in the
          ternatives.   sense defined by (R3d2b).

.
.
.

and so on

Reflection on what we have been doing should also make it clear that, *whenever* we develop a "higher-level" derivative concept of rational action defined in terms of justified belief that a lower-level concept of rational action is satisfied, we could develop a parallel same-level derivative concept of rational action defined in terms of a justified belief that a lower-level concept has *the best chance* of being satisfied by an alternative open to us. Thus in (R3d2b) we could substitute for the definiens: *S* is justified in believing that *X* has the best chance of being rational in the sense defined by (R3d2a). In (R3d1b) we could substitute for the definiens: S is justified in believing that X has the best chance of being rational in the sense defined by (R3d1a). We can, therefore, recognize a fascinating array of permutations on indefinitely many derivative concepts of rational action. Again, there is no need to *choose* between these different derivative concepts of rational action. It seems to me that, once one clearly makes the distinctions, one can probably see that in principle all could find expression explicitly or implicitly in our thought about reasons for acting. Given the limitations of our finite minds, we almost surely have no need for derivative concepts past a certain level of complexity, but the above framework allows us to generate derivative concepts as needed.

Recognizing all of these important and interesting derivative concepts of rational action is consistent with insisting on the logical priority of our first-order concept of rational action defined by (R3). The derivative concepts of rational action are all parasitic on the concept defined by (R3). Furthermore, it is, I believe, (R3) that defines the subject matter of our first-person deliberations concerning the rationality of action. *Whatever* analysis of rational action one proposes, one will encounter these questions I have raised concerning the rationality of an action for an agent with justified false belief about the rationality of his action or justified belief that his action has the best chance of being rational. The solutions I have suggested are, I believe, both interesting and original ways of dealing with what is surely a perplexing set of problems. Recognizing the derivative concepts of rational action which this solution involves raises interesting possibilities for the way in which one responds to skeptical worries that arise within the context of (R3)'s account of rational action, skeptical concerns that we shall address later.

Although I have explained the above ambiguities and derivative concepts with reference to the value adjusted possible consequence analysis of rational action, it should be obvious that the same distinctions can and should be made in connection with the *metaethical* view, value adjusted possible consequence generic utilitarianism. Once we have defined a concept of morally right action in terms of the value adjusted possible consequences of that action with respect to the exemplification of intrinsic goodness and badness, we again face the question of whether a person is doing what she morally ought to do when she has a justified but false belief that her action is morally right in the primary sense. When we allow that there is a sense in which an agent ought to do X if she justifiably believes that this is what she ought to do in some more fundamental sense, we also presumably allow that there is yet another sense in which she ought to do X if she justifiably believes that she ought to do X in the first-level derivative sense. And again, we can introduce as many derivative concepts of right action as we can distinguish relevant higher-level metabeliefs. Furthermore, just as we allowed a derivative sense in which X can be rational for an agent by virtue of that agent's justified belief that X has the best chance of being rational, so we can allow a derivative sense in which S morally ought to do X by virtue of her justifiably believing that X has the best chance of being the thing she ought to do. If S is justified in believing that she ought to do X in this derivative sense, then there is another derivative sense in which she ought to do X; if she is justified in believing that she ought to do X in *this* derivative sense then there is another derivative sense in which she ought to do X, and so on for as many derivative senses of right action as one cares to distinguish.

Later, when we explore the epistemological implications of allowing these derivative concepts, we do so for both views about rational action and their metaethical analogues (still leaving open the question of whether and how to unify these two analyses).

Acting Rationally

In the preceding discussion we have been concerned with understanding what it is for an action to be rational, where we view that question as logically prior to the question of whether an agent acts rationally, that is, acts *with* appropriate reasons. Action X can be the rational thing for an agent to do even if that agent does not do X. Moreover, intuitively, someone can do what he has the most reason to do and still be acting irrationally because it wasn't his reasons that moved him to act—he didn't act *for* or *with* those reasons. What is it for an agent to act rationally? The most straightforward suggestion might be that an agent acts rationally in doing X if he acts *because* he had the most reason to do X, where we understand these reasons in the sense defined by (R3). If we adopt this suggestion, however, it may be very difficult to act rationally. It is certainly not clear to me that the mere existence of probability relations between an agent's available evidence and possible ends that might be satisfied by alternatives ever *causes* an agent to act. Rather, it seems more likely that it is a rational agent's *beliefs* about the rationality of his action that cause him to act. We could say, then, that S acts rationally in doing X when S is justified in believing that his action is rational (in the sense defined by [R3]), and it is this justified belief that causes him to act. But as you recall, this is just another way of saying that S is acting rationally in doing X when S does X because he had the most reason to do X in the sense defined by (R1d1a). Of course, if we allow that S acts rationally when he acts because he had reason to act in the sense defined by (R3d1a), there is no reason not to allow yet another sense in which S acts rationally if he acts because he has reason to act in the sense defined by (R3d1b), (R3d1c), (R3d1d), and so on. And the same would hold true for actions that result from the agent's having reasons in the derivative senses defined by our (R3d2) series. If I do X because I rationally believe that it has the best chance of being rational in the sense defined by (R3), there is surely a sense in which I am acting rationally. Every sense of rational action we defined in the preceding section, then, can give us a corresponding sense of acting rationally. For every concept of rational action, there is the corresponding concept of an action caused by the agent's having reason to act in the sense captured by that concept.

This distinction between rational action and acting rationally is paralleled again by the metaethical distinction between the morally right thing to do and acting morally. For every derivative concept of morally right action we distinguish, we can recognize a corresponding sense in which an agent is acting morally when she acts because that action is morally right.

Summary

In this chapter I have presented and defended the outline of an act consequentialist analysis of rational action. The version of act consequentialism which seems most plausible in capturing a concept of rational action relevant to an agent making choices is value adjusted possible consequence act consequentialism.

We found that, once one introduces probabilities into the characterization of rational action, it is necessary to recognize the possibility of ambiguities arising in connection with second- and third-person evaluations of rational action. In particular, we saw that in evaluating the rationality of another's actions I can understand the relevant probabilities relative to *my* epistemic perspective or relative to the perspective of the agent whose action I am evaluating. This ambiguity is obviously present in the analogous act consequentialist analyses of morally right action.

We also noted that we can evaluate the rationality of the actions an agent takes (or fails to take) concerning the accumulation of relevant evidence. This introduced the possibility of further ambiguity. We no doubt occasionally characterize an agent's action as irrational because we view the decisions he made vis-à-vis the accumulation of relevant evidence to be irrational.

Finally, though I defend the concept of rational action defined by (R3) as the concept that defines the primary object of our deliberations concerning what we rationally ought to do, I suggested that we must recognize some rather subtle ambiguities and derivative concepts arising from this approach to understanding rational action. If one can rationally but falsely believe that an action is rational in the sense defined by (R3), it seems to me that there is *another* sense in which the action is rational by virtue of the existence of that rational belief. And if one can rationally but falsely believe that one rationally believes that one's action is rational in the sense defined by (R3), then there is yet another sense in which that action is rational, and so on.

Even if one doesn't rationally believe that X is rational in the sense defined by (R3) but one does rationally believe that X has the best chance of being rational in the sense defined by (R3), there is still another derivative sense in which X can be the rational action to take. And the possibility of justified (false) beliefs about the rationality of action in this derivative sense begins another continuum of derivative concepts of rational action.

All of these concepts of rational action can be used to define corresponding concepts of acting rationally. For each sense in which an action can be rational, we can allow a sense in which an agent acts rationally if he acts because of the relevant reasons. The concept of acting rationally is clearly parasitic on the concept of there being reasons for an agent to act, and I again emphasize that all of the derivative concepts of rational action are parasitic on the first-level concept of rational action defined by (R3). Everything said about rational action has its corresponding claim with respect to analogous act consequentialist analysis of morally right action.

I have presented the above account of rational action presupposing a highly controversial framework in which the concept of an "arational" end plays a crucial rule. In the next chapter we must try to defend this approach against potential objections. Doing so gives us a natural opportunity to make some remarks about the ancient controversies concerning egoism and altruism.

CHAPTER 5

The Evaluation of Goals and the Egoism/Altruism Controversy

The concepts of rational action defended in the last chapter are defined in part by reference to an agent's ends or goals. But surely, many will argue, such an account is incomplete unless one specifies conditions for the rationality of an agent's ends. Goal-oriented behavior, the argument goes, is only as rational as the rationality of the agent's goals. In order to assess this claim, we must become clearer about the concept of a goal or end relevant to the analysis of rational action.

INTRINSIC VALUE

In the last chapter we tentatively suggested that X is a goal or an end for S if X is something that S values intrinsically. I often use the terms "value", "want", and "desire" interchangeably in the subsequent discussion, but it is important to emphasize that one needs a very broad conception of want and desire if one is to use that concept to define the goals that in turn define rational action. The term "desire" (and even the term "want") is sometimes used to describe a particularly strong, driving force. And though some of the things we value intrinsically may be desired intensely, there is no a priori reason to deny that at least some of things we value intrinsically are valued in a rather calm "dispassionate" way. I think that most people probably value or want the happiness of even people they don't know, but as I shall indicate later, I don't think they value or want this happiness very much. It is also the case that the terms "desire" and "want" are used in such a way as to preclude my now wanting or desiring something that has already occurred. On the other hand, I can obviously value that which is in the past. I don't think these semantic differences between the occasions appropriate for using one expression of interest or value rather than another reflect any deep metaphysical distinction between the "positive" intentional states described. In what follows I use whichever expression seems most natural given the context, and when I am discussing the views of others I tend, for simplicity, to employ their favored terminology.

What is it to want something or value something *for its own sake?* The vast majority of things we want in life we want only because we believe that they will (or might) get us other things we want. Indeed, as we shall see, the thesis that people want only their own happiness intrinsically and value everything else instrumentally is not a wildly implausible thesis even if it is in the final analysis probably false. But precisely how should we try to capture the difference between intrinsic and instrumental wants? Because one's answer to this question may be restricted to some extent by one's philosophy of mind, I shall briefly outline the analysis of intentional states I believe to be correct. As was true at other junctures in this book, I do not think the reader needs to accept the details, or even the general outline, of this account of valuing to accept the main thrust of the theory of rational action I defend, and for that reason I shall explore alternative analyses of intrinsic value which presuppose different philosophies of mind.

I have defended elsewhere (Fumerton 1985) the following general analysis of occurrent intentional states. Beliefs, fears, hopes, desires all have a propositional *content.* The grammatical structure of sentences describing intentional states suggests that these states have an *object,* but if one tries to make one's ontology fit the surface grammar of these sentences, one's ontology will be encumbered by such problematic categories as nonexistent (nonoccurrent) states of affairs. When Jones believes that there are unicorns or desires world peace, there are no *facts* that can serve as the objects of this belief and desire. A fact can make a belief true and can satisfy a desire, but the belief is what it is whether or not it is true, and the desire is what it is whether or not it is satisfied. If one cannot find room in one's ontology for nonexistent facts to serve as the objects of false belief and unsatisfied desire, *and* one thinks that belief and desire are at least logically prior to language (so that linguistic items cannot be the primary objects of intentional states), one might embrace a so-called adverbial theory of consciousness. On the specific view I have defended, every intentional state involves the having of a thought that defines its propositional content. Thoughts are *nonrelational* properties of the mind, but they have a sui generis intentional feature that makes them different from all other properties. Thoughts can *correspond* to facts. Correspondence is a sui generis relation that holds between the content of true belief and the fact that makes it true, the content of satisfied desire and the fact that satisfies it. False beliefs and unsatisfied desires have contents that fail to correspond to anything.

On the view I once held, the having of a thought constitutes a *belief* (as opposed to, say, a desire) when the subject stands in the "believing" relation to the thought (another sui generis relation). The having of a thought constitutes a desire when the subject stands in the "desiring" relation to the thought. It now seems to me better to construe belief and desires as *kinds* of thoughts. An analogy might be helpful. When I believe that there are unicorns and want there to be unicorns, there is in each case a property I exemplify, the property of thinking of there being unicorns. If we compare this property to the property of being a triangle, then the property of believing that there are unicorns will be analogous to the property of being a red triangle and the property of desiring that there are unicorns will be analogous to the property of being a blue triangle.

We might formally represent the analysis of occurrent true belief and satisfied desire this way (where s = the subject, $\ulcorner P \urcorner$ = the nonrelational property of thinking that P, the superscript ^{1} indicates that the thinking is a believing, the superscript ^{2} indicates that the thinking is a desire or want, P = the fact that P, and C = the relation of correspondence):

$$^1 \ulcorner P \urcorner s \, . \, \ulcorner P \urcorner \, C \, P$$
$$^2 \ulcorner P \urcorner s \, . \, \ulcorner P \urcorner \, C \, P$$

False belief and unsatisfied desire can be represented this way:

$$^1 \ulcorner P \urcorner s \, . \, \sim \exists x \, (\ulcorner P \urcorner \, C \, x)$$
$$^2 \ulcorner P \urcorner s \, . \, \sim \exists x \, (\ulcorner P \urcorner \, C \, x)$$

Something like the above account of intentionality is, I believe, the only way we can acknowledge the fundamental sui generis character of intentionality within the framework of a relatively "clean" ontology. The account, however, would obviously be anathema to most contempory philosophers, who seek to account for reference and aboutness in terms of such "natural" relations as nomological connection. Such views are attractive to many if for no other reason than that it will be easier to accommodate reference and intentionality within a straightforward physicalist ontology.[1] I have never seen a version of a causal theory of reference, however, that comes even close to handling the problem of meaningful terms that fail to refer, a causal theory of intentionality that can cope with the existence of false thought.

Of course, I cannot hope to convince the reader of the preceding analysis of intentionality with the rough statement of the view presented here. The full statement and defense of the view requires a separate, book-length treatment. I summarized the view so I could state within the framework I accept some options for the analysis of intrinsic valuing. The two options I am most interested in involve defining intrinsic desire in terms of what causally sustains it and defining intrinsic desire as a species of desire. Let me consider each in more detail.

On the first option, we might understand instrumental and intrinsic desire as involving the *same* intentional state of desiring. The difference is that we have an instrumental desire for X only because we believe that X will (might) lead to some Y which we desire. When we desire X intrinsically, we desire X and would desire X even if we had no beliefs about its consequences. Thus if I value my pleasure intrinsically, I value it and would value it even if I didn't believe that my pleasure had any other consequences at all. One could also develop a broader concept of intrinsic desire which takes into account not only what causally sustains the desire but also the causal *origin* of the desire. In *this* sense we desire X intrinsically only if we desire X and would desire it even if we do not now have and never have had any beliefs about its consequences. The two concepts are, of course, different. Many would argue that that there are some things we start out wanting only as a means but end up wanting for their own sakes. As Mill points out in *Utilitarianism* (p. 46), the miser might start out wanting money for the things it will buy but

---

1. Some philosophers, such as John Searle, would argue that the sui generis character of the intentionality of mental states is perfectly compatible with physicalism, however. See Searle 1983, chap. 10.

ends up just wanting to have money for the sake of having it. If such a person truly would want money even if he were to have no beliefs about the consequences of his having money (material wealth, power, prestige, etc.), he could have an intrinsic desire for money on the first counterfactual analysis but not on the second.

The other approach to analyzing the distinction between instrumental and intrinsic desire is dialectically more attractive, phenomenologically more tenuous. On this view, when one desires X instrumentally, the content of one's desire includes the anticipated consequence. Thus the more perspicuous way to report the instrumental desire for X is to describe it as the desire for $[X\text{-as-a-means-to-}Y]$. The intrinsic desire for X includes nothing beyond X in its content.

I think the main difficulty with this view is that it seems to make it too easy to determine what one desires intrinsically. Among the things one would like to account for with an analysis of the distinction between instrumental and intrinsic desire is the vast disagreement that has existed for thousands of years over what people value intrinsically. As I shall argue later, the dispute over the rationality of egoism just is a dispute over whether people desire intrinsically the well-being of other people. Now on the counterfactual analysis of intrinsic desire, we can easily explain how someone might not know what she intrinsically desires. We can explain why it might be very difficult for us to determine what things we desire for their own sakes. After all, we have no privileged access to the causes of our mental states, including, of course, our desires. Mother Theresa is obviously aware of the fact that her work with the poor makes her happy, and it is surely *possible* that her awareness of that connection causally sustains her desire to help others. Of course, it is equally possible that it is satisfaction of her intrinsic desire to help others that causes her to be happy helping other people. But my point is that she might not know—nobody might know—which of the two descriptions of her motivation is correct. Again, it seems to me a virtue of an analysis of intrinsic desire that it can explain why the question of what we desire for its own sake can be an enormously difficult empirical question even for ourselves to answer.

Now the second analysis we considered can, to a certain extent, also accommodate a subject's error with respect to what he desires intrinsically. As Moore pointed out in trying to explain how we might be mistaken in thinking that something is intrinsically good, we sometimes must successfully isolate in thought the subject matter of a judgment in order to reach correct conclusions about it.[2] And this method of isolation is not always easy to follow. Suppose that there is some X and I believe that X leads to Y. Suppose also that I desire Y and that I desire X either instrumentally or both intrinsically and instrumentally. On the analysis considered above, the question of whether my desire for X is intrinsic is a question concerning the "focus" of the intentional state. If the "light" of the desire shines on X *considered by itself*, I desire X intrinsically. But because I believe that X leads to Y, which I desire, I will also desire X instrumentally as a means to Y. And one might argue that the "light" of that instrumental desire "overlaps" the "light" of the intrinsic desire. To determine whether or not one desires X intrinsically, one needs to think about X in isolation from one's beliefs about its effects in order to see whether the desire is really focused on X considered in and of itself. But it is not clear that the human mind can so easily erase from imaginative consciousness deeply ingrained beliefs about consequences. Mother Teresa might still be deceived as to the nature of her desire to help others.

As long as one accepts the metaphor of instrumental desires potentially overlapping intrinsic desires so as to make their discernment problematic, I think it is difficult to find any convincing reason for adopting the one rather than the other analysis of intrinsic desire, and since nothing much hinges on the issue, I will not try to settle it here. It should also be obvious that one need not accept the details of my account of intentional states to make the distinctions discussed above. Certainly, one can make them within the framework of an act/object analysis of intentional states where the relevant objects might be, for example, possible states of affairs or nonexistent facts. One's options, however, might be more limited within the context of a behavioristic analysis of such states as desire. Suppose one tries to understand the desire for X as a disposition to act so as to produce X under certain circumstances.[3] On such a view, what would be the difference between instrumental and intrinsic desire? Here it is not clear to me that the proponent of this view has any alternative to a counterfactual analysis of the distinction. Unless one reintroduces the concept of intrinsic desire by identifying the relevant disposition as the disposition to produce X

2. See Moore 1903, chap. 6, sec. 112.
3. Pure behavioristic analyses of intentional states are, of course, enormously problematic. Note that in the example given here the locution "so as to" clearly constitutes a disguised reference to yet another intentional state of the agent.

for its own sake, one could only appeal to the causal connection between the behavioral disposition that constitutes desire and the behavioral dispositions that constitute beliefs about consequences in order
to explain the difference between instrumental and intrinsic desire.

Behavioral analyses of desire introduce another difficulty, which Darwall discusses in his evaluation of what he calls desire-based accounts of
practical rationality. Darwall points out that on a behavioristic analysis
of preferences it may turn out that preferences are intransitive.[4] It is
logically possible for Jones to be so constituted that, given a choice, he
would choose B over A, C over B, and A over C. If desire is defined in
terms of disposition to choose, then Jones will want B more than A, C
more than B, and A more than C. But theses of rationality such as the
one I defend typically presuppose that desires are transitive. In any
event, it is surely easy to show that a person with the intransitive desires
described above would be particularly vulnerable to a kind of exploita-
tion that would make him appear irrational. As Darwall and Davidson,
McKinsey, and Suppes (1955, p. 145) point out, if Jones desires money
and is willing to "pay for his preferences," I will be able to get Jones to
give up A, which he already has, by selling him B, which he prefers to A.
But I will also be able to get him to give up B by selling him C, which he
prefers to B. And I will in turn be able to sell him A, which he prefers to
C. Jones ends up where he began but is poorer to boot.

Now Darwall brings up the inherent irrationality of intransitive
desires as a way of arguing for his view that desires are the sorts of things
that require *justification*. I can rationally desire B more than A only if I
judge there to be more reason to want B than A (if I judge that B is
better than A); I can rationally desire C more than B only if I judge there
to be more reason to want C than B; and I can rationally desire A more
than C only if I judge there to be more reason to want A than C. But
intuitively, I am inconsistent if I think that B is better than A; C better
than B, and A better than C (p. 76). This seems right, but only because
we suppose that there is a "scale" of goodness and if something B
occupies a higher place on that scale than A, and C occupies a higher
place on that scale than B, then obviously C occupies a higher place on
that scale than A. But it seems equally clear to me that on my account of
intrinsic desire (as opposed to a behavioristic account), one can appeal
to the same metaphor in arguing for the *impossibility* of someone intrin-

4. See Darwall 1983, p. 68.

sically wanting B more than A, C more than B, and A more than C. Desires, like beliefs, admit of degrees of strength. Just as desire is a sui generis intentional state, so the intensity or strength of a desire is also a sui generis notion. But if my desire for B considered in and of itself is stronger than my desire for A considered in and of itself, and my desire for C considered as an end is stronger than my desire for B considered as an end, it follows that my desire for C considered as an end is stronger than my desire for A considered as an end. Rational people are moved by their awareness of the varying strengths of their goals or ends, but nothing logically follows about how a person will actually act in any given situation because there is nothing logically impossible (or even unusual) about people acting irrationally.

Although I reject an analysis of valuing that identifies it with a disposition to behave in a certain way, I would accept the view that intentional states in general, and wants, desires, and valuing in particular, can be either occurrent or dispositional. When I describe my neighbor as believing that, fearing that, or wanting it to be the case that interest rates will rise I am obviously not implying that my neighbor is presently exemplifying the thought of interest rates rising. The formal analysis of dispositional intentional states is more problematic than it might at first seem to be. If one accepts something like the analysis of occurrent intentional states I proposed above, the most obvious candidate for an analysis of dispositional intentional states is an analysis employing subjunctive conditionals whose consequents refer to occurrent intentional states. Thus one might say that Jones dispositionally wants X if he would occurrently want X were he to consider it (Jones dispositionally believes P if he were to occurrently believe P were he to consider it, dispositionally fears X if he were to occurrently fear X when contemplating it, and so on). The difficulty with counterfactual analyses of dispositional mental states, however, is that they seem insensitive to two logically distinct hypothetical situations. Intuitively, Jones might be so constituted that he would desire X *for the first time* were he to consider it, even though it was not true in any sense that he wanted it all along. Similarly, there may be many propositions that I might believe were I to consider them (because they would strike me as perfectly reasonable) but which I do not now either occurrently or dispositionally believe.

If one were interested in capturing the ordinary use of terms like "want" and "desire", there are some ways in which one might try to modify a subjunctive analysis. One might insist that dispositional desires must have been occurrent desires at some time or at least follow from other desires that were at one time occurrent. Or one might maintain that Jones has a dispositional desire for X only if he would *spontaneously* value X were he to consider it. Neither of these approaches seems quite right, but fortunately, I do not think we need worry much about capturing the ordinary sense of dispositional wants or desires in order to develop a concept to use in defining the concept of rational action. I am prepared to stipulate that I use the locution "Jones values X intrinsically" to describe the fact that he either occurrently values X intrinsically (in one of the senses discussed above) or would value X intrinsically were he to consider it. If this is not quite the ordinary concept of a dispositional desire, so be it. It seems obvious to me that, from the perspective of a rational agent trying to bring about things he intrinsically values, the consequences of an action which are relevant are those that he would value were he to consider them. If there is some Y that might result from X and Jones values Y in the sense that he would care about it were he to consider it, then this is obviously something Jones would want to consider in evaluating the question of whether this action was rational. Ignorance of this fact might lead him to error in his conclusions vis-à-vis the rational course of action to take. But if this is true, then it is the concept of dispositional desire analyzed using the relatively straightforward subjunctive discussed above which should be used in the analysis of rational action.[5]

Now I stress again that I may be creating terminological strain from the perspective of ordinary usage. Certainly, the ordinary use of the term "goal" might be incompatible with the idea of an agent's having goals that she doesn't know anything about. But if we define an agent's goals in terms of what she values intrinsically and we define an agent's intrinsic values so that they include what she would value intrinsically were she to consider it, it is obviously possible for an agent not to know

5. Richard Foley has suggested to me a reason why one may want to add a qualification to what I say here. One may, he suggests, want to distinguish subjunctive conditionals grounded in one's intrinsic nature from those with an "external" ground. Suppose, for example, that there is an evil demon who would cause me to value intrinsically the suffering of Jones (and only Jones) should I ever consider it. Would we want that "subjunctive fact" about me to count as a consideration relevant to what would be rational for me to do? Perhaps not, in which case we would have to make a vague distinction between the "subjunctive facts" about what I would value which flow from my nature and those that do not.

what some of her goals are. But my concern is not with the analysis of ordinary concepts of wanting, valuing, desiring, and goals. My concern is with the concept of rational action. It may be that, in straining the ordinary use of the above expressions, I am at the same time increasing the plausibility of the overall account of rational action defined in terms of what the reader may regard as technical concepts. Theories that take wants or desires to determine at least partially the rationality of action have always been suspect partly because the question of what it would be rational for an agent to do seems so much more complicated than questions concerning how we can get what we want. But the ordinary meanings of "want" and "desire" have precious little to do with a fully analyzed concept of rational action. Usually, when we describe a person's wants we are *not*, in the first place, describing her intrinsic wants, but it is only intrinsic wants or values that enter into our analysis of rational action. And as we have just noted, the subjunctives that define the most useful notion of dispositional intrinsic valuing might fail to capture a concept that finds expression in ordinary usage. The philosophically technical question of what we intrinsically desire is difficult to answer—much more difficult to answer than the everyday question of whether one wants to play golf today. But the difficulty of answering such questions nicely mirrors the difficulties we intuitively feel are involved in assessing the rationality of alternative actions open to us.

Having freed ourselves from the chains of ordinary language and the concepts that find expression there in our search for the building blocks of a plausible analysis of rational action, we might do well to consider still further modifications of a concept of valuing relevant to the analysis of rational action.

The intrinsic wants, desires, or valuings we have considered so far might be called *contemplative* wants, desires, and values. We have been talking about an intentional state that characterizes a person when he is merely thinking about a given state of affairs. But it seems possible that I might want something X for its own sake when imagining its occurrence, even though I would feel quite differently were I to find out that X has actually occurred. It seems, in other words, possible simultaneously to exemplify two dispositional properties: the disposition to value X on contemplation of it and the disposition to disvalue it on the realization that it has occurred. It is not easy to describe uncontroversial examples of situations in which these dispositions are present, in part because it is not easy to describe uncontroversial examples of things we desire intrinsically. One might, however, consider the contemplative desire one has to see one's enemy suffer. I suspect that it is a relatively common human characteristic to want to see one's enemy suffer only to be repelled by the actual knowledge that this contemplative want is satisfied. As I say, this is not an uncontroversial example. I myself think it more plausible to construe the situation as one in which what one wants intrinsically is the *pleasure* one expects to get from seeing one's enemy writhing in pain, where one's disappointment results from the fact that one didn't get the anticipated pleasure. But in any event, it is surely logically possible for an agent to be so constituted that he would value X in the imagining of it and not-X were he to realize that it had occurred.

Let us call the attitude one has toward a given state of affairs on awareness that it has occurred a cognitive valuing.[6] Should we identify the intrinsic values of an agent which define the rationality of his actions as his contemplative values or his cognitive values?

As long as we are considering contexts in which an agent is making a choice, the distinction may not in fact make a practical difference if we assume that one's contemplative attitudes are the best indicator of one's cognitive attitudes. But just as the distinction between probable consequence and actual consequence utilitarianism remains despite the fact that one's choices won't be affected by which view one endorses, so even assuming a one-to-one correspondence between the having of a contemplative desire and the having of a cognitive desire, there will still be a conceptional distinction between a concept of rational action defined in terms of the one rather than the other.

One might thing that the issue could be settled by the following thought experiment. Suppose one knew that one had a contemplative intrinsic desire for Y but a dispositional cognitive intrinsic disapproval of Y. One knew, in other words, that if one were to become aware of Y's occurrence, one would ultimately disvalue it. In deliberating on some course of action X, should one take the fact that X will probably lead to Y as a reason for doing X or a reason against doing X? It seems obvious to me that one should hold the latter view, and thus it might seem that what one is really concerned with vis-à-vis producing what one intrin-

---

6. Note, again, that in describing the attitude one has toward a state of affairs that has already occurred it is odd to use the terms "desire" or "want", and so I use the term "value" instead. As I indicated earlier, however, I do not think this marks any fundamental distinction between the positive intentional attitudes denoted by these terms.

sically values is producing what one would intrinsically value with full awareness that it has occurred. The thought experiment, however, is complicated by the fact that, in addition to the contemplative desire for Y, one might have a contemplative desire that one's cognitive values be *satisfied*. In the hypothetical situation discussed above, one might argue, one's knowledge that X leads to Y is a strike against X because one realizes that one's contemplative desire for having one's cognitive desires satisfied will be frustrated by X. One might also construe the situation as one in which the individual realizes that the frustration of his cognitive values will cause unhappiness, a state he contemplatively disvalues. And again, this could accommodate the intuition that his awareness of X leading to Y is a strike against X.

Although the issue is rather complicated, it seems to me that in the final analysis a value that would not be sustained through the realization that it has been satisfied is too ethereal to give us a reason to act. In acting rationally, we are trying to produce a world in which we can *live*. We are not just trying to produce a world we like to imagine. And if the two diverge, it is only the stable values that would survive our knowledge of their satisfaction which can give us reasons for acting.

Richard Foley has suggested to me yet another way in which one might restrict the dispositional cognitive desires relevant to understanding reasons for acting. We do want to produce a world in which we can live, but why, Foley asks, should we view as relevant the fact that our action might bring about some Y which we would disvalue if we were to consider it when, in fact, it is extremely unlikely that we would ever be aware of or consider it? In other words, why not let our reasons for acting be defined only by things we dispositionally value where there is a reasonable chance that the dispositional value would become occurrent? Of course, if one accepts Foley's initial suggestion, it would be natural to extend it and introduce a mechanism for adjusting the strength of a dispositional value relevant to understanding reasons for the *probability* of its becoming occurrent. The resulting view could be characterized as a value "doubly adjusted" possible consequence consequentialism. We would, in effect, discount the value of possible consequences twice—once for the probability that the state of affairs valued will occur and once for the probability of the dispositional value becoming occurrent.

Although the above view is extremely interesting and has some plausibility, I suspect that for many it derives its plausibility from implicit hedonistic presuppositions. I suspect that many would be initially sympathetic to the suggestion that one can discount things we care about only dispositionally when the disposition would never be actualized because they really believe that only happiness and unhappiness are, respectively, valued and disvalued. And this presupposition is coupled with the view that ignorance is bliss. If one were an egoistic hedonist, one clearly would have no reason to take into account the fact that an action would lead to some result if that result would never impinge on one's consciousness. If, for example, I try to avoid making other people suffer only because it makes me unhappy to think of them suffering and I come to realize that I can easily avoid this result by not thinking of them, I might rationally discount the effects of my actions on others. But if I value intrinsically, even only dispositionally, some consequence of an action, then I think that my *complete* self, that is, the self defined by both occurrent and dispositional properties, still has a reason to perform the action that might bring about that result. Still, I am not certain about this conclusion, and I would stress that it would be an easy matter to accommodate within Chapter 4's framework the concept of end defined in terms of intrinsic dispositional value, where the weight of a dispositional value relevant to defining a reason is adjusted for the probability of its becoming occurrent.

FUTURE DESIRES AND REASONS FOR ACTING

The question of whether it is cognitive or contemplative desires that enter into the analysis of reasons for acting is superficially similar in some respects to the issue of whether the values that define the reasons I have for acting are only those values I now have, or whether they include future wants or values as well.[7] But though the questions are superficially similar, they are really quite distinct, and I would here side with those who argue that it is only one's *present* attitudes that can define the rationality of one's present actions. This might seem at odds with the decision to let cognitive attitudes define an agent's goals, but it is not. Suppose that I know that in twenty years I will become a sadistic

---

7. See the discussion of this issue in Nagel 1970, chap. 8, and Brandt 1979, pp. 81–87.

monster. I might now have not only a contemplative but a cognitive intrinsic aversion to the future suffering of other people. I might be so constituted that I would now disvalue the suffering of other people in the future if I now knew that they would in fact suffer. And this present desire seems to give me a powerful reason to do what I can to make sure that my future cognitive desires are frustrated. Of course, I will almost always have *some* reason to ensure that my future cognitive desires are satisfied insofar as I have a present desire for my future happiness and I realize that my future happiness is at least causally linked to the satisfaction of my future desires. It is this fact that makes plausible the idea that what one knows one will want bears on the rationality of present decision making. But as we have just seen, that intuition can be accommodated quite nicely within an account of practical rationality that always makes rational action a function of one's present goals or ends.

SUMMARY

The rationality of one's actions is in part a function of one's goals or ends. I have suggested that we understand goals or ends in terms of one's cognitive intrinsic values, values that can be either occurrent or dispositional. I have offered a general analysis of intentional states and a particular analysis of intrinsic valuing. Having made these distinctions, I will for simplicity continue to refer to an agent's wants, values, or desires but with the understanding that, unless otherwise indicated, I am using these concepts in the technical sense relevant to their employment in an analysis of rational action.

A critical component of my egocentric conception of practical rationality is the view that an agent's goals or ends (together with epistemic considerations) are the ultimate court of appeal in assessing the rationality of action. There is no higher court to which one can appeal in assessing the rationality of one's goals or ends (one's intrinsic values). What one intrinsically values is a brute empirical fact no more rational nor irrational than the fact that one has black hair, five fingers, or two arms. This is my position, but it is a view that many philosophers would reject along with the conception of rational action which rests on it. Many philosophers insist that there must be standards for evaluating the rationality of an agent's goals or ends, and we must turn to some of their arguments now.

CAN ONE'S INTRINSIC WANTS BE IRRATIONAL?

We must stress at the outset that we are concerned only with the question of whether *intrinsic* wants can be irrational (or rational, for that matter). Critics of my view will inevitably get considerable mileage out of the fact that we are perfectly comfortable with evaluating the rationality of wants and desires as these are ordinarily understood. My neighbor Jones with the six kids has an irrational desire to have a Corvette as the family car. My wife has an irrational desire to live in Toronto; my daughter has an irrational desire to be a test pilot; and my son has an irrational desire to be a television sports announcer. My critics have an irrational desire to show that intrinsic desires can be irrational. But the desires or wants we characterize as irrational are typically *instrumental* desires or wants. We often characterize an instrumental want as irrational if we think that the beliefs it involves are irrational. If I want X as a means to Y, and have no reason to believe that X might lead to Y, then there is a perfectly clear sense in which one can say that I am irrational for wanting X. But beliefs about consequences do not enter into the having of an intrinsic desire, and consequently there are no *present* irrational beliefs that can infect the rationality of an intrinsic desire.

Brandt on Intrinsic Desire

In *A Theory of the Good and the Right*, Richard Brandt offers what is surely one of the most sophisticated attempts to distinguish rational from irrational intrinsic desires. Essentially, his conclusion amounts to the claim that a person's intrinsic desires are rational if they "would survive or be produced by careful 'cognitive psychotherapy' for that person" (p. 113). Intrinsic desires are irrational if they "cannot survive compatibly with clear and repeated judgments about established facts." But despite the sophistication of Brandt's view, with its heavy reliance on the conceptual apparatus of cognitive psychology, it is not clear what the *argument* is for taking facts about what would cause intrinsic desires to appear or disappear to be relevant to the question of whether these desires are rational or irrational. There is, of course, the prevalent idea that psychologists and psychiatrists are "experts" on deciding when something is "wrong" with a person, and I suppose one might be tempted to think that, if a psychiatrist has the inclination and the ability to get rid of a character trait through the methods of cognitive psychology, then there must be something defective about that character trait. But this is surely not the kind of reasoning that a philosopher would take seriously, nor do I think that Brandt makes any such overt appeal to the atuhority of cognitive psychology. Rather, it seems to me that the force of Brandt's argument rests virtually entirely on a number of thought experiments. He considers examples of intrinsic desires that he says could be extinguished through cognitive therapy and expects us to agree with him that these desires are, for that reason, irrational. Now I defer entirely to Brandt on the empirical causal questions concerning how one can produce or inhibit desires—I have very little knowledge of cognitive psychology. But I will try to diminish the force of Brandt's examples by pointing out plausible alternative ways in which his hypothetical situations could be described so as to eliminate whatever intuitive force they have as support for his conclusions.

A Derivative Concept of Irrational Intrinsic Desire

Before we go on, however, we should emphasize a point that I have made elsewhere and that Brandt accepts as well.[8] It should be obvious that, given any consequentialist account of practical rationality, it may turn out that a person would be acting rationally if he acted so as to remove some intrinsic desire. One intrinsic desire might conflict with others in the sense that it might be impossible to satisfy it without frustrating others. And the having of a desire that is constantly unsatisfied might itself frustrate the satisfaction of other desires such as the desire for "peace of mind." If the situation involves one desire that is at odds in this way with more, or stronger, desires, the individual might do well to get rid of it, if possible. An example might be helpful. Suppose that I am a hedonistic sadist. I intrinsically desire producing pain and suffering in other people, but I also have normal desires concerning more mundane pleasures. I enjoy music, golf, tennis (especially hitting my opponent in the face with an overhead), and so on. Given this society and its laws, and more generally, given human nature, it might be extremely difficult for me to satisfy my sadistic intrinsic desires and at the same time satisfy my desires for these more mundane pleasures. Sadists who satisfy their sadistic desires often end up in prison, where it is notoriously difficult to maintain a hedonistic lifestyle.

8. See Fumerton 1980, p. 267, and Brandt 1979, p. 111.

And even if practicing sadists manage to avoid formal punishment, their victims will no doubt try very hard to prove Hobbes's rationale for abiding by the golden rule.[9] Sadistic behavior directed toward others will likely lead to retaliation, and unless one's sadism is coupled with masochism, this can bring about some nasty repercussions. Now I imagine it would be rather distracting if one constantly must quell one's sadistic inclinations, and consequently, I can well believe that our hypothetical sadist would be much better off if he could rid himself of his sadistic desires. He might well have good reason to seek psychiatric help. Conversely, he might well be irrational for not taking steps to remove the intrinsic desire whose presence is causing so much difficulty. In keeping with our imprecise descriptions of the world, we might well "transfer" the irrationality of our sadist's inaction to the intrinsic desire that remains because of that irrational inaction.[10] But now that the situation has been fully described, it should be obvious that there is no clear sense in which we should regard intrinsic sadistic desires as any more or less rational than any other intrinsic desire. We evaluate the rationality of our actions by reference to our goals or ends, and there is no higher court to which we can appeal in evaluating the rationality of our goals or ends. But the court of ends has jurisdiction to preside over the rationality of actions related to the production and removal of goals or ends.[11]

Now that all that is said, it should be evident that Brandt's task, as he well realizes, is to show that intrinsic desires can be "intrinsically" irrational by virtue of the fact that we could get rid of them in certain ways. Let us look at some of the examples he gives of irrational desires.

Brandt's Examples of Irrational Intrinsic Desires

One kind of intrinsic desire that Brandt calls irrational is an intrinsic desire that has its causal source in false belief, where the desire would

9. See Hobbes, part 1, chap. 15. As I read Hobbes, the golden rule is just commonsense egoistic advice. Treat others the way you want them to treat you, because by and large they will treat you the way you treat them. The more obnoxious you are, the more obnoxious behavior you will get from others.

10. When Plato in *The Republic* argues that sexual desire, for example, is irrational, it may be that he, too, is simply arguing that the consequences of not doing all one can to eliminate or at least subdue this desire are bad.

11. It is also formally possible for one to have a second-order intrinsic desire that one not have a certain first-order desire satisfied. This would simply be another case of having desires that cannot both be satisfied, and again it might be rational to take steps to

disappear were the subject made vividly aware of the truth. He gives the examples of a student who wants to become an academic because he (falsely) believes that his parents would be disappointed if he did not, and someone who has an aversion to the taste of a certain food because he (falsely) thought it would make him ill (p. 115). Again, let us suppose that the relevant desire/aversion would disappear were the person exposed to the truth through "cognitive psychotherapy." Are the above desire and aversion irrational?

It is important to take seriously the rather strained hypothesis that these desires are supposed to be intrinsic. I should have thought that the most natural description of the would-be academic is someone who wanted to become an academic *as a means* to pleasing his parents. The person with a distaste for that food had the aversion because it was thought of as a *source* of disease. If the individuals are described this way, then, given our earlier account of intrinsic value, neither the desire nor the aversion would be intrinsic. But suppose that, although the relevant desire/aversion had its causal *source* in a belief about consequences, it is no longer causally sustained by beliefs about consequences. You recall that we earlier considered the possibility of restricting intrinsic wants to those wants that are not now sustained by beliefs about consequences and were not originally *produced* by beliefs about consequences. And given that very restrictive sense of intrinsic desire, it would be almost impossible to construe the wants and aversions Brandt discusses as genuine intrinsic wants or aversions. But let us stay with the broad conception of intrinsic want or aversion.

If it is indeed true that the desire to be an academic would cease to exist were the student no longer to believe that its satisfaction would please his parents, and if it were similarly true that the aversion to that food would cease to exist were the subject to bring to mind repeatedly and vividly the fact that it is harmless, why should we not conclude that these beliefs about parents and food are causally *sustaining* the respective desire and aversion? And thus why should we not conclude that the desire and aversion are not genuinely intrinsic?

Brandt might well reply to these suggestions by arguing that, given the conception of cognitive psychology he has in mind, it is not enough to rid oneself of the relevant false beliefs. I might now know that the

---

eliminate one of the desires. Note, however, that in calculating which, if either, desire one should try to remove, both preside on the court of appeal along with all of the agent's other ends.

food I dislike doesn't cause illness, but until I repeatedly bring that thought before my mind in the way that I presume a therapist helps one do, I might not be able to get rid of the aversion. But does that really imply that the aversion was *intrinsic?* The issue is complicated by the complexity of the human mind. Belief occurs at many different levels. When I am moved to tears by the suffering of a character in a film, do I believe that the character is really suffering? In one sense, obviously not. But in another sense, I am clearly in a state very much like belief. I have heard that one will not lose money betting people that they cannot hold their hands to the outside of a glass jar as they watch the scorpion inside strike. At one level one obviously believes that the scorpion will do one no harm, but at another level there is clearly the *expectation* of pain, an expectation so vivid as to cause one to move one's hand. The cognitive psychotherapy Brandt talks about seems to me to be a way of ridding oneself of vestiges of a belief that (in part) causally sustains a desire. But insofar as this is true, there is no reason to view the desire as genuinely intrinsic. And we have already acknowledged that there are surely senses in which instrumental desires can be characterized as irrational.[12]

Another kind of desire that Brandt thinks is often irrational he calls *artificial*—desires produced by various forms of "unnatural" cultural conditioning. The contrast seems to be with a "naturally" produced desire that results from representative experience of its object (pp. 116–17). I am not sure I really understand what the various examples Brandt gives all have in common, but let us consider his example of the person who has a desire to achieve because he thinks it brings respect if not affection, "a belief which is partially false, since achievement is apt to produce irritation" (p. 119). Again, Brandt's own description of the desire, with the implication that its irrationality has its source in the cognitive error of a belief that sustains it, clearly suggests that we would more plausibly construe the desire as an instrumental desire, and the kind of irrationality it has as the kind of irrationality that an instrumental desire can have. And again, the proof that the desire is causally sustained by the belief *on Brandt's assumptions* is that the desire would disappear were all vestiges of the belief fully and completely purged.

---

12. Even when these cases are construed as instrumental desires, it is not clear to me that Brandt has given convincing examples of irrational instrumental desires. As I indicated in previous discussion, unless the instrumental desires rest on unjustified (not merely *false*) belief, I am not sure that there is any epistemic irrationality that infects the instrumental desire.

Not all of Brandt's examples of irrational desires can so easily be assimilated to instrumental desires. He considers, for example, desires and aversions produced by various forms of deprivation, where what is relevant is that the desire would cease to exist were the subject made vivdly aware of the fact that it was caused by that deprivation. Thus he suggests that a very strong desire for attention brought on by early childhood neglect might be irrational provided that a therapy that forces vivid awareness of those childhood experiences would make the abnormally strong desire for attention wane. Here, it isn't beliefs about the consequence of achieving attention which are causally sustaining the relevant desire. Indeed, we may assume that the subject with the putatively irrational desire had no beliefs about his childhood or beliefs about the consequences of getting attention from others.

In this case we must address head on the suggestion that there is a sense in which the desire in question, if intrinsic, is irrational. Why should we think that a desire is irrational just because there is a procedure we could go through which would rid us of the desire? In general, of course, no one would argue that desires we can get rid of are for that reason irrational. If I castrated myself, I imagine I could get rid of my desire for sexual pleasure, but it has never even occurred to me that my desire for sexual pleasure is for that reason irrational. Brandt, of course, will agree and will point out that the difference is that the desire for sexual pleasure doesn't survive as a result of a cognitive *defect,* where cognitive defects are construed very broadly so as to include not just unjustified beliefs but false beliefs and even the absence of certain true beliefs (as might be the case with the deprived child). But Brandt's thesis is both stronger and weaker than the thesis that desires resulting from unjustified, false, or absent, true beliefs inherit the defects of the agent's cognitive states (or lack thereof). I may have all true beliefs about the origin of my extremely strong desire for attention where the desire nevertheless survives only because I don't go to the effort of repeatedly and vividly bringing to mind the facts of deprivation that cause my desire. Desires, in other words, can be irrational even if there is no error of commission or omission in my cognitve representation of the world which is causing the desire. Moreover, it is surely a strange feature of Brandt's view that the fact that a desire is inextinguishable is a sign of rationality. If the underlying thrust of Brandt's position is that desires are irrational insofar as they are produced by cognitive defects, then why should a desire be any the less rational just because it was so effectively produced by a cognitive defect that I can't get rid of it? If a desire is rational because it is impossible to get rid of, why should we not think of a desire as rational because it is very, very difficult to get rid of? Indeed, why would a person take any interest in whether he could or could not get rid of an intrinsic desire or aversion that Brandt has decided to define as irrational?

In a most illuminating discussion of this question, Brandt suggests that (1) desires and aversions that are irrational in his sense are as a matter of empirical fact desires and aversions to which people have an aversion (p. 157), and (2) desires and aversions that are irrational in his sense are "apt to be costly, or to stand in the way of benefits, in one way or another" (p. 157). On both counts, people have reason to prefer eliminating irrational desires and aversions. But notice that this suggests rather strongly that what is *wrong* with the having of irrational desires/aversions is the trouble they cause. But now we can accommodate any intuitions that seem to support Brandt's position by returning to the original sense in which I have admitted (and Brandt admits) that intrinsic desires might be irrational. It is a feature of *any* plausible account of practical rationality that one might have reason to take steps to remove desires that cause trouble, and we can view a person as irrational for not taking those steps. Furthermore, we can, in a derivative sense, characterize the desire that remains as a result of this irrational inaction an irrational desire. But the critical question is whether that desire while *present* should be ignored in calculating reasons for acting, including reasons for acting so as to eliminate certain desires.

Suppose that my love of Christmas carols has its causal source in all sorts of false beliefs about there being a God who had a son who was born in a manger with assorted shepherds, wise men, and angels around. For all I know, a therapist might be able to eliminate my desire to hear music of that sort by inundating me with the true facts about Christianity. It seems to me that on Brandt's view my liking of Christmas carols would be irrational, but it also seems to me that the presence of that like gives me a very strong reason to go to the Christmas carol concert given by the local high school. The whole point of Brandt's introducing the concept of an irrational desire/aversion is to develop a concept of rational action that takes into consideration only those goals or ends defined by *rational* desires. To be sure, Brandt is uneasy about the reader misunderstanding his view and acknowledges that insofar as an unsatisfied irrational desire might make one unhappy one may have a reason to satisfy it (p. 161). But this admission is consistent with the view I think he is committed to, that the having of an irrational intrinsic desire for X cannot, in itself, give one a reason for pursuing X. The only reason one has for trying to satisfy irrational desires is as a means to satisfy the rational desire for pleasure. But if we think about it, this is surely a reductio of the position. If I intrinsically like the sound of Christmas carols for *whatever* reason, that gives me *a* reason to buy recordings of Christmas carols. If I have an intense aversion to pork because I was raised in a religion with all kinds of irrational and false beliefs about God's preferences in our eating habits, I still have a good reason to avoid ordering the pork chops on the menu. The desires Brandt calls irrational are defective, as he himself implicitly admits, only insofar as they cause trouble. My intense desire for attention caused by my deprived youth frustrates the satisfaction of many other desires I have. My intrinsic desire to become an academic when I get no pleasure from living the life of an academic cannot be satisfied without frustrating my equally intense desire for happiness. People may well have strong reason to get rid of these desires, but as long as they have them, they continue to preside along with their other goals or ends on the court of appeals that defines the reasons they have for acting.

I have made it clear that I am in general unsympathetic to Brandt's views concerning the possibility of intrinsic desires/aversions being inherently rational/irrational, but it may be useful to recall that we have earlier distinguished contemplative intrinsic desire from cognitive intrinsic value. I have suggested that we should define the goals or ends that (partially) define our reasons for acting in terms of the attitudes we would have on knowing that the state of affairs contemplatively desired has occurred. And to this extent I can agree in a sense with Brandt's suggestion that the only desires that give people reasons to act (what he calls *rational intrinsic desires*) are those that "have developed from sensitive interaction with the world, from discovery of what one likes or dislikes at first hand" (p. 156). As is evident from the above discussion, however, Brandt builds far more into the concept of his rational intrinsic desires than that they be able to survive the awareness of their objects obtaining. And it is this broader conception of the required "tenacity" of a "reason conferring" desire that creates the counterintuitive consequences I have discussed.[13]

13. In "The Definition of Rational Desires," Robert Shope presents some objections to the *conditional* analysis of rational desire. Shope, in effect, raises intuitively plausible counterexamples of desires that would disappear or be lessened by consideration of certain facts, which desires are, nevertheless, perfectly rational. He offers the example

DARWALL ON IRRATIONAL DESIRE

In *Impartial Reason,* Darwall appears to be another philosopher determined to maintain that intrinsic desires can be rational or irrational.
In offering his initial account of rational action,[14] Darwall seems to
reject the view that the only thing that can give an agent a reason to act is
ultimately a fact that involves reference to that agent's desires (wants,
values). But many of Darwall's arguments against what he calls the
DBR thesis (desire-based reason theory) focus on a very narrow conception of desire, far more narrow than the concept of value on which
we are relying. At least sometimes (see pp. 39–40) Darwall's argument
seems designed only to show that an agent can have reason to act where
that reason does not derive from some desire or value that either is, or
has been, occurrent. And it should be obvious by now that I have no
quarrel with such a claim.

In the course of developing his own account of reasons for acting,
Darwall talks more about preferences than desires, but it seems clear
that he thinks that even intrinsic preferences can be rational or irrational. Again, I should remind the reader that I have already admitted
that *instrumental* desires or preferences can be irrational, and I have also
admitted that there is a *derivative* (somewhat misleading) sense in which
intrinsic desires/aversions whose presence causes difficulties can also be
irrational. But the "irrationality" of a troublesome intrinsic desire/
aversion can be traced wholly to the irrationality of inaction that fails to
eliminate that desire. There is also *another* sense, which we have not yet
discussed, in which we can allow the intelligibility of raising questions
about the reasons for wanting something intrinsically.

In *Language of Morals,* Hare argues that judgments about the goodness of something are always *supervenient* in the sense that it always
makes sense to ask *why* the thing in question is good, where the answer
to that question involves picking out some property or properties that

---

(p. 333) of a desire for food at a party when that desire would be weakened by remembering a past occasion on which that food caused indigestion. Shope suggests that, in trying
to distinguish rational from irrational desires, one might focus not on the truth of certain
counterfactuals but on the factors that causally sustain desires. He concludes his article,
however, with some problems that would need to be solved in order to complete such an
analysis.

14. The initial account gets modified radically so as to abandon its act consequentialist
character. We say more about Darwall's mistaken attempts to leave act consequentialism
later.

the thing in question has. "What makes this a good car?" we ask, and we expect an answer that identifies the relevant "good-making" characteristics. It is a good car because it is safe, doesn't use much gas, and so on. In the same sense in which we must logically identify some feature of a thing in virtue of which it is good, one must also be prepared to identify some feature of a thing which is the "ground" for wanting or valuing it. If I claim to value something X, there must be a "reason" for valuing X, but only in the sense in which there must be something about the thing, some feature of the thing at which the value is directed. There is nothing more profound about this thesis, however, than that, phenomenologically, there is nothing to a thing other than its properties. I am not arguing here (although I believe it) the *ontological* thesis that one should construe a thing as a "bundle" of properties. But even if one has dialectical reasons for introducing bare particulars or substrata, one is hardly acquainted with such entities over and above their properties. Even if there are bare particulars, one cannot value one bare particular a more than another b, except insofar as one values some aspect or property of the one particular more than the other. We might crudely talk about having intrinsic desires for things or states, but it is always more precise to describe the object of the intrinsic desire as the exemplification of some property or properties. It is for this reason that, when one identifies something X as the object of some intrinsic want, there must always be something about X (some property or feature of X) which is the reason we want it. But this is really just a convoluted way of saying that intrinsic value has as its object the exemplification of properties and is obviously irrelevant to the issue we have been discussing vis-à-vis the question of whether an intrinsic desire can be intrinsically rational/irrational.

The fact that if we want something we always want it in virtue of some property or characteristic it has provides the only sense in which wants are universalizable. When the master rhetorician Hare first introduces his concept of universalizable value, he argues that it is no more problematic than the sense in which any descriptive term is universalizable.[15] If we view something as good *in virtue of* the fact that it has some

15. See Hare 1963, chap. 2. By the time he is finished, of course, it turns out that the universalizability of moral judgments involves far more than the willingness to treat like situations the same. There are restrictions placed on what can count as a proper universal imperative that one must accept in making a moral judgment. And (this is the crucial point) in accepting the universal imperative, one must accept its consequences in all *imagined* situations, including those in which one "puts oneself in the other person's shoes." All of this amounts to making *impartiality* a condition for universalizing.

characteristic *F*, then we must view anything else that has that characteristic *F* as equally good (ceteris parisbus). But similarly, if we intrinsically value something *X* where what we value about *X* is that it is *F*, then we are obviously going to value anything else that has the property *F* as well. Again, this thesis is no more mysterious than the fact that it *is* the exemplification of *F* which is intrinsically valued. As we shall discuss shortly, this innocuous feature of the "universalizability" of value gives the altruist her best (but not very good) chance of placing logical constraints on the kinds of states one can rationally take an interest in.

Now at least sometimes Darwall seems to be claiming nothing more problematic than that value (preference) is supported by reason in the trivial sense in which there is always some feature or property of the thing valued in virtue of which it is valued:

> Even intrinsic preferences can be based on reasons. If one thing is rationally preferred to another, certain facts about the former, when considered rationally, lead the agent to prefer it. The sort of rational consideration may simply be that involved in reflective awareness. Facts that lead us to an intrinsic preference when we consider them reflectively provide reasons, at least presumptively, for that preference. (pp. 88–89)

Although Darwall clearly holds that intrinsic preferences can be held "rationally criticizable," the bulk of his discussion about the rationality of intrinsic preferences concerns the concept of comparing the relative strength of the reasons "supporting" one intrinsic preference rather than another. Darwall starts out with the claim that "facts that when we are reflectively aware of them move us to have (or maintain) an intrinsic preference for something are presumptive *reasons* to prefer it" (p. 87). But this thesis can be construed in different ways. As I indicated above, I *suspect* that it is just a convoluted way of asserting the trivial thesis that there are reasons why we have an intrinsic desire for a thing in the sense that there is some property or character of the thing whose exemplification is the object of the intrinsic preference. One can, however, construe the claim much more broadly—one can interpret it as identifying as a reason supporting an intrinsic preference *any* fact awareness of which *causes* the intrinsic preference. Thus if I happen to be so constituted that my awareness of the moon in the night sky causes me to want to eat cheese, the moon being in the sky would be a (justificatory) reason for wanting to eat the cheese! When clearly stated, this view is, of course, too absurd to require refutation.

In discussing the way in which we assess the relative strength of reasons supporting one conflicting preference over another, Darwall, in the same spirit as Brandt, suggests that what we must do is reflectively consider the reasons for the respective preferences at the same time. Darwall construes the "weight" of the respective reasons as a function of which preference one would act on were one to consider reflectively all of the relevant facts. Reflective awareness involves *vivid* representation of the relevant facts (p. 94) undistorted by temporal or spatial perspective (p. 95). The reader recalls, however, that we have already distinguished cognitive value from contemplative value and we have decided that it is only the former that defines the concept of an end relevant to the analysis of rational action. By doing so, we have accommodated much more neatly whatever insight underlies Darwall's attempt to correct for "errors" due to "vivacity" of imagination. Of course, we do not want the vivacity with which we imagine the imminent pain of the dentist's drill to overshadow the more difficult-to-imagine future suffering of a destroyed tooth in deciding whether or not reason, all things considered, recommends a visit to the dentist. But as I have suggested, the way to turn counterfactuals to one's advantage here is to construe the relevant strength of value or disvalue as that which would occur on realization that the object of the value or disvalue obtains.

That said, the only sense in which the reasons for an intrinsic desire for X can be greater than the reasons for another intrinsic desire for Y is that there are properties F whose presence in X are intrinsically valued, and properties G whose presence in Y are intrinsically valued, where the exemplification of F is valued more than the exemplification of G. What other *facts* are relevant to consider in "deciding" whether to prefer X to Y? By definition, if it is awareness of causal or logical consequences of X which would lead us to want it more than Y, we are no longer discussing an *intrinsic* preference for X over Y. And as we have seen in connection with Brandt, causal connections that obtain between the awareness of other sorts of facts and desires are unrelated to the question of whether there is anything irrational about those desires, at least if the irrationality of a desire is supposed to make it impotent vis-à-vis giving us reasons to act.

TURNING THE TABLES

Of course, if one thinks that there is objective value, yet another way is available of trying to distinguish between the rationality and irrationality of intrinsic desires. Robert Audi (1983) and Derek Parfit (1984), for example, argue explicitly or implicitly that what makes at least some intrinsic desires rational is that their objects have value. (Parfit claims that some desires are intrinsically irrational and others are rationally required—the intrinsically irrational desires are those whose objects are in no way *worth* desiring; the rationally required desires are those whose objects are worthy of support. This "worth" is presumably not to be defined subjectively.) I have relatively little to say about this suggestion beyond what I said at the close of Chapter 3. Obviously, in order to endorse such a view, one must convince oneself that there is such a thing as objective value or worth. Furthermore, one must convince oneself that things that have this property are thereby rational to pursue even if as a matter of contingent fact one finds oneself completely and utterly indifferent to this objective property identified as value. The oddness of supposing that I could have reason to pursue as an end something to which I am completely and utterly indifferent seems to me so great that it is difficult for me to take the view seriously, but I would also concede that, dialectically, it is the strongest alternative to the Humean position I defend. One can claim, for example, that human happiness is objectively good (no matter whose it is) and that anyone who doesn't desire it intrinsically is irrational. A person is irrational (the argument goes) if he does not desire that which is intrinsically good. Sadists have irrational desires because they desire human suffering, which is intrinsically bad. The fact that the sadist doesn't care about another's pain is irrelevant to the rationality of his sadistic behavior, because the sadist *should* care about another's pain. And this is true because pain is intrinsically bad and, by definition, one (rationally) should disvalue that which is intrinsically bad. The dialectical strength of this position comes from its unequivocal rejection of the relativism and subjectivity of rationality that so permeates the Humean approach. It is difficult for the opposing sides in this controversy to know how they should even begin to resolve their radical disagreement. As I said earlier, if the court of phenomenological appeal fails, I can see no alternative but to develop the most plausible positive account of rationality and morality within the relativist framework and hope that its clarity and plausibility simply win over the opposition.

Closely related to the view that the *rationality* of desire is to be defined in terms of the value of its object is a view that would *identify* the recognition that something has objective value with a kind of desire. This may be Aristotle's view in *Nichomachean Ethics,* and a version of it is defended by Butchvarov (1989).[16] Essentially, the view amounts to the claim that at least one sort of desire is a species of belief or knowledge. We can accommodate the intuition that there is an intimate connection between *recognition* of intrinsic value in X and the presence of a desire for X without *defining* value in terms of desire. The recognition itself (so the view goes) constitutes a kind of desire.

However ingenious this move might be, however, it surely seems to rest on an ad hoc conflation of an otherwise perfectly straightforward distinction between two kinds of intentional states. In general, belief or knowledge is logically and ontologically distinct from desire. If our knowledge that something is yellow does not constitute a desire for that thing, why should one take seriously the claim that our knowledge that something is intrinsically good constitutes a kind of desire for that thing? The thesis seems to me to rest on a completely mysterious decision to take knowledge of one objective property and identify that knowledge with desire!

Both the attempt to identify *rational* intrinsic desire with desire for what has objective nonrelativized value and the view that one can identify one kind of desire with knowledge of what has intrinsic objective nonrelativized goodness are so far dialectically removed from the approach I find plausible that it is difficult to find common ground on which to debate. Again, if phenomenological appeals to the absence of a plausible candidate for objective nonrelativized value fail, there may be no alternative but to present the most plausible positive account one can within the framework of relativism.

EGOISM AND RATIONALITY

One of the longest-running controversies in ethics concerns the question of whether rational behavior requires egoistic behavior. I consider the question here because it is a useful way of emphasizing certain consequences of our account of rational action and the concept of an agent's goals or ends on which that account rests.

What a person intrinsically values is a contingent fact about that person. In their famous dispute, Philippa Foot and Hare disagree over whether there are logical constraints placed on the kind of thing one can intrinsically value, and it should be obvious by now that I agree emphat-

16. See especially chap. 3.

ically with Hare, who follows the Humean tradition.[17] "S intrinsically values X" never asserts an impossibility (unless "X" itself is a term that carries with it the implication that X is disvalued).[18] Given the concept of rational action we have been developing, and the contingent character of questions about what one intrinsically values, it should be evident that it is a contingent question as to whether any given individual acts rationally by acting egoistically. The correct answer to the question concerning the rationality of egoism is, therefore, simple. Some people act rationally by acting egoistically; some people do not. If Thomas Nagel in *The Possibility of Altruism* really wanted to show only the *possibility* of altruism, we could wholeheartedly agree with him. It is all too evident, however, that Nagel and other critics of egoism want to place logical restrictions on what one can *reasonably* value. They want to argue not for the possibility of (rational) altruism but for the impossibility of (rational) egoism. Before we examine some of these concerns more closely, let us become clearer about the empirical character of questions concerning the rationality of egoistic behavior.

Given the framework within which we have been working, the simplest and most natural way to define an egoist is in terms of her goals or ends. An egoist is someone who intrinsically values only her own happiness or well-being. We can define an altruist in any number of different ways. On the one extreme, we have the direct opposite of an egoist, the person who intrinsically values only the well-being of others (an altruist [1]). I assume, however, that philosophers interested in defending the rationality of altruistic behavior more often have in mind Mill's conception of the ideal person as one who "as between his own happiness and that of others . . . [is] strictly impartial" (1957, p. 22). That is to say, an altruist in this sense (altruist [2]) is someone who intrinsically values his own happiness or well-being and, to the same extent and in the same way, the happiness or well-being of others. The philosophical debate is sometimes carried on as though the choice was between egoism and altruism (2), but if some people are not egoists, it seems to me much more likely that they would fall somewhere in between egoism and altruism (2). Thus it is possible, for example, that I value intrinsically my own happiness and value in the same way and to

17. See Foot 1958–59.
18. Thus, for example, "I approve of murder" *might* involve a contradiction if one can successfully argue that the term "murder" is used by someone to designate an act of killing of which one disapproves.

the same extent the happiness of *some* other people (my family, my friends, perhaps my fellow citizens). Or, I may value intrinsically the well-being of all other people but to varying degrees. Thus I may care very much about my children's happiness, somewhat less for my friends' happiness, still less for the happiness of people whose lives do not obviously touch my own.

In characterizing the egoist (and her altruistic counterparts), I have been using the expressions "well-being" and "happiness" more or less interchangeably. Although I shall not attempt to defend in detail a particular view here, it is, of course, important to clearly define this "happiness" that the egoist seeks (and the corresponding pain that she seeks to avoid). There is a bewildering array of analyses of pleasure or happiness, and some of these *define* pleasure in part by reference to desire. Such definitions raise the possibility of making it *analytic* that people desire only their own pleasure. But if we consider the more plausible desire-based accounts of pleasure, we shall see that even on these views it remains a contingent question as to what people intrinsically desire and even a contingent question as to whether people desire their own pleasure intrinsically. Thus Brandt, for example, defines pleasure as a state of a person which that person would want to prolong.[19] The virtue of such an account, of course, is that it accommodates our inclination to identify such a wide range of states as pleasures. On such an account, it will be a contingent question as to which particular states of mind we will desire to prolong, but it will also be a contingent question (although an odd one) as to whether one will intrinsically desire one's pleasures. To want one's pleasure, on a view like this, is to want to be in a state that one would want to prolong were one in it. And it is at least conceivable that someone might not want to be in such a state (perhaps as a result of religious conditioning that condemns certain sorts of pleasures).[20] And it is even more obvious that such a view would not prohibit me from having an intrinsic desire for the happiness of others.

Despite the attractiveness of desire-based accounts of happiness, I am more inclined to views that identify pleasure and happiness as states

19. See Brandt 1979, p. 40. William Heald (1985) has a most interesting and detailed discussion of this kind of analysis of pleasure.
20. This is obviously true of contemplative desire but is also true, I think, of cognitive desire. I might be a religious fanatic who, even in the throes of sexual pleasure construed as a sensation I want to prolong, manages to maintain the second-order desire that I not be in the position of being in a state like this that I want to prolong.

analogous to sensations. In the literature, a great deal is made about the alleged disanalogies between pain, which, it is often admitted, *can* be assimilated to sensation, and pleasure, which cannot. But the dissimilarity seems obvious only when one compares certain intense physical pain with more nebulous intellectual pleasures such as the pleasure of listening to Beethoven. In fact, of course, there are intellectual pains just as there are intellectual pleasures. A character in one of Woody Allen's movies describes the horror of death as worse than spending an evening with an insurance salesman. And whether or not death is all that bad, one can surely conjure up the kind of intellectual suffering he had in mind.

What do the extraordinarily diverse things we find pleasurable and painful have in common in virtue of which they are pleasurable and painful? I suspect that the answer may lie with the so-called hedonic tone theory, the view that there is a sui generis intentional state of enjoying that accommodates a wide range of states and activities, where its opposite defines the activities we call painful. The enjoyment or pain differs from case to case, and the relationship between different "enjoyings" can best be described using the familiar idea of family resemblance. To accept the view, one must convince oneself that one can find phenomenologically these ethereal states of mind, but I am not sure they are all that difficult to discover. In any event, I will not pursue the matter further, as I do not think that the following discussion rests on accepting either of the above two concepts of pleasure or happiness. Although some of my remarks may seem to presuppose the view that pleasure is a state of mind, I am confident that I could rephrase them to accommodate any plausible alternative conception of pleasure or happiness.

On any defensible conception of pleasure and happiness, it seems to me that it will be a contingent question as to whether people intrinsically desire only their own happiness and thus a contingent question as to whether one acts rationally only insofar as one acts so as to maximize one's happiness.[21] Notice that we have defined an egoist in terms of her goals or ends. We have *not* defined an egoist as someone who acts in the way that would be *rational* given her egoistic ends and the available evidence concerning the possible effects of action on her happiness. I

---

21. I use the misleading concept of maximizing happiness for convenience. It should be evident that on my view a person with egoistic ends takes into account the value adjusted possible consequences of his action with respect to his own happiness.

have indicated already that I do not assume that people, in general, act rationally, and I make no exceptions for egoists. As we shall shortly point out, failure to appreciate this point may give some objections to egoism an undeserved appearance of force.

We have already noted that, given our conception of an agent's goals or ends, it may be difficult for an agent to determine what his goals or ends are. Philosophers who argue that everyone is an egoist have a relatively easy time constructing hypotheses that are consistent with outward human behavior and that, if true, would support an egoistic conception of human nature. Consider again the example we discussed before of Mother Teresa and her life, which appears to be devoted to other people. If Mother Teresa isn't an altruist, it is hard to see how *anyone* will satisfy the concept. Yet it is surely possible (indeed, *likely*) that Mother Teresa is so constituted that she knows she will get pleasure from helping other people; she knows that she will suffer psychologically from ignoring the plight of others; and she believes that she will experience all the rewards of an afterlife, a belief that itself, no doubt, produces still more pleasure. It is also possible that, even if she doesn't realize it, the *only* things she values intrinsically are these various pleasures she believes she will experience. Given the fact that at least some of these pleasures are so causally bound to the helping of others, it may be difficult or impossible for her to be sure that she would value the well-being of others even it she were to hold no implicit beliefs about the effects of helping others on her own happiness. Of course, while the egoist can provide a plausible egoistic construal of Mother Teresa's behavior, the altruist can equally well offer a plausible altruistic construal of her behavior. Mother Teresa will probably tell you that she values the happiness of others intrinsically, and for all I know she may be right.

Some would argue that, if our conception of an egoist leaves open the possibility of Teresa being an egoist, that only shows that we have an implausible understanding of the distinction between egoistic and altruistic behavior. And there is something to this observation. Even if we should decide that all people have as their ultimate goal or end their own happiness, we would still want to make a sharp distinction between people like Mother Teresa, who get pleasure from helping other people, and people like Jack the Ripper, who get pleasure from hurting other people. Moreover, I would have no objection to using the terms "egoist" and "altruist" to mark the distinction. But in the philosophical context, it is fairly clear that for thousands of years philosophers have understood the distinction in terms of the *ultimate* ends of an agent in acting, and in this sense we can meaningfully raise the question of whether Teresa and Jack had the same ultimate end: their respective happiness.[22]

Because I believe it is ultimately an extremely difficult empirical question as to what people value intrinsically, I am not sure that philosophers who know next to nothing about the empirical world are in a terribly strong position to answer this fascinating question about human nature. Still, philosophers are rarely shy about offering a priori solutions to empirical questions, and some offer "thought experiments" designed to establish that at least some people are not "pure" egoists. These thought experiments typically request the reader to imagine himself or others in hypothetical situations in which he would realize that he would not act egoistically. Some of these situations are realistic; some fanciful. Thus at least some people pay large insurance premiums so as to guarantee a comfortable life for their children in the event of untimely death. Still others can be convinced that they would sacrifice their lives for their children's lives if they faced a situation in which these were the only options.

Obviously, even if it is agreed that people behave in the ways just described, this will not faze the philosopher determined to construe human nature as fundamentally egoistic. People do, after all, get pleasure *now* from thinking of their children growing up happy and prosperous. And parents would, no doubt, be aware that deciding to abandon their children would only lead to a life of utter anguish and despair. Egoists can surely kill themselves rather than suffer excruciating physical pain, and it seems obvious that there are kinds of psychological suffering every bit as severe as the most horrible of physical pains. To block these sorts of egoistic "reconstructions" of human behavior, the egoist's critic sometimes appeals to more exotic thought experiments involving more unrealistic hypothetical situations. Suppose, for example, that a being I firmly believe to be omnipotent offers me a life guaranteed to be as full of happiness as a human life could be. The only

22. There is, of course, an ambiguity in "same end". In one sense two egoists do not have the same end. *S*'s end is *S*'s happiness. *R*'s end is *R*'s happiness. In another perfectly clear sense they have the same kind of end. Both are interested in their respective states of pleasure. One must presuppose the first sense of "different end" to understand Plato's famous competition argument in *The Republic* (349a–350c).

condition is that I agree to execute my immediate family. As part of the hypothesis, we assume that I have absolute trust in this being's word and his powers. I believe, for example, that he will manipulate the environment so that my inevitable successes will not become too predictable, thereby making life too boring. I further believe that he will *immediately* destroy all memory of both the agreement and my decision to execute my family after I have fulfilled my side of the contract. My old memories will be replaced by those of an even more pleasant family which idolizes me in ways that I don't think my present family will ever quite manage. The rhetorical question is then asked: What would you do? And the assumption is that at least a great many would confidently reply that they would turn down the offer of the omnipotent being.[23]

Assuming that this prediction of human behavior is correct, does it show that people are not egoists? I don't think so. The *most* it would show is that people are not *rational* egoists. In the hypothetical situation, we still realize that we will suffer the most *intense* psychological agony we can imagine before gaining our ultimate rewards. And human nature being what it is, we all know that it can be extraordinarily difficult to endure short-term suffering for long-term gain. The person who cannot bring himself to visit the dentist, the smoker who cannot bring herself to quit, the student who cannot forgo the hot date to study for the final are all familiar examples of people who cannot hurdle the initial short-term suffering for the long-term gains that they could reasonably expect. Does this indicate that these individuals are not egoists? Hardly. Indeed, the examples I just gave are of individuals who seem primarily concerned with *their* happiness and suffering. And the pain the smoker can expect to endure on the road to good health *pales* in comparison with the almost unimaginable suffering the omnipotent being will require us to endure at the moment of making the critical decision. I conclude that this kind of hypothetical situation is no more effective than other standard thought experiments designed to block egoistic construal of human nature.

My guess is that I do intrinsically value the well-being of my family and friends and probably, to some small extent, even the happiness of the billions of people I don't even know. I suspect the same is probably

---

23. Hubin (1980) discusses a similar hypothetical situation. He is concerned not to refute psychological egoism, however, but to argue that a person's well-being does not necessarily consist in the satisfaction of his desires (the assumption being that a person might well desire to turn down the offer, get his desire satisfied, and not be better off).

true of most other people, with the main differences between individuals being a matter of the *degree* to which they value the well-being of others. It certainly wouldn't surprise me enormously, however, if the true counterfactuals about my values entail that the only thing I really intrinsically value is the various kinds of satisfaction I get from knowing that my family and friends are and will be happy.

Obviously, many philosophers remain convinced that there is some sort of incoherence involved in an egoist's values. One underlying source of this conviction, I believe, is the idea that there is no *reason* to treat one's own happiness as being different from the happiness of another.[24] If I intrinsically value my own happiness, *consistency* requires that I value the happiness of others. But what does it mean to charge an egoist with having inconsistent values?

One line of argument we shall postpone for later discussion, as it invokes the claim that rationality involves rules whose general acceptance can be rationally willed. Our evaluation of rule consequentialist conceptions of rationality and morality occupies most of the next chapter. There is another kind of objection to *ethical* egoism which we might briefly consider here, given our intention eventually to conceptually link morality to rationality. In a rather bad-tempered attack on the consistency of ethical egoism, Brian Medlin (1957) argued that, if one thinks one ought to promote one's own well-being, one is committed to thinking that everyone ought to promote his own well-being. Furthermore, believing that another person ought to do something involves *wanting* him to do it, and perhaps (if one goes as far as Hare) even helping him to do it. But when an egoist gets involved in a situation in which her self-interest conflicts with another's self-interest, she must, consequently, want herself to come out on top while she simultaneously wants that other person to come out on top. And if one is a prescriptivist in Hare's sense, the situation is even worse. Universalized ethical egoism commits one to doing the impossible. It commits one to accepting the imperative "Act so as to come out on top" while one also accepts the imperative "Let him act so as to come out on top." In a world that is difficult enough, one does not need a moral theory that commits one to doing the impossible.

Medlin's attack was directed as ethical egoism, but for now I am

24. Although they justify this claim in importantly different ways, this is the underlying structure of the arguments presented by Gewirth 1978, Moore 1903, Nagel 1970, and Parfit 1984, to mention just a few.

interested in exploring its implications for the thesis that one can act rationally by acting egoistically. It should be clear how I would respond to an argument analogous to Medlin's directed at the rationality of egoistic behavior. First, it does not follow that if I think I ought to act egoistically, I must think that everyone ought to act egoistically. I may have only egoistic ends while I realize full well that at least some other people have altruistic ends. I *am* (trivially) committed to the view that anyone like me in the relevant respects (i.e., anyone who is also an egoist) should (rationally) act egoistically. And this admission is probably enough for Medlin to proceed with his argument. But it is abundantly clear that the "ought" of rationality carries with it no implications as far as wanting people to do what one judges them to have the most reason to do.[25] Still less does our conclusion that someone rationally ought to do X require us to act so as to help him succeed.

Now if one should end up divorcing the "ought" of morality from the "ought" of rationality, and one further commits oneself to the view that accepting second- and third-person moral judgments about what others ought to do entails wanting people to act in the way one thinks they ought to, or acquiescing in any action that a person takes consistent with one's judgment that he is doing what he ought to do, then *of course* one is going to have trouble defending ethical egoism. Hare's meta-ethics, for example, with his technical concept of universalizability and his understanding of what accepting a moral judgment involves, would, in effect, require an ethical egoist to be *impartial* as between his pursuit of his happiness and others' pursuit of their happiness. The reason you have to put yourself in another's shoes to see whether you can accept the consequences of your behavior is to make sure you sympathetically take account of the effects of your action on others. And it doesn't take a genius to realize that one will encounter tensions trying to be an *impartial self-interested* person. The obvious moral to draw is that an egoist should ignore morality so conceived and simply refrain from making moral judgments, secure in the knowledge that he will encounter no conceptual difficulty defending his behavior as *rational*. One will have to live with Medlin's livid denunciation of the egoist who retreats from the impartial moral perspective to endorse what he calls individual egoism:

> Should he retreat to individual egoism his doctrine, while logically impregnable, is no longer ethical, no longer even a doctrine. He may wish to

25. Recall our discussion of this question in Chapter 2.

quarrel with this and if so, I submit peacefully. Let him call himself what he will, it makes no difference. I'm a philosopher, not a rat-catcher, and I don't see it as my job to dig vermin out of such burrows as individual egoism. (p. 59)

But a philosopher who gets this exercised at his opponent's maneuver is almost always just admitting (in a grouchy sort of way) the success of that maneuver.

It may seem to some unnecessary to dwell on Medlin's argument when it has surely been successfully refuted many times over, but it will be useful later, in recognizing a similar mistake made by Darwall in objecting to act consequentialist analyses of rational action, to recall Medlin's fundamental error.

By far the most promising attack on the consistency of an egoist's values involves the trivial sense we have recognized in which there are reasons even for intrinsic preferences. We have admitted, you recall, that phenomenologically at least, and probably ontologically, there is nothing to a thing over and above the exemplification of certain properties. This holds true for people, the argument goes, just as surely as it holds true for other things. When I value something intrinsically, it is always in virtue of my valuing the exemplification of some property. Now if I desire intrinsically my happiness, then *what* I desire is the exemplification of that property, happiness. And insofar as what I value is the exemplification of that property, I presumably value it no matter *where* it is instantiated.[26] An analogy might be helpful. I like a particular ice cream *a* because and only because of its flavor *F*. If there is another dish of ice cream *b* with precisely that same flavor *F*, then I must value it in the same way that I value *a*. After all, my valuing *a* just is my valuing the exemplification of *F*, and *F* is exemplified in both *a* and *b*. Similarly, if I value my happiness, it is presumably because I value the exemplification of happiness. But, then, how could I fail to value your happiness when that same property is exemplified? As I pointed out earlier, even if there *are* substances or bare particulars or, in this case, bare selves, it is hard to see how the fact that one "bare" self rather than another is present in the state of affairs of someone's being happy could make a difference as to whether it is an object of value.

However dialectically attractive this argument might initially seem, there is obviously something wrong with it. The difficulty becomes

26. Darwall presents this argument on p. 163, but although he seems to endorse it, he strangely enough doesn't try to rest his defense of "impartiality" on it.

evident once one realizes that the argument really purports to show not that one *shouldn't* have egoistic values or that having egoistic values involves inconsistency, but rather that one *cannot* have egoistic values. And the easiest way to refute this thesis is to take a good look at one's fellow human beings, who certainly behave as if they value the happiness of themselves and their loved ones more than they value the happiness of others. Moreover, if it is *impossible* to have egoistic values, then it is more than just a little ironical that philosophers like Gewirth and Nagel spend so much time trying to figure out how to convince people not to be egoists.

But given that there is something wrong with the above argument for the impossibility of having egoistic values, how should we diagnose the mistake? The obvious answer, I think, is that one must recognize that my concept of myself just is the concept of the bearer of certain properties. I am arguing neither for nor against the idea that there is such a thing as an individual essence or haecceity in the sense that Chisholm (1976) once recognized. But just as I single out everything else in terms of uniquely exemplified properties, so I single out myself as the person who has properties X. Properties X may include my haecceity (if there is such a thing), or memory experiences, or appearance, or whatever you think the most plausible candidate for such a property is. Now as an egoist, when I value intrinsically *my* happiness, what I value intrinsically is the exemplification of the property happiness *conjoined with X*, not the exemplification of happiness per se.

Someone like Nagel could argue, no doubt, that it is surely only the fact that happiness is good that gives one a reason to want it. And if the exemplification of happiness is good, it is good whether it is exemplified in you or in me. But such a response *presupposes* that a desire for the exemplification of F is rational only if F is good. And when all is said and done, I think that Nagel's defense of altruism rests on Audi's and Parfit's conception of the rationality of intrinsic desire being a function of the goodness of its object. In short, the argument goes, we have a reason to desire happiness only insofar as we can rationally regard the exemplification of happiness as being *objectively and nonrelativistically* good. As I indicated at the close of Chapter 4 and in discussing this conception of rational intrinsic value, we reach here one of those fundamental crossroads in philosophical thought where each party to the dispute has a difficult time arguing for his position. I can only repeat the rhetorical question. Do we want goodness and reasons for acting to be the kinds of things a person can be completely and utterly indifferent to? Can I have a reason to do something even if I take no interest whatsoever in the thing that is supposed to give me a reason to pursue it? If one accepts the Humean intuition that this violates the fundamental concept of reasons for acting, one has already abandoned the possibility of reintroducing objective goodness as a property whose presence in an object gives us reason to intrinsically value that object.

Parfit attempts to buttress his argument against egoism (the self-interest theory) by employing an elaborate argument that appeals to our intuitions about what it would be reasonable to care about or take an interest in. Parfit appeals to an exotic thought experiment in which we are to imagine ourselves "splitting," amoeba-like, into two different people, each of whom satisfies all of the ordinary criteria for personal identity through time. If we call these future halves of me A and B, and we call my present self C, we could argue, appealing to the transitivity of identity, that neither A nor B could be identical with my present self C since at most only one could be identical with C and it would be gratuitous to claim that it is one rather than the other.[27] Nevertheless, Parfit argues, it is obvious that I would have reason to care about the well-being of these future individuals who bear the "R" relation to me (where the "R" relation just is the ordinary criterion for personal identity). It follows, therefore, that people have reason to care about the well-being of at least some individuals other than themselves.

Now given my unqualified Humean position on the arationality of intrinsic value, I reject, of course, the suggestion that it would be *irrational* not to care about these future individuals. I don't even see that it is *irrational,* although it is decidedly odd, not to care intrinsically about one's future self given the metaphysical supposition that there is something that in the strict sense of identity survives through time. In order to construe paradigmatic egoistic behavior as rational, it is true that we must assume that the egoist values intrinsically her future well-being. If Parfit is right, and A and B in the future are not me, and if I value intrinsically the well-being of A and B, then I am not an egoist and I will be acting irrationally if I act as an egoist. Would we value intrinsically the well-being of A and B if we were C? Probably. Does this mean that we value intrinsically the well-being of individuals other than our present and future selves? Perhaps. One could, of course, argue just

27. See Parfit 1984, chap. 12. Compare Parfit's views about this kind of hypothetical situation with Chisholm's in *Person and Object.*

as plausibly that in the far-fetched situation of fission we should say that the future A and B are both identical with C. It's true that we would have to give up the principle of transitivity of identity, but if one thinks that identity through time isn't strict identity, one would probably be just as well off restricting the principle of transitivity of identity to strict identity. When all is said and done, it seems to me that there is only a terminological difference between saying that A and B bear the R relation to me and saying that A and B are both identical to me *in the loose sense of identity relevant to evaluating the identity of things through time.*

In any event, without surreptitiously introducing the concept of objective reasons for desires, one cannot even argue that an individual is irrational for not caring about his future self, let alone his fissioned halves. But if one has the concept of objective, nonrelative reasons for having intrinsic desires, one surely does not need the complicated argument Parfit presents to argue against the rationality of an egoist's desire. One can simply claim that human happiness is objectively "worthy" of being desired and is, therefore, by definition rational to desire no matter whose happiness it is. On the view I defend, as long as there is a difference between a future self and a present self, or a fissioned half of a present self and a present self, then that difference can differentiate a desire for one's present self's well-being and a desire for one's future self's (or fissioned half's) well-being. In the completely unrealistic situation in which one doesn't care a fig about one's future self's well-being, one wouldn't have any reason to act so as to protect that future self. In fact (and this *is* just a brute psychological fact), everyone does care about his future well-being and probably would care about the future well-being of his fissioned halves. It does not seem to be a brute psychological fact that all people care about the well-being of other people (or people who do not bear the R relation to themselves), and that is why it may be rational for some people to act egoistically while it is irrational for others to act egoistically.

CHAPTER 6

Objections to Act Consequentialism

We have examined some controversies concerning the analysis of rational action, but to this point we have presupposed the general framework of an *act* consequentialist view. However we understand the concept of an agent's goals or ends, and whether we construe as fundamental, actual, probable, or possible consequences of alternative actions, or justified belief about actual, probable, or possible consequences of alternative actions, we have been supposing that the consequences are those of the particular hypothetical act in its specific circumstances. This is what makes the view I defend a version of *act* consequentialism. As readers familiar with the literature know, act consequentialist analyses of rationality and, even more so, of morality, have been objected to on several grounds, and we must explore some of these objections now.

Because we are postponing until the last chapter a detailed effort to conceptually link our analyses of practical rationality with the concepts of morality, we shall continue to take as our primary concern practical rationality. If I am right about the conceptual connections between morality and rationality, however, the kinds of objections we must consider to act consequentialist analyses of rational action arise also in connection with act consequentialist analyses of morally right action. It will be useful, then, to consider these objections as they are raised against analyses of both rational and morally right action. Even if the concept of morally right action is distinct from the concept of rational action (perhaps because we cannot conceptually tie moral goodness to wants or goals), I am convinced that act consequentialist analyses of these respective concepts stand or fall together when faced with the sorts of objections we are about to consider.

As was pointed out in Chapter 2, the main alternatives to act consequentialist analyses of rational/right action are *rule* consequentialist analyses. And it is arguments designed to support rule as opposed to act consequentialist analyses of rational/right action that primarily occupy us later in this chapter when we focus on the implications of the prisoner's dilemma, the voter's paradox, and other attempted reductio's of act consequentialism. But let us begin with some epistemological concerns that act consequentialism might understandably raise.

Act Consequentialism and Skepticism

One might argue that, if an act consequentialist analysis of rational/ right action entails that one can never know or justifiably believe that an action is rational/right, we have a reductio of that analysis. In Chapter 1 I warned against philosophers making unwavering commitment to the rejection of philosophical skepticism. In fact, I believe that an extensive and fundamental skepticism with respect to almost all of what we unhesitatingly believe may well be the correct *philosophical* position to take. But even if this were true (and I certainly don't expect the reader to believe it), I would concede that a plausible analysis of any concept should accommodate our *beliefs* about what we know or justifiably believe. And people do seem to *believe* that they can reach justified conclusions concerning what they rationally/morally ought to do. I accept, therefore, the responsibility of showing how, on my analysis of rational action, people would believe that they can justifiably reach these conclusions given "commonsense" (perhaps mistaken) beliefs about what counts as reasonable sources of evidence. When I later talk about what we can or cannot justifiably believe, then, it will be elliptical for justifiably believe *given the presuppositions of common sense.*

Do act consequentialist analyses of rational/right action fail the test of accommodating our "commonsense" beliefs about the possibility of knowing what we ought to do? The answer obviously depends on what sort of act consequentialism we are talking about. We have already pointed out in Chapter 4 that *actual consequence* analyses of rational/right action are going to have a terrible time explaining why anyone would think they could know rational from irrational, right from wrong, action. Again, the consequences of having a child extend at least indefinitely, if not infinitely, into the future, and we do not even *pretend* that we can see indefinitely into the future. How, then, can we compare the hypothetical consequences (in terms of satisfied ends or goodness) of alternative actions to determine which would be the rational/right action to take? I argued earlier that one might be able to place a reasonable "bet" on one alternative rather than another, but only in the sense that one might be able to reasonably conclude that one alternative has a better chance of being rational/right than each other alternative considered by itself. As we also noted, however, this is a far cry from being able to rationally conclude of this alternative that it would be the rational/right action to take.[1]

Probable consequence act consequentialist analyses of rational/right action would make epistemological issues ever so much easier to deal with. The only consequences we need to consider on this view are those that are *probable* relative to our evidence. There is a sense, then, in which the less we know or justifiably believe about the consequences of alternatives, the easier it will be to reach conclusions about what we rationally/morally ought to do. The arguments for moving to value adjusted possible consequence consequentialism were decisive, however, and it is no use lamenting how much simpler our epistemological lives would be if we were to accept a false analysis of rational/right action.

At first it may seem that value adjusted possible consequence analyses of rational/right action are no better and perhaps even worse than actual consequence analyses at avoiding radical skepticism. Whereas on an actual consequence view one must worry about the indefinitely many effects that would actually occur as a result of taking one action over another, on the *possible* consequence view one must worry about the even larger class of possible effects that might result from an action, where these possible effects extend into an infinite future. And if we take

---

1. Of course, an actual consequence consequentialist can introduce *derivative* concepts of rational action analogous to the derivative concepts of (R3) which we defined in the last chapter. Such derivative concepts would *not* define rational action in terms of hypothetical actual consequences.

seriously the implications of lottery examples, we cannot make life easier for ourselves by restricting the relevant possibilities to those that are "realistic," that is, to those that have at least a reasonable chance of occurring. It seems obvious that when the stakes get high enough we should insist on the necessity of taking into account *extremely* unlikely, but still possible, outcomes. I hope, for example, that the president of the United States still keeps in mind the possibility of starting a third world war by some action he contemplates even when he thinks there is a chance of only a one in a hundred thousand that it will happen. But if we must take into account even very improbable consequences, how can we even begin to cope with calculating the rational/right thing to do? I am considering having a child. The child might turn out to be the next Mother Teresa but also might turn out to be the next Adolf Hitler. I want to go to the grocery store. But I might run over someone on the way. That person might be a person who would find the cure for cancer or might be a person who would eventually find a way to blow up the world. The most trivial action I contemplate has potentially enormously important consequences.[2] It is difficult to see how a possible conse-quence consequentialist could concern himself with questions about what he ought to do and at the same time make it through the day without having a nervous breakdown. How, then, could a possible consequence consequentialist use his view in making decisions as to what he rationally/morally ought to do?

The solution to keeping possible consequences "manageable" is, in part, to find a way to justify not worrying about certain sorts of ex-tremely unlikely possibilities. Again, as the lottery example indicates, one cannot achieve this end simply by ruling out as irrelevant highly unlikely possible outcomes. But one can let highly unlikely possible outcomes *cancel each other out*. In most cases, a highly unlikely beneficial possible outcome will be matched by a highly unlikely but possible calamitous outcome. It is possible that the child I am thinking of having will destroy the human race, but there is a roughly equal possibility that she will save the human race. In my calculations, therefore, these respec-tive possibilities may be safely ignored. There is, indeed, a small chance that I will accidentally kill someone driving to the grocery store, but there is an equally small chance that I will encounter some situation in which I can save a life, perhaps by resuscitating an accident victim.

2. Donagan (1977) raises this sort of objection against act consequentialism. See p. 201.

Moreover, the extremely unlikely but possible fortuitous and calamitous consequences of one action typically exist, or have their counterparts, for *alternative* actions. In such an event, the unlikely possible consequences of alternative actions again cancel each other out. My decision to live in California might result in my death in a freeway accident, but my decision to stay in Iowa might result in my death from contaminated drinking water.

Notice, by the way, that we have here a solution to some rather formal concerns involving decision making under risk. As long as we are considering *possibilities,* I suppose one might worry, for example, that there are possible outcomes of our actions that have an *infinite* amount of positive or negative value. As an egoist, for example, one might worry that there may indeed be a hell in which one would suffer for an infinite amount of time for that brief affair one is contemplating. If one assigns, as one might, an infinite amount of disvalue to an infinite amount of suffering, one will be left with an infinite amount of disvalue even after it has been discounted for the improbability of its occurring. And though some theologians might be happy with this result, it is disturbing to us atheists that the possibility of an omnipotent, omnivengeful God should decide a priori the rationality of violating that possible God's possible commandments. The solution, again, is to let this infinitely bad possible consequence of eternal suffering be cancelled by the equally possible eternal suffering that *might* result from inadvertently violating the possible commands of a God that might want people to have occasional affairs.

In short, far-fetched possibilities are not irrelevant simply because they are far-fetched, but rather they are irrelevant because they are typically cancelled by virtue of the fact that there are analogous unlikely consequences that might occur no matter which action one takes.

Still, in deciding what one morally/rationally ought to do, wouldn't one need to canvass all of the indefinitely, or even infinitely, many possible outcomes in order to ensure that they do indeed cancel each other out, and wouldn't this again preclude the possibility of reaching rational conclusions about what one ought to do? The answer has two parts. First, thought experiments of the sort we have just been discussing allow us to generalize. We learn to recognize that there are kinds of possibilities that re-arise in situation after situation which cancel each other out in the way discussed. These kinds of possiblities may have infinitely many instantiations, but in inductively eliminating the relevance of this kind of consequence, one ipso facto eliminates the relevance of the many different instances of the kind. Furthermore, there is obviously room for the use of *rules of thumb* in making decisions, and this, coupled with the preceding consideration, really does accommodate, I think, the intuition that deciding questions of practical rationality and morality is not beyond the pale of human cognition (as it is ordinarily conceived). As Mill pointed out, rational people have had ample time to reflect on the possible consequences of kinds of actions—lying, for example—and we can certainly reach inductively supported conclusions that in the vast majority of cases lying would be irrational. And surely no one would argue that this inductively supported conclusion could not be rationally relied on in reaching conclusions about what one ought to do in situations in which one must choose quickly and unreflectively.

Still, suppose one faces an extremely unusual situation without much in the way of precedent, where again a choice must be made relatively quickly. One begins assessing the possible outcomes, trying to discount the value of those that have value for rough and ready assessments of probability. One simply cannot, however, reasonably expect to have considered all the relevant possibilities. Indeed, one might be able to confidently predict at the time of choosing that one has failed to consider all sorts of relevant possibilities. In situations such as this, would rational action be precluded or, at the very least, be a matter of pure chance? More generally, how does failure to take into account possible outcomes affect the rationality of action?

In answering this question, we should again recall that interesting ambiguity in the concept of rational action discussed earlier. At one level, the intentional object of our deliberations concerning rational action is, I believe, captured by value adjusted possible consequence consequentialism. But we also recognized another sense in which a person may be said to act rationally if he acts with the justified belief that his action is rational in the primary sense defined by (R3). We then took this derivative concept a step further and argued that there is certainly a sense in which a person is acting rationally if he acts with the justified belief that his action is more likely to be rational (in the primary sense) than any of the alternatives open to him.

Now in this *derivative* sense of rational action, there are at least two senses in which a person who has failed to survey all of the relevant possible outcomes of alternative actions can still end up acting rationally. First such a person can, of course, simply choose a certain action X which, through sheer luck, turns out to be the action that maximizes value adjusted possible utility (satisfaction of ends for rationality, goodness for morality). In other words, one's actions can, through chance, be rational/right in the primary sense of these concepts defined by (R3) and its moral analogue—the primary sense that defines the object of our concern when we deliberate on questions of rationality/morality. But second, we can invoke our derivative concepts of rational action and a strategy discussed earlier in connection with a move that the actual consequence consequentialist might make. Having surveyed as many possible outcomes as time permits, we can make our rough and ready calculations concerning the relative merits of alternative actions vis-à-vis *envisioned* possible outcomes. Suppose that of the available alternatives, X, Y, and Z, X would clearly be the rational/right action to take if, contrary to fact, the only possible outcomes were those *considered*. Since, by hypothesis, we have not considered the other possibilities, we have no reason to believe that *they* favor any one of the alternatives over another. On that basis, then, we can justifiably conclude on the data we *have* had time to consider that X is more likely than Y and more likely than Z to win the "contest" of rationality/morality were *all* possibilities considered. The situation is precisely analogous to that bet on coin tossing discussed earlier. If after a few tosses one coin has turned up heads more than the others, and we have no reason to believe of subsequent tosses that one coin will turn up heads more than another, it is more likely, relative to the observations we have made, that the coin ahead after a few tosses will be the ultimate winner. Similarly, if after some value adjusted possible outcomes for the alternatives X, Y, and Z have been considered, X has an early lead, and we have no evidence concerning the relative merits of possibilities not yet considered, then relative to the available evidence, X is more likely than either Y or Z to be the rational/right action. And if we act with the justified belief that this is so, then we are acting rationally in that important derivative sense of rationality we developed earlier (R3d2a).[3]

Now one might worry that this strategy for reconciling rational action with the obvious limitations of the human mind concerning the evaluation of possible outcomes makes it *too* easy for an agent to act rationally. Indeed, one might worry that a person who accepts the view

3. We can obviously envision similar ways in which still higher-level derivative concepts of rational action could be satisfied.

I have been defending would be encouraged to adopt a rather "happy-go-lucky" attitude toward decision making. In debating the relative merits of alternative actions open to me, why wouldn't I simply stop the process of considering possible outcomes as soon as one of the alternatives developed an early "lead" vis-à-vis the possibilities already surveyed? I have argued that I would be justified in believing at that stage that the action with the early lead has the best chance of being rational, and I have argued that if I act with that justified belief I am acting rationally in at least an important derivative sense. But surely we want to allow that at least for important decisions a rational person must carefully evaluate as many possible outcomes as time permits.

This is, of course, correct. But we have already indicated in Chapter 4 how we should accommodate this point. You recall that I argued that we must distinguish the rationality of seeking further evidence on which to base our evaluation of probabilities from the rationality of an action relative to the evidence the agent has available. We made that distinction by way of clarifying the evidence base relative to which we should identify the possibilities and probabilities that define rational action in the primary sense. But we can make a similar distinction in connection with this derivative sense of rationality we have just been discussing. An agent who considers relatively few possible outcomes before acting may be acting rationally in our derivative sense relative to the justified belief she has when making her choice. But there is nothing to stop us from evaluating the rationality of her decision to act without considering further possible outcomes. Typically, if an agent makes an important decision without considering many possible outcomes, we can conclude that she acted irrationally (in our primary sense) for not thinking more about the possible effects of her action, even if she acted rationally relative to the justified belief she had while acting.

The distinction is, of course, a subtle one, and in ordinary thought about such matters, we no doubt ignore it. We may well call a person's action irrational by virtue of the irrationality of the decision-making procedure (in this case, the contemplation of possible outcomes) leading up to the action. But though ordinary discourse may obscure the distinction between questions concerning the rationality of the deliberative process from questions concerning the rationality of the action it results in, we should have no difficulty as philosophers making the distinction. Of course, a great many factors would go into the question of when one should stop the process of calculating the rationality/ rightness (in the primary sense) of an action before making one's choice. The question is to be answered like any question about what one ought to do, that is, its answer depends on the valued adjusted possible outcomes of choosing at a particular stage in the consideration of alternatives. Time is certainly always a factor. Choices often must be made relatively quickly. The more likely it is that crucial foreseeable consequences depend on one's decision, the more energy it is presumably worth spending trying to take into account these possible outcomes. But the "wear and tear" on the human mind is certainly a negative factor to take into account in deciding whether even important decisions should be made only after exhaustive and *exhausting* surveys of possible outcomes.

One might worry at this point that we are flirting with a vicious regress when we distinguish the rationality of the decision-making process from the rationality of the action it eventually produces. Certainly, if in considering the question of whether we ought to do *X*, we must deliberate on the question of whether we ought to discontinue evaluating possible outcomes of *X*, the first step in a regress might appear to have been taken. For in deciding whether we ought to discontinue evaluating possible outcomes of *X*, we would need to consider the possible outcomes of discontinuing the evaluation of possible outcomes of *X*. But this would in turn raise the question of when we ought to discontinue evaluating the possible outcomes of discontinuing our evaluation of the possible outcomes of *X*, and so on ad infinitum. But our account does not require that a rational agent *deliberate in this way*. Usually, we simply decide to make our choice between *X* and its alternatives after considering some of the possibilities that occur to us. That decision, nevertheless, might be rational or irrational in our primary sense of rationality, where its rationality depends on what the possibilities and probabilities are relative to our evidence but where the relevant possibilities and probabilities need *not* be considered by us. Of course, we *may* start thinking about the question of when we should stop evaluating possible outcomes, and this *may* lead us to consider questions concerning the possible outcomes of discontinuing our evaluation of possible outcomes. And we may even take the process of conscious deliberation to still higher levels. But I stress again, nothing in our account requires that an agent deliberate about possible outcomes in order for the primary concepts of rationality and irrationality to apply.

ACT CONSEQUENTIALISM AND PROCRASTINATION

I mentioned earlier that some philosophers worry that act consequentialist analyses of rational/right action make every decision a momentous one, for the actual and possible consequences of every action, however insignificant that action might seem, go on and on. I have tried to argue that there are no serious epistemological difficulties generated by this observation, at least within the context of commonsense epistemological presuppositions. It has always seemed to me that, if anything, the difficulty with act consequentialism might be precisely the opposite. I have long been a most reprehensible procrastinator, and I have occasionally worried that my sometimes disastrous procrastination is a direct outgrowth of my act consequentialism. Put crudely, though it sometimes seems obvious that it would be rational for me to do something *sometime,* it is often difficult for me to conclude that there is any *particular* time at which it seems rational to engage in that behavior. This is especially true of unpleasant chores. Thus, for example, suppose I decide that it would be best for me to clean out my garage *sometime.* From the fact that I ought to clean out my garage sometime it does not follow that there is any *particular* time at which I ought to begin work on the garage (though it does follow that I should begin work on the garage sometime).

As an act consequentialist, I presumably evaluate the wisdom of beginning work on the garage at any particular time by looking at the value adjusted possible consequences of this action compared to alternatives. Life being what it is, we procrastinators will assure you, it is notoriously easy to come up with alternatives to work which would seem to win the battle of potential consequences. And one of the main reasons for this is that it *always* seems reasonable to argue that it is highly unlikely that postponing the unpleasant activity, say, two hours will have any negative consequences. In the whole scheme of things, I think *correctly,* it surely wouldn't make any difference if I waited until after the football game to clean out the garage. But of course, after the football game I can equally well argue that the consequences of waiting until after my tennis game would hardly matter one way or the other (and I do enjoy my tennis). Furthermore, after tennis, I very much enjoy just lying around the rest of the day, and it is hard for me to see how waiting another day to begin work on the garage would really make any signifi- cant difference. The consequences of not starting work on my garage at any particular time *always* seem to be insignificant, and given that I can always think of something I'd rather be doing at that particular time than working on my garage, I always do something else instead. And this procrastination seems to be rational, given act consequentialism, even though acting in accord with the principles of act consequential- ism will have as its consequence that my garage never gets cleaned out, something that (for the sake of argument) is bad.

We have been talking so far about procrastination with respect to unpleasant projects that have no deadline. A similar problem, however, arises with respect to the sort of project that does have a deadline. It is bad if I don't get my income tax returns filed by April 15. Sometime between now and April 15 I ought to begin work on my taxes (a most unpleasant activity). Still, it doesn't follow that there is any particular time at which I ought to begin work on my taxes, and delaying such work a few hours *almost* never seems to have any serious consequences. Now this case is different from the last in that there will presumably be some time when further procrastination definitely has disastrous conse- quences—namely, the time when it will be physically impossible to complete the tax forms by the deadline. Still, the vast majority of times are such that it is hard to see how not doing the taxes at those times has any serious consequences. And even if there is a "moment of truth" at which I begin work on my taxes or fail to get them done, it may well be that I would never have any reason for believing that I am at that very point. Assuming that as an act consequentialist I can rationally pro- crastinate when I rationally believe that the consequences of not doing the unpleasant activity are insignifianct, we still get the result that an act consequentialist will rationally engage in persistent procrastination, procrastination that we may assume will, in the long run, probably have bad consequences (when, for example, the many procrastinated projects all pile up, making it impossible to complete them).

I have tried to illustrate a potential problem by focusing on pro- crastination. It should be obvious, however, that it is not isolated in this way. The same reasoning that might seem to encourage an act conse- quentialist to constant procrastination can also lead to bankruptcy. I certainly realize as an act consequentialist that I shouldn't spend far more than I earn (the likely consequences of this being, in the long run, unpalatable). When it comes to evaluating the rationality of any *particular* relatively inexpensive purchase, however, it seems difficult to see how *it* will have consequences that are particularly disastrous compared with the pleasures involved in owning the item. Being another twenty dollars in debt is hardly going to make any significant difference one way or the other. Of course, if I continue to make decisions on particular purchases this way (the way the act consequentialist recommends), I'll be in a very awkward situation in no time at all.

One might think the solution to these problems is to recognize that to be rational one must live by *rules,* which then determine the rationality of particular decisions. We discuss rule consequentialism later in this chapter, so I will not attempt to deal with this suggestion in any detail here. Notice, however, that the rule consequentialism necessary to resolve the above difficulties is far weaker than the rule consequentialism discussed in Chapter 2. For one thing, we have as yet no argument for evaluating the rules by which we govern our lives in terms of the consequences of people *in general* acting in accord with these rules. Rather, the view I am imagining suggests only that each individual must guide his decisions by formulating rules, which he in turn evaluates by looking at how his life would turn out were he to live in accord with those rules.

There is certainly a sense in which I would admit that, in evaluating alternative actions open to one, one must take into consideration actions as they form a part of a general *strategy.* I indicated earlier that we should become clearer about the notion of alternative actions that our account of rational action presupposes. John Pollock (1983) worries about this question and suggests that, rather than compare isolated acts and their consequences, we should be comparing what he calls "maximal strategies". To discover whether or not one should do A, one should consider strategies designed to maximize expected value which incorporate A with strategies designed to maximize expected value which incorporate some other action instead of A. I won't go into the details of Pollock's account, which gets quite technical to deal with some formal paradoxes involving potentially unlimited value.[4] The

4. One such problem involves a case similar to one suggested by Burks (1977, p. 192). What should you do if a God promises to produce for you as many units of value as the number you give that God? If you come up with the number 20, he will give you 20 units

rough idea, however, could be restated in connection with the resolution of another problem, a potentially vicious regress.

To calculate the probabilities of various consequences of an action A, I will presumably have to calculate the probability of my doing certain other things, X, in conjunction with A. But if I am a committed consequentialist, I will only be able to determine if I will do something else X, if I know what I will conclude vis-à-vis the possible and probable consequences of X. But the consequences of X will depend, no doubt, in part on what else I do along with X. But to know what else I will do with X I will have to know what conclusions I will reach vis-à-vis the consequences of these other actions, and so on. There appears to be a problem here only because we are thinking of decision making as though it applied to each act in a chain of actions. In fact, of course, we do no such thing. In deciding whether I ought to walk to the grocery store, I do not ask myself at each step whether I ought to take the next step. I decide, if you like, on a chain of actions that for want of a better expression form a strategy, and the consequences I concern myself with are the consequences of that strategy.

Pollock himself suggests that the idea of comparing strategies to determine the rationality of actions they incorporate is "reminiscent of rule utilitarianism" (p. 413). But it really isn't conceptually linked to the idea of rule consequentialism at all, particularly if one allows that at any given time it can be rational to interrupt a strategy that was originally rational to pursue in order to pursue an alternative. Act consequentialists are surely aware that narrowly defined actions are at best tiny nonredundant parts of conditions that are nomologically sufficient for their effects.[5] To calculate the effects of one's actions, one is going to

---

of value. If you come up with the number 100, he will give you 100 units of value, and so on. Intuitively, any number you decide on will be the wrong one to have decided on because there was another act, namely, giving God that number + 1, which would have produced more value. Is this really a problem for that account I have been defending? I don't think so. The moral to draw is that in far-fetched hypothetical situations one may have to reconcile oneself to the possibility that, no matter what one does, one will not do the best thing. Interestingly, at least one philosopher (Kretzmann forthcoming) would argue that the impossibility of doing the best thing might be offered as an excuse for a God producing this world instead of some better world. It is surely true that God could have created a better world than this, but that would be true of any world God created. God could no more be blamed for producing this world than we could be blamed for instructing God to give us n units of value rather than $n + 1$ units of value.

5. I have tried to analyze the concept of a nonredundant part of a nomologically sufficient condition (an NRPSC) elsewhere. See Fumerton 1976.

have to do so in the context of presuppositions about what else is going to happen, where these other conditions include both the actions of others and additional actions of oneself. One looks beyond the moment, in other words, in deciding whether or not one ought to do *A,* but that does not suggest that one looks to exceptionless rules whose correctness is defined by hypothetical questions concerning the consequences of always acting in accordance with them.

Now I brought up this whole question of understanding the relevant concept of alternative action in terms of strategies because it might seem to help with our puzzle concerning procrastination and deficit spending. The twenty-dollar expenditure in isolation might not seem to have any significant consequences, but one must think of the expenditure of this twenty dollars as part of a strategy that either does or doesn't include other similar purchases. If it doesn't include any other similar purchases, then indeed, there may be no bad consequences that result from pursuing this strategy, but if it does, then the likely consequences may include whatever happens to one after one goes deep into debt. In fact, however, for all its utility, I do not think Pollock's concept of comparing maximal strategies helps with the problems we are now discussing. And this is so because of that point we stressed earlier. A rational person must be able to rationally decide to abandon a strategy that was initially rational, and furthermore, a rational person must calculate when to begin a strategy. But this latter issue, of course, simply reraises the problem of procrastination. I have determined that I will eventually follow the strategy of avoiding deficit spending. But it is not clear to me that the consequences of beginning that strategy after my next twenty-dollar purchase are likely to be significantly worse than the consequences of pursuing that strategy before the next twenty-dollar purchase. But after that purchase, I can reraise the issue of whether it might be best to postpone beginning my strategy of a balanced budget after yet another twenty-dollar purchase, and so on.

I think one needs a more straightforward solution to the problem of procrastination for an act consequentialist. Specifically, I think one needs to construe the problem as simply a more general instance of the sorites paradox.

The fact that it is notoriously difficult to keep a straight face and identify the height at which a person becomes tall does not mean that there isn's a perfectly useful notion of being tall. And similarly, the act consequentialist might argue, the fact that it is difficult to isolate any particular time at which postponing work on the garage is bad doesn't mean that there is no time at which further procrastination is bad. I think this response is essentially correct. However, one must carefully distinguish the sense in which it is "hard to say" that further procrastination will be bad from the sense in which it is "hard to say" when another thousandth of an inch would make a person tall. Some distinctions can usefully be made.

In general, the sorites prolem does not seem to be an epistemological problem. One can *know* all there is to know about the heights of everyone alive and the height of some particular person and one will still have a hard time saying *exactly* how much that person would have to grow in order to be tall. Part of what seems to characterize sorites sorts of situations is that as we progress along the relevant continuum we becomes less and less sure as to what we should say until it finally becomes obvious that the problematic concept applies. The problem of procrastination for an act consequentialist might not *seem* to be of this sort, for we have been arguing that one can *always* confidently assert that another hour's postponement of the unpleasant activity will amost certainly not have any untoward consequences.

It might be useful here to contrast the case of procrastination with what seemed to be a similar problem, the problem of repeated but individually insignificant deficit spending. You recall that, just as in the case of procrastination, each purchase considered individually did not *seem* to have any terrible consequences, even though it is obvious that if one continues to act in this way the results will be disastrous. Here, it does seem that the problem is just a familiar sorites problem and can be justifiably ignored by the act consequentialist. Having a *large* debt is (for the sake of argument) undesirable, and one is incrementally approaching a large debt with each minor purchase. It will, of course, always be hard to say that the next purchase will make the debt large, just as it will always be hard to say that the next thousandth of an inch will make the person tall. But we do feel progressively more uneasy that we are getting to the negative consequence of a large debt with each individual purchase, just as we feel progressively more sure that we have got a tall person as he continues to grow. But just exactly how is procrastination different from this? The answer lies in construing the problem of procrastination as more epistemological in character than a typical sorites problem. Let me explain by first returning to the case of procrastination involving a deadline.

I know that the consequences of not getting my tax forms filed by April 15 are bad, but it is hard for me to identify any particular time at which postponing work on my taxes is likely to have any significant effects. The situation is complicated, however. The probability of an action causing future difficulty obviously depends in part on the probabilities of other future events occurring. One can always safely assume that life will bring with it its usual quota of minor day-to-day crises that need to be quickly resolved. The potential procrastinator, if rational, must take this into account. He must not succumb to the irrational procrastinator's temptation to think of the future as an "uncluttered" span of time, any moment of which would be available as a starting time for work on one's taxes. The closer April 15 approaches, the more likely it is that completing my taxes will require some significant sacrifice on my part in terms of either neglecting another necessary evil or forfeiting some significant pleasure.

Now it *may* be that there is *no* time at which I am justified in believing that further procrastination will bring about such a hardship. It may be that there is no time at which a rational person could conclude that it is now or never to begin work on taxes. But as act consequentialists we must not slip into the error of supposing that one needs to find *probable* consequences that would justify our starting work on our taxes. I have argued earlier that people have a terribly difficult time remembering that the rationality of an action is not solely a function of consequences that are *probable* relative to the agent's evidence. And it may be that the tendency of many people to procrastinate is a symptom of this rather pervasive failing. Certainly, if you are a probable consequence consequentialist, you may end up being the kind of procrastinator who eventually gets yourself into a lot of trouble. If your policy is to postpone unpleasant but eventually necessary activities whenever it *probably* won't get you into trouble, your policy will, ironically, eventually get you into trouble. But as we argued, plausible act consequentialism takes into account *possibilities*. As the deadline approaches, it becomes more and more likely (albeit perhaps still unlikely) that the project you are putting off will not get completed, and as a value adjusted possible consequence consequentialist, you must keep assigning a higher and higher adjusted value to one of the possible consequences of further procrastination: not completing the project or completing it only at the cost of some other considerable loss. When the adjusted negative value becomes high enough, it might well outweigh the more certain but comparatively less significant pleasures you would get from, for example, an afternoon of tennis.

How does this treatment of the problem of procrastination for projects involving a deadline differ from simply treating the problem as just another instance of the classical sorites puzzle? Well, as I suggested earlier, I think you could treat the puzzle of how to avoid procrastination from an act consequentialist's perspective as a *species* of sorites paradox. The difference is that classical sorites puzzles do not seem to be epistemological in nature. The difficulty of marking some specific point along the continuum of height at which a person becomes tall does not seem to derive from a lack of information (about, say, average heights). The act consequentialist will be hard pressed to identify *the point* at which one shouldn't engage in further procrastination of an unpleasant activity, but the continuum presenting the difficulty is the vague *epistemic* continuum of ever-increasing probability that some untoward unpleasantry will result from any additional postponement. These probabilities are incrementally increasing, and it will be impossible to identify (with a straight face) the moment at which an incremental increase in the probability of some future possible bad effect of further procrastination so alters the consequentialist calculations as to drop the adjusted value of procrastination below the alternative. But *this* should be no more disturbing to a philosopher than the fact that she can't identify (with a straight face) the specific height at which a person becomes tall.

Originally, then, it didn't seem possible to reduce the problem of procrastination for an act consequentialist to a sorites paradox because it seemed we could always confidently claim that further procrastination, in all probability, wouldn't cause any harm. Given value adjusted possible consequence act consequentialism, this claim turns out to be perfectly compatible with deciding that further procrastination would be wrong, and I argued that we could reduce any remaining difficulty involving pinpointing the time at which one should no longer procrastinate to the familiar sorites problem of a continuum, this time an epistemic continuum of incrementally increasing probabilities.

But what about procrastination involving projects without deadlines? How can a value adjusted possible consequence act consequentialist rationally talk himself out of procrastinating unpleasant activities of this sort? Once again, I think the act consequentialist faces a problem no more serious than familiar sorites puzzles. The relevant continua, however, vary from case to case. Let me illustrate with just two examples.

In some cases one can construe the problematic continuum that can seduce an act consequentialist as the same sort of continuum involving incremental increases in probabilities with respect to untoward consequences of further procrastination. Thus, suppose the reason I think it would be a good idea to organize my garage *sometime* is that I envision the possibility of needing to find something relatively quickly in some kind of crisis—say, a difficulty with the plumbing in my house which requires me to be able to find the necessary tools. Now it is perfectly true that I can always reason at any particular time that waiting another day to being work on this project is unlikely to have any ill effects, but we have already seen that this, by itself, does not provide a value adjusted *possible* consequence act consequentialist a reason for postponing the work. Moreover, in cases of this sort, it would not involve the gambler's fallacy to reason that the longer I have "got away" with such procrastination the more likely it is that a problem will arise, the solution to which is facilitated by an organized garage. Things do wear out, and the longer you have avoided one of the many household calamities that inevitably will come your way, the more likely it is that such a calamity will occur. As time goes by, therefore, there arises more and more consequentialist reason to begin the project, even though postponing it a day is never *likely* to make a significant difference. These reasons may eventually outweigh the more certain but rather low-level gratification one gets from, say, lying on one's couch daydreaming for a few hours.

Another familiar sort of procrastination involves a different sort of incremental increase which the act consequentialist must not ignore. For the past ten years I have been meaning to organize and file the many philosophical papers I have acquired. These papers currently constitute several enormous piles on the bookshelves of my office. I'm sure I'll find a sympathetic ear in most readers when I emphasize the degree to which this project strikes me as unpleasant. Indeed, as I look back on my wayward life, I wish that I had taken a few moments every week to file the papers that came my way that week. I didn't because I hate filing and I always reasoned that waiting for a few more papers to accumulate before I began filing would hardly make a difference. As the size of the project grew, however, it became evident that somewhere along the way I acquired too many papers to file without the kind of major effort that would test the very limits of my capacity to do this kind of work. And here we have found another continuum that a potential procrastinator who is an act consequentialist must treat carefully. The act consequentialist must know himself, and if the unpleasant project that he puts off is one that *grows* in unpleasantness the longer he puts it off, the more likely he will arive at some point along the continuum at which the project has become so enormous as to defy the practical possibility of completion (or allow completion only at some enormous cost). As I look at the inch of remaining space on my bookshelves, I realize that I have been the victim of a sorites continuum involving just that sort of incremental growth in the difficulty of completing what was originally a relatively insignificant task. Having identified the relevant continuum, however, I now understand that the problem has no special implications for the plausibility of act consequentialism, and I am convinced that my temptation to procrastinate has no special connection to my value adjusted possible consequence act consequentialism.

I feel I should conclude this discussion of procrastination from the perspective of an act consequentialist with an important qualification. It is, I have been supposing, important to find an act consequentialist justification for not always procrastinating with respect to at least some unpleasant but necessary projects. At the same time, I am anxious not to be too hard on procrastination. I suspect that there are as many people who don't procrastinate enough as who procrastinate too much. The person who insists on doing her taxes a whole week before they are due on a beautiful afternoon in which she could be satisfying a desire for all the pleasures associated with a game of golf is probably as irrational as the person who consistently procrastinates. The higher the adjusted value one assigns to the pleasures associated with the alternative to unpleasant but eventually necessary work, the more rational it is to postpone the unpleasant work even if that decision does involve risks. After all, it *is* never likely that waiting will have these possible ill effects. Moreover, a good act consequentialist is perfectly entitled to factor into his calculations some other relevant possibilities. When the benefits of an unpleasant activity are not immediate, the possibility that one might die, for example, after completing the project and before reaping the benefits is a perfectly appropriate factor to weigh in deciding when to begin work on the project.

It is important for us act consequentialists to argue that our view does not commit us to the rationality of a policy—inevitably disastrous—of persistent procrastination. But that doesn't mean we shouldn't take advantage of our view to justify putting off the spring cleaning on the kind of weekend nature obviously intended for a game of golf.

NEWCOMB'S PARADOX AND DOMINANCE REASONING

Before we leave our discussion of some of the epistemological implications of our accounts of rational action, it might be appropriate to consider another potential objection to that account, an objection that has its source in our heavy reliance on epistemic probability. At least some philosophers would argue that there is a conflict between concepts of rational/right action defined in terms of maximizing the accumulated value of value adjusted possible outcomes (call these *maximizing accounts*) and so-called dominance reasoning accounts of rational/right action. (For simplicity, I discuss the issue only in connection with the concept of rational action.) According to the Dominance Theory, an agent's action is rational if the alternative he selects would produce the optimum outcome no matter what else happens.

A puzzle developed by William Newcomb is supposed to illustrate that a dominance principle can conflict with a maximizing principle. In the hypothetical situation described by Newcomb, you have a choice between taking an opaque box *A*, which you know contains either a million dollars or nothing at all, or taking *A* and another box *B*, which you know has one thousand dollars in it. We assume for the discussion that the having of money has value. As I understand the hypothesis, you also know that the contents of *A* have already been determined. At the time of making your choice, there either is or is not the million dollars in *A*, and your choice is not going to affect causally the outcome. So far, it seems pretty obvious that dominance reasoning, and plain common sense, would dictate that you take both boxes. How could you go wrong? But suppose, further, that you know that there is some being who has determined the contents of *A* and who has placed a million dollars in *A* if and only if he has predicted that you will choose *A* alone. Furthermore, you have observed that of the thousand people who in similar situations have selected both *A* and *B*, only one found a million dollars in *A*, whereas of the thousand people who selected only *A*, nine hundred and ninety-nine found a million dollars in the box. You might certainly conclude on this evidence that the probability of becoming a millionaire by selecting only A is much higher than if you were to select both A and B, and thus that selecting only A would be the rational course of action according to a maximizing account of rationality.

Does a dominance principle conflict with a maximizing principle? It seems to me that it clearly does not and that Newcomb's paradox attempts to generate a puzzle out of an essentially incoherent hypothetical situation. Specifically, it seems obvious to me that it cannot be more likely, relative to your evidence, that selecting A alone will make you a millionaire, if you also *know* that your choice does not affect the contents of A. If you know that the million already either is or is not in box A, and it won't either appear or disappear as a result of your choice, then you also know that the statistical evidence is misleading vis-à-vis the probability of your choice *affecting* the question of whether or not you will become a millionaire. One must remember that the view we are defending is possible *consequence* consequentialism. We have relied heavily on epistemic probability, but the epistemic probabilities that define the primary sense of rationality are the probabilities that our action will have certain *consequences*. If I *know* that my choice of A will not affect the contents of A, then the probability of becoming a millionaire *by* choosing both A and B is identical to the probability of becoming a millionaire *by* choosing A alone.

Would I in fact choose both A and B rather than A alone? I certainly would if I were absolutely convinced that the choice of boxes would not causally affect their contents, as the hypothesis states. Of course, it is difficult to imagine being convinced in that way. For one thing, even if I were convinced that the contents of box A was already determined, it is not absolutely clear that the idea of backward causation is completely unintelligible. On the contrary, when we read fictional accounts of people who have uncanny abilities to predict the future—say, a psychic who unfailingly predicts the exact date of important leaders' deaths—we commonly attribute the imminent death as the *cause* of the earlier premonition. Now I don't know whether it is really intelligible to suppose that a disaster today can cause a premonition yesterday, but as long as I can wonder whether such a hypothesis is intelligible, I can wonder whether my choice of A can cause the predictor to have placed in A a million dollars. And if I assign any significant probability at all to that hypothesis on the basis of the statistical evidence described earlier, I *can* view there being a million dollars in A as a possible consequence of my choosing *A*, a consequence whose adjusted value is so high that it will no doubt make it rational for me to choose *A* alone. But I repeat that if I *know* that the contents of *A* would be unaffected by my choosing *A* alone, I would surely choose both *A* and *B*, knowing that I am bound to be a thousand dollars richer for my choice.

What is the connection between maximizing principles and dominance reasoning? I have argued that the two have the same consequences vis-à-vis which course of action is rational, but what are their conceptual connections? The answer, I believe, is obvious. Dominance reasoning is just a special instance of choosing in accordance with the principles of maximization. Specifically, if one knows that of the alternatives, *X*, *Y*, and *Z*, *X* will have the best consequences *no matter what*, then one can deduce that the added value of the value adjusted possible consequences of *X* will be higher than the added value of the value adjusted possible consequences of alternatives to *X*, no matter what probabilities one assigns to the various possible outcomes.

One can illustrate the point with another famous hypothetical situation that we discuss at length later—the prisoner's dilemma. You and I are captured by the enemy, are asked to confess, and know the following: if you confess and I remain silent, you go free and I am executed; if you remain silent and I confess, you are executed and I go free; if we both confess, we spend ten years in prison; and if we both remain silent, we spend two years in prison. Our respective actions do not *causally* influence each other. For the sake of argument, we suppose that I care nothing about your well-being and rank the possible outcomes concerning my well-being in the following order of preference: going free, spending two years in prison, spending ten years in prison, and being executed. It is easy to see that dominance reasoning entails the rationality of confessing. I am better off no matter what else happens by confessing. But our value adjusted possible consequence consequentialism entails the same result. I may have no idea what you are likely to do and consequently no idea what the likely consequences of my confessing are, but because confessing dominates remaining silent, I can reason that the value adjusted possible consequences of confessing will be greater than the value adjusted possible consequences of remaining silent. The probabilities of the various outcomes depend on the probability of your confessing or remaining silent, but I can assign *any* probability to the variable of your confessing, and as long as I suppose

the same probability in calculating the possible consequences of confessing and remaining silent, it is easy to see that the strategy of confessing will satisfy maximizing criteria.

Counterexamples and Act vs. Rule Consequentialism

Perhaps the most serious attacks on act consequentialist accounts of
rational and moral action come from those philosophers who argue that
rational and moral action must be defined by the correct *rules* of rationality and morality. As we indicated in Chapter 2, consequences are
still relevant for the rule consequentialist, but only insofar as one defines
the correct rules of rationality and morality by reference to the hypothetical actual, probable, or possible consequences of people in general
acting in accordance with these rules.

I believe that the main source of argument for the view that rationality and morality are "rule defined" is argument by counterexample. In short, act consequentialism is said to have certain strongly
counterintuitive consequences that rule consequentialism can avoid. In
discussing this sort of objection, I would still like to consider act
consequentialist accounts of rationality and morality together. I will do
so by simply considering objections to act consequentialist accounts of
what one *ought* to do, leaving open the question of whether "ought"
is or is not ambiguous as between the "ought" of morality and the
"ought" of rationality. At the same time, it should be noted that at least
some of the counterexamples I discuss are probably intended to appeal
primarily to our *ethical* intuitions. We must remember, however, our
earlier conclusion concerning the priority of judgments about rationality over judgments about morality *should* the two conflict. If morality is
defined by rules but rationality is not, then so much the worse for
morality. I am only interested in arguments for rule consequentialism if
they apply equally to consequentialist accounts of both morality and
rationality.

The literature has by now a rich heritage of counterexamples to act
consequentialism. Put very crudely, I think it is fair to say that critics
believe that act consequentialist accounts of what you ought to do will
entail that you ought to violate conventional morality and conventional

views about rationality more often than philosophical sensitivity will tolerate.[6] And as we have admitted in Chapter 2, it *is* a feature of *all* act consequentialist accounts that there is no *kind* of action which might not turn out to be rational/moral, at least if action kinds are defined independently of their actual, probable, or possible consequences. There may arise circumstances in which, according to an act consequentialist, one ought to break promises, lie, steal, cheat, kill, and generally wreak havoc with the ten commandments of the Judaeo-Christian tradition. But abstract concerns of this sort will not cut any ice with us act utilitarians, for we obviously think that there can arise circumstances in which one ought to break promises, lie, steal, cheat, kill, and violate the rules of conventional morality. To be sure, many people probably violate conventional morality more often than they should, but then, some people probably don't do so nearly enough. The person who is never prepared to lie, for example, is probably a menace to his friends, himself, and society. There is simply no point in telling your wife that you can't stand the haircut she just got, at least until it grows out and she can do something about it. In general, I suspect, it is true of most people that they ought to be kind (for Hobbesian reasons, if not for altruistic reasons), and kindness in many cases often requires some relatively harmless lying.

As I said, one cannot evaluate the force of the charge that act consequentialism conflicts in unacceptable ways with conventional morality/rationality in the abstract. One must evaluate particular arguments designed to draw out counterintuitive consequences of act consequentialism. Let us consider some representative examples of these arguments and explore the ways in which the act consequentialist might respond.

The institution of promising is a favorite topic for the act consequentialist's critics, probably because authority figures have conditioned most of us from an early age not to break promises *unless we have very good reasons*. The difficulty with act consequentialism, the argument goes, is that one does not need very good reasons at all in order to

6. See, for representative examples, Warnock 1971, Hodgson 1967, Lyons 1965, chap. 5, and Williams in Smart and Williams 1973. Some of these authors are concerned primarily with attacking consequentialist conceptions of morally right action, and even within this subclass of consequentialist views their concern is often primarily with hedonistic utilitarianism. I suspect, however, that they would be equally dissatisfied with the act consequentialist analysis of rational action I defend above.

conclude that one ought to break a promise. Consider a familiar sort of example. I visit my Aunt Mary on her deathbed. From under the mattress she pulls out a roll of thousand-dollar bills and tells me that it is her desperate wish that the money goes to her late husband's favorite charity (call it *A*). She asks me to *promise* that I'll make sure the money gets there, and to make her last moments of life pleasant, I do. As is usually the case with such scenarios, the promise is made in private, I know that no one else knows about the money, and Aunt Mary immediately dies. All this ensures that I don't have to worry about the effects of my breaking the promise on the attitudes others have toward me as a promise breaker. Let us also suppose (to keep the moralists happy) that I am an impartial altruist and I agree, in fact, with Aunt Mary that the money ought to go to a charity. But after a little investigation, I discover that charity *B* is marginally more effective than charity *A*. What should I do? Act consequentialism would seem to entail that I should give the money to charity *B*. But apparently a lot of people would argue that that would be wrong. It would be immoral and (here I am extending the usual sort of argument) irrational to break that promise I made to poor Aunt Mary.

  Now as with all such alleged counterexamples to act consequentialism, one can always simply dismiss the knee-jerk reactions of rule-bound moralists who cannot get used to the fact that adults must recognize that there are all kinds of exceptions to those "exceptionless" rules they were taught when they were children. And I must confess, I have difficulty appreciating the moral revulsion so many seem to feel at the thought of double-crossing my late Aunt Mary. Still, if you do want to conclude that I ought to keep my promise to Aunt Mary, there are any number of ways you can rationally reach that conclusion within the framework of act consequentialism. You recall from Chapter 2 that our act consequentialism certainly does not preclude the intrinsic value of an act, if it has any, from being considered along with the adjusted value of the other possible consequences of the act. And one can always "juggle the books" until the numbers come out the way your "intuition" wants them to come out. We can assign very large intrinsic value to the act of keeping a promise and very large intrinsic disvalue to the act of breaking a promise, and if the numbers are large enough, a great many horrible potential consequences would have to be associated with keeping a promise before these negative possible consequences outweigh the intrinsic value of keeping the promise. Everybody in his right mind wants to agree that if you can get *enough* accomplished by breaking a promise then that is what you ought to do. The only question is whether relatively insignificant gains can sanction the breaking of a promise, and one can assign one's intrinsic disvalue to the breaking of a promise so that things work out pretty much the way one wants them to.

Now if one had a view that allowed objective nonnatural goodness and badness to attach to various states of affairs, I suppose there is no telling what sorts of things intrinsic goodness and badness might attach to. If I held a view like that, and I didn't like the idea of people breaking promises, I suppose that dialectically I could generate the conclusions I wanted by "intuiting" the presence of intrinsic badness in the breaking of a promise. On my own view, of course, the intrinsic disvalue (for me) of breaking a promise would have to derive from the fact that I intrinsically disvalue breaking a promise, and to be honest, I can't say that I do. I am afraid I would have to say the same thing about dishonesty in general. I simply do not find intrinsically abhorrent the idea of lying. Furthermore, I suspect the same thing is true of many philosophers. Consequently, despite the *formal* ease with which act consequentialism can accommodate the intuition that one needs very strong reasons to break promises (or, more generally, lie), I am not confident that many are in a position to *honestly* make the moves required.

One certainly can, however, appeal to other considerations to explain why it might be true that even with my attitude I ought to keep my promise to Aunt Mary. For one thing, the consequences of becoming a *known* promise breaker in this society are really quite significant. To be sure, we have stipulated that in the hypothetical situation, I am certain that no one else knows about the money or the promise. But here Hare's advice discussed earlier must be kept in mind. These hypothetical situations are *highly* artificial. In fact, we could *not* know that Aunt Mary hadn't told someone else that she was about to make her request of me. And God only knows it is difficult, given human nature, to keep secrets. After my fourth glass of wine, I might end up bragging about my act consequentialist decision to forget about the promise I made to Aunt Mary.

Furthermore, I may well have to end up living with a guilty conscience. This may strike one as an odd concern. After all, if I do what I should do (given my views), why would I have a guilty conscience? The answer, of course, is simple. Society does a very good job of conditioning people not to be dishonest. For all I know, Harman is right, and we really do imagine father figures (superegos) hovering over us ready to scold us for our transgressions against those rules we learned when we were very young.[7] It is certainly true, for example, that long after some people realize the idiocy of some of the sexual taboos they learned in their youth they still feel very uncomfortable engaging in behvaior they were taught to feel bad engaging in. If, in fact, one is caused by one's upbringing to feel bad engaging in certain sorts of behavior, then that is a significant factor to take into account in deciding whether or not to behave in that way.

Still, the critic will charge, there is something "fishy" about this attempt to accommodate the intuitions of the counterexample within the framework of act consequentialism. For one thing, we seem to be supposing that all of those people who have conditioned us to feel bad lying or breaking a promise have themselves been acting irrationally. If they had any sense they would have *told* us that we were to use our discretion in deciding when to lie or break promises. This point involves the more general question of whether a society of act consequentialists could even have an institution of truth speaking, promise keeping, or anything else that requires people to have rational expectations about another's behavior.[8] In fact, I think act consequentialists could rationally act so as to create the kinds of expectations necessary for communication to take place and for the existence of institutions such as promising to survive. Act consequentialists certainly could, for act consequentialist reasons, set up Hobbesian sanctions against people who lie and break promises, even when in the absence of such sanctions, the people in question ought to lie and break promises. Of course, for the external sanctions to work, one would need someone to enforce them rigidly, and the critic will again charge that one would at least need someone who is not an act consequentialist to enforce these sanctions in the required way. But this presupposes that an act consequentialist cannot herself decide to act in ways that will create useful expectations on the part of others. Certainly, it seems to me that an act consequentialist can have good reasons to do whatever is necessary to convince others that she will make them pay for promises casually broken. And one way to convince others of this would be to adopt an extremely harsh pattern of behavior toward promise breakers, a pattern of behavior from which others can inductively infer the likelihood of

7. Harman 1977, pp. 60–61.
8. For this criticism see, again, Hodgson 1967, especially chap. 2.

their getting some of the same in similar situations. In short, I may have good reason to create in you expectations that I will react in a certain way to some aspect of your behavior *no matter what*. And the only way to do this might be to act in fairly rigid and exceptionless ways vis-à-vis other people behaving in a similar fashion.[9] I have more to say about the ways in which a society of act consequentialists might come up with the rules that "define" conventional morality in the last chapter.

Let us emphasize that, even if act consequentialists would recognize that there are all kinds of situations in which people should lie and break promises, there is nothing in act consequentialism that implies that we should inform people of this fact. More generally, there is nothing in act consequentialism that implies that we should encourage people to be act consequentialists. We certainly don't tell children that they ought to tell the truth unless they get more good done by lying than by telling the truth. It would probably be irrational to give them this advice even if it is true. The last thing we would want is children trying to figure out on their own the value adjusted possible consequences of alternative courses of action. They wouldn't be very good at making the relevant calculations and, consequently, would probably fare better just acting on the rule "Tell the truth." If they are intelligent, or take the right philosophy course from the right professor, they will eventually figure out that the rule was intended only as rule of thumb, but in the meantime it is probably best that they don't think about such things. And frankly, I am not sure that the same isn't true of people in general. Fortunately, in writing a book like this I can safely assume that no one except professional philosophers and their students are likely to read it, and most of them aren't likely to believe the views I defend, anyway. If there were any realistic chance of converting the entire world to act consequentialism, I would certainly have to think twice about doing so. It may turn out that it would be best to convert most people to some form of irrational rule consequentialism. Whether it would or not depends on the possible consequences of people becoming conscious act consequentialists. The more likely it is that people will mess things up trying to be act consequentialists, the more likely it is that I shouldn't try to persuade these people to become act consequentialists.[10] Having

9. For similar replies to some of Hodgson's concerns, see Mackie 1973 and Regan 1980, chap. 4.

10. I may even be able to conclude on act consequentialist grounds that it would be rational for me to try to make myself into something other than an act consequentialist. If

said all this, I wouldn't be at all surprised to find that we might have to live the rest of our lives with annoying conditioned responses to behavior prohibited by "exceptionless" rules that have been inculcated in us for as long as we can remember.

The range of replies to the above counterexample applies to many other putative counterexamples to act consequentialism. These, of course, vary from case to case. It might be useful to consider a few other examples.

Most of us were brought up to think that we shouldn't litter. But it is often difficult to see how the empty bottle I am thinking of tossing into the woods will make any significant difference one way or the other. To be sure (as we are often reminded), it would be bad if *everyone* felt free to toss garbage wherever it was most convenient, but as act consequentialists we are trying to avoid this sort of appeal to the consequences of people generally acting in a certain way, an appeal that would only support the rule consequentialist's position that what we ought to do is a function of rules, whose correctness is determined by the hypothetical consequences of people following them. Of course, in *fact,* there are *laws* prohibiting littering, laws that an act consequentialist in power might have good reason to bring into being. Given the existence of these laws, act consequentialists have the Hobbesian threat of the sovereign's sword hanging over their heads as they contemplate littering. The counterexample must now build into the hypothetical situation the supposition that the litterer knows that no one capable of directly or indirectly imposing sanctions will discover his act of littering. It is easy enough to imagine this being *probable,* but as value adjusted *possible* consequence consequentialists we will certainly never be in a position to rule out the important possibility. Furthermore, if we suppose that most of us do have at least some degree of altruism, or are the kinds of egoists who enjoy seeing others happy, we cannot eliminate the *possibility* that our unsightly garbage will marginally detract from an otherwise pleasant day for some other person. Anyone with a degree of

---

I realize that *I* am likely to mess things up badly if I go around trying to calculate the consequences of my actions, I might reasonably decide that I would be better off trying to convince myself of rule utilitarianism or some other mistaken ethical theory. Even this, however, does not show that there is anything *theoretically* wrong with the act consequentialist's conception of rational action. For an excellent and detailed defense of act consequentialism against the charge that it is a "self-defeating" theory, see Parfit 1984, chap. 1.

aesthetic sensibility knows how repugnant the sight of man's handiwork can be intruding on nature's beauty. Moreover, we can always construe the problem with littering as involving yet another sorites continuum. A lot of litter is very bad. It is certainly always unlikely that my litter will create the quantity of litter that is bad, but then it is always unlikely that a millionth of an inch added to the height of a man who is not tall will make him tall. As long as I think of a great deal of litter as bad, there is the *possibility* that my addition to the present amount of litter will yield the undesirable result. All these factors, together with the undeniable effects of conditioning (which act consequentialists in power certainly have good reasons to use), give act consequentialists many reasons to behave in the way that they "intuitively" feel they ought to behave vis-à-vis the question of littering.

The act consequentialist's critics also have a field day hypothesizing situations in which the act consequentialist would allegedly be forced by his theory to conclude that one ought to kill some innocent people in order to save many more lives. (Again, let us assume, as most do in the context of moral theory, that human life, in general, has value.) The force of these sorts of counterexamples is particularly difficult to evaluate, however, as most people, I assume, agree in principle that in some circumstances one *ought* to sacrifice innocents for the greater good of humanity. You don't have to support the firebombing of Dresden or even, perhaps, the bombing of Hiroshima to agree that the allies in World War II were acting quite correctly when they bombed munition factories located in major cities. And yet everyone knows that, given the accuracy of such bombing runs, it is virtually certain that innocent people, including young children, would be killed. If we are not prepared to sacrifice the lives of innocent children, we surrender the world to people far more unpleasant than ourselves who won't think twice about doing so.

Still, despite the plausibility of the *general* thesis that one ought to sacrifice the lives of a few to save the lives of many, there are hypothetical situations in which our "moral intuitions" recoil at the thought of such behavior. The literature contains many exotic examples. One that is representative is discussed briefly by Harman (1977, pp. 3–4), and I paraphrase a version of it here. Suppose that five patients enter the hospital for treatment. Four are critically ill and need *immediate* transplants of, respectively, a heart, kidneys, a liver, and a spleen. The fifth is in for treatment of poison ivy. Now, the reductio goes, as act consequentialists, why shouldn't we conclude that the physician in charge ought to take the relatively healthy victim of poison ivy and simply divvy up his vital organs to the other four? The net gain would be four lives at a cost of only one. I imagine the potential donor wouldn't be thrilled with the decision, but even he should recognize that an altruistic physician was doing the right thing. Of course, we would all agree that the physician should not behave in this way, and thus we have a reductio of act consequentialism.

Again, we must surely be struck by the coarseness with which this hypothetical picture is drawn. In fact, there are laws prohibiting physicians from behaving in such ways, and the existence of these laws and the sanctions associated with them give the physician ample act consequentialist reasons not to behave in the way envisioned. To eliminate these considerations, one would have to suppose that in the hypothetical situation, the physician *knows* that no one will find out about her actions and it doesn't make sense to suppose that there is no epistemic possibility of being found out. But why pass such laws? If the people who pass laws were act consequentialists, why wouldn't they pass legislation *encouraging* physicians to make this kind of four-for-one trade? Here, the answer is simple. If you were sick, would you go to a hospital for treatment of the flu if you knew that there was an outside chance that someone would choose you as organ donor of the week? Of course you wouldn't. You would take your chances at getting well without a doctor's care. And if the law encouraged physicians to behave in the way described above, people in general would stay away from hospitals, thus, no doubt, causing the spread of all sorts of dangerous diseases and subsequent human suffering. Act consequentialists who can do so have reason to pass laws that give act consequentialists reasons to refrain from certain sorts of behavior. They also have act consequentialist reasons to enforce these laws in a relatively exceptionless way, for it is through such enforcement that one inductively establishes for others the likelihood of punishment that *gives* them their reasons for obeying the laws.

On questions concerning the legitimacy of killing innocents to save others, I am convinced that I can accommodate those "moral intuitions" I agree with in ways similar to those discussed above. In all frankness, however, I should admit that I think people are notoriously irrational about such matters. If the United States bombs suspected terrorists, it takes only one mutilated baby on the evening news to cause many people to bemoan the immorality of the action. Given human nature, the probability of destroying lives of children is surely a strong reason to avoid the action that has this probable consequence. But it is equally obvious that there can be reasons that outweigh this concern. The chance of saving many many more innocent lives by dissuading terrorists from engaging in terrorism may be just such a reason. The person who won't kill innocents for potential great gains is, I believe, analogous to that individual who can't bring himself to hurdle the short-term pain of the dentist's drill in order to alleviate much greater long-term suffering. Both behave in ways that are, perhaps, psychologically understandable. But both are deplorably irrational.

THE VOTING PARADOX AND PRISONER'S DILEMMA

I want to single out two alleged counterexamples to act consequentialism for special attention, in part because the options for dealing with them can be made quite stark and in part because they provide a useful context for presenting and discussing the implications of rule consequentialism.

Although I am sure it will disturb some moralists, I have found over the years that the standard counterexamples to act consequentialism which focus on the alleged implications of the view concerning the violation of conventional morality have little impact with students. When the hypothetical situation is defined *in detail,* most shrug their shoulders and ignore the late Aunt Mary's wishes. The thought of lying does not seem to conjure up the moral horror that it did for a Prichard or a Ross, let alone a Kant. Indeed, I suspect that young people, particularly, have far too casual an attitude concerning the possible consequences of violating conventional morality.[11] I have found, however, that the voting paradox still seems to make almost everyone extremely uneasy about the implications of act consequentialism. Despite the gradual erosion of some of the tenets of conventional morality, almost all people still think they ought to vote. Come election time, we

11. Bloom (1987), of course, traces this to the pervasiveness of moral relativism among the teachers of our youth. But this is silly. If one can't convince someone on the view I defend to stick with conventional morality for the most part, one probably isn't going at it the right way. Of course, I would have no interest in defending the kind of rule worship that someone like Bloom probably longs for.

are inundated with advertising praising the merits of voting and disparaging the character of those who do not participate in the electoral process. Former presidents appear on television in earnest conversation with idealistic young people lamenting the fact that there are so many misguided souls out there who "think that their votes don't make a difference." But from an act consequentialist's perspective, the truth is that your vote is *extremely* unlikely to make a difference of the sort that the former president has in mind. In national elections (when people *strongly* believe that they ought to vote) your vote has only a *tiny* probability of affecting the outcome of the election. If you live in Illinois and a candidate received one more vote than his opponent, when winning Illinois would give him one more electoral college vote than his opponent, your vote *still* wouldn't affect the outcome of the election, for you know that someone somewhere in Chicago will "recount" the vote until it turns out differently. Although I don't really know what the probabilities are, it certainly seems to me that there is a better chance of my accidentally killing someone on the way to the polls than my vote deciding the outcome of a national election. Thus even if I felt confident that I knew which politician would make the best president (and I often don't), the possibility of electing the person I want *as a result of my vote* seems so remote that it is one of those far-fetched possibilities that I argued earlier we can safely ignore. And the same is true of the probability of my affecting the "perception" of the election results. Even if the election is not decided by my one vote, I suppose I might hope to affect to some extent the public perception of the margin of victory. But again, let us face reality. Almost no one ever even reads the final results. And even if the matter was of general interest, does anyone really believe that if Reagan beat Mondale by 50,233,987 to 33,479,243 instead of 50,233,987 to 33,479,244 someone is going to conclude that it wasn't really such a "blow-out" after all? Given that all this is obvious, and given that it might take a considerable effort to get to a polling place and stand in line to vote, why should an act consequentialist bother to vote?

In Chapter 3 of *Reasons and Persons,* Parfit warns of making mistakes of "moral mathematics." The alleged errors he discusses are, for the most part, not *mathematical* errors at all, but he does warn against ignoring very small probabilities of bringing about potentially significant results. Specifically, he argues in the case of voting that, *if* one candidate is clearly better than another and *if* that candidate would clearly benefit many more Americans than the opponent, then you may have a reason to vote despite the fact that it is extremely unlikely that your vote would make a difference. He goes on to justify that claim by pointing out that, according to the experts, the odds are not more than a hundred million to one against your vote making the difference *if* the election is close and *if* you live in a populous state with a great many electoral votes. As possible consequence consequentialists, we would certainly agree with Parfit that one must in principle factor into one's calculations even very remote possible consequences. We could even agree that, *if* all of the presuppositions of his argument are correct, one may have a very slight reason to vote, assuming that one had nothing very interesting to do that day. But of course, the presuppositions of the argument are rarely satisfied. In the last several presidential elections the preelection polls made it clear that one candidate was a prohibitive favorite to win the election. And speaking for myself, it was hardly clear that one candidate rather than the other would make things significantly better for many Americans. That is not to say I didn't have views as to who would improve matters the most, but I wasn't foolish enough to suppose that there was any great likelihood of my views being correct. As one factors in *these* probabilities, the adjusted value assigned to the possible consequence of winning the election for candidate A starts dipping back down toward o. Furthermore, this solution of Parfit's to the voting paradox is hardly going to make the residents of Wyoming happy. I'm sure they wanted to think that they had just as much reason to vote as Californians and that that reason was a *powerful* reason—not the kind of reason that might just barely survive the diminishing value of the extremely unlikely consequence of affecting the outcome of the election.

Some philosophers would argue that an act consequentialist can resolve problems like the voting paradox by introducing the concept of a contributory cause. Essentially, the idea is that although my vote does not by itself make the difference in the health of an election or the victory of the best candidate, it nevertheless *contributes* along with all the other votes to that end. But as Regan (1980, p. 13) points out, it is surely ingenuous to suppose that one can define the relevant consequences that an act consequentialist must consider in terms of "contributory" consequences and still remain within the spirit of the view. Surely the attractiveness of act consequentialism derives, at least in part, from the idea that one chooses between alternative actions based on how the world will be as a result of acting one way rather than the other. And the fact remains that the world in which I don't vote, given the behavior of others, will be insignificantly different vis-à-vis the outcome of the election or the general perception of the election as "healthy."[12]

Just as with previous counterexamples, there are dialectical moves available to the act consequentialist who wants to abide by the conventional wisdom that one ought to vote. As we noted earlier, it is *always* the case that *formally* one can simply assign intrinsic value to the act of voting itself and assign a high enough value that it outweighs any of the inconveniences involved. Again, speaking for myself, I can only say that it strikes me as very odd that someone might value intrinsically the ceremony of pulling a lever beside a politician's name. God only knows when and how people find intrinsic objective value, but again, I would think one has to grit one's teeth rather hard to insist that the act of voting is intrinsically good.

More plausibly, one might argue that for many there is a very real (though, I think, odd) kind of pleasure, almost childlike pleasure, associated with the ceremonial expression of approval for a person you like and disapproval for a person you dislike. This pleasure associated with an act of voting might be thought of as analogous to the pleasure one might get from throwing darts at a picture of the politician one dislikes most. The throwing of the darts is, presumably, not designed to accomplish anything other than a curious cathartic feeling of satisfaction. Now I certainly do understand the value of pleasure, and if people get pleasure from voting (for whatever odd psychological reason), I suppose they have a good reason to vote.

---

12. In his list of moral mathematical errors, Parfit includes the errors of not taking into account the consequences that I can bring about *together* with others (p. 77) and not taking into account imperceptible benefits and harms. I suspect that the principles Parfit introduces in this context are really disguised efforts at something like the rule consequentialism we shall discuss later, and he clearly needs an argument for departing from more straightforward consequentialism. It is, however, interesting to note that even Parfit is willing to recognize that one has no reason to join a group that is acting so as to produce certain benefits when one believes that, if one were to join the group, the group would be "too large." He then goes on to define a group's being too large in terms of its being true that "if one or more of its members had not acted, this would not have reduced the benefit that this group gives to other people" (p. 83). The reference above to mere belief is too weak to make the principle plausible, but my concern here is only to call attention to the fact that I certainly do believe that the group voting in national elections is "too large" by this criterion relative to the outcomes of deciding the winner and producing a respectable turnout.

On the opposite side of the coin, there is, again, the feeling of guilt associated with not voting which those in power have successfully inculcated in many people. Those millions of dollars spent on advertising no doubt have had some effect, and as act consequentialists, people in power might have good reason to spend money they control in precisely this way. *They* can hope to affect the behavior of large numbers of people, and it is arguably better if most people vote than if they do not.

Of course, there might be a bit of a problem in a democratic government getting act consequentialist legislators to vote for the policies that have these good effects. But here the elections are typically much smaller, and the possibility of affecting the outcome of the election is correspondingly much greater (although still usually very small). In any event, the probability is sufficiently high that even given its adjusted value it is a significant factor. Moreover, the legislator's job depends on showing up for votes. However rational or irrational the condemnation of nonvoters might be, it is real and must be factored into the decision of whether or not to vote.

Do any of the above actually explain why most people vote or at least think they ought to vote? I suspect not. And the main reason for this suspicion is that no one has the nerve to *cite* these as their reasons for voting. Most of the people I know who think they ought to vote resent the suggestion that the rationality of their action might be analogous to the rationality of our hypothetical dart thrower. Nor do they think that they ought to vote because they are trying to avoid feelings of guilt. Rather, they seem to sincerely believe that they would feel guilt for not voting because they think they ought to vote. Of course, we do not have to take what people say at face value. People might not know why they think they ought to vote. But neither can we simply dismiss the relevance of their apparently sincere testimony.

My own view as to why people vote will hardly strike many readers as plausible. In fact, I suspect that the cause of people voting either has nothing to do with their judgments about reasons for voting or, if it does, involves wildly irrational beliefs about voting. It wouldn't surprise me if, at some level, people really do believe that there is a reasonable chance of their vote affecting the outcome of the election. I have a hunch that at least some people have "bought" the idea that their vote does indeed make a difference. They believe it in the way in which some people believe that they have a reasonable chance of winning their state lottery. Or perhaps better, they believe it the way you think you can influence your favorite team's field goal to go through the uprights by swaying your body in the relevant direction as you watch the flight of the ball on television. Do people really believe that their exhortations shouted at the television screen make a difference to their heroes? At some level, obviously not, but this doesn't stop people from shouting encouragement. The encouragement to a politician offered by the act of voting is analogous to the encouragement offered to the images of one's athletic heroes moving on that screen. I suspect its psychological cause is the same and the respective acts are equally rational (irrational).

Do I have any positive evidence for this rather odd hypothesis? Not a great deal, but I ask you to reflect on the following facts. People are more likely to vote in national elections they take to be close than in elections in which one candidate seems to be far ahead. And the most obvious explanation for this phenomenon is that they really think that in the "close" elections there is a more significant chance that their votes will make the difference. Of course, there *is* a more significant chance that their votes will make the difference, but the probability is still so incredibly small that it is only by postulating an irrational belief about the probability that one could explain these familiar judgments about the rationality of voting in close elections.

Consider, too, the recurring controversy over whether television coverage of presidential elections should be allowed to project the winner before the polls close in California. Many object to this practice by pointing out that it would *discourage* voters in California from coming out to vote. Presumably, the idea is that, if they already know it is extremely likely that Jones will win no matter how they vote, they won't think they have any reason to vote. And I suspect that this *is* exactly the conclusion many people would reach. But they could only reach this conclusion if they already held the curious belief that their votes had some significant probability of making a difference, a belief that is, of course, highly irrational.

It is also a familiar empirical fact that people are more likely to vote in elections the more strongly they feel about the respective candidates. Again, one can explain this as a symptom of a dim awareness of the adjusted valued of the possible outcomes (in this case getting the person you strongly like elected). But it still seems obvious to me that the minuscule value that remains to the possibility of affecting the outcome is so small on any realistic assessment of probabilities that one can only understand this act of voting as involving the bizarre belief that there really is some realistic probability of a single vote accomplishing this goal of affecting the outcome of the election. The advertising campaigns themselves advise you that your vote does make a difference. Politicians tell you when they shake your hand that they need *your* vote. They seem to be appealing to an act consequentialist's perspective, albeit in a way that makes absolutely no sense, given the facts about the relevant possible outcomes and their respective values.

Suppose, then, that you are not a victim of delusions with respect to the causal efficacy of your vote. Suppose also that you get no pleasure from the ceremony of voting and have succeeded in avoiding any guilt that others have tried to make you feel from not voting. If you are an act consequentialist, why should you vote? The answer, I believe, is that you shouldn't. It seems to me to be manifestly irrational for such a person to vote. If you cannot bring yourself to accept this conclusion, then I really do think you need to find an alternative to act consequentialism. I might add parenthetically that if I had the power to do so I would make it illegal for people not to vote and I would impose sufficiently tough sanctions that act consequentialists like myself would *have* act consequentialist reasons to vote. I do think it is likely that it would be bad if people in general did not vote. I just think that individuals of the sort described above are irrational to vote. One should immediately recognize, of course, that I am asserting the thesis that individuals acting rationally can produce a world far worse than one that could have been produced by irrational behavior. And this takes us very naturally to the prisoner's dilemma.

Some philosophers, myself included, think of the prisoner's dilemma as simply a way of making obvious the fact that individuals acting rationally can produce a world far worse than could have been produced by irrational behavior. Other philosophers try to use the prisoner's dilemma as a reductio of views about morality and rationality which have this result. Let us remind ourselves of our version of the dilemma. While on a spy mission, you and I are captured by the enemy, and a sadistic but philosophical chief of interrogation gives us the following information. If we both confess to our spying, we will each spend ten years in prison. If we both remain silent, we will each spend two years in prison. If one confesses while the other remains silent, the one who confesses will go free while the one who remains silent will be executed. For simplicity, both prisoners are usually supposed to be egoists and, indeed, egoists who do not even concern themselves with the happiness of others as a means to their own happiness. On some versions of the dilemma we are allowed to communicate before making our decision, and on others we are not. I don't think it makes the slightest bit of difference. Assuming that I rank the possible outcomes, from best to worst, as going free, spending two years in prison, spending ten years in prison, and being executed, what should I do? Dominance reasoning certainly seems to suggest that as an egoist I ought to confess. No matter what you do, I am better off confessing. No matter what we have agreed to do, whether you keep or break whatever agreements we have made, I seem to be better off confessing. I argued earlier that dominance reasoning is just a special case of maximizing reasoning, and it seems obvious that, no matter how I rate the probabilities of your confessing or remaining silent, it will turn out that I ought to confess *as long as my confessing does not affect those probabilities.* If it is rational for me to confess, then it is presumably also rational for you to confess (assuming that your value system parallels mine).[13] We seem to have, then, a paradigm of a situation in which two individuals acting in an ideally rational way produce for themselves a world (in which they spend ten years in prison) worse than a world they could have produced (spending two years in prison) were they to act in some alternative way.

It should be emphasized that one does not need the presupposition that people are egoists in order to generate a prisoner's dilemma sort of choice. And for this reason it would be a mistake to try to use the dilemma as a reductio of egoism per se. One could suppose, for example, that both you and I care nothing for our own well-being but value intrinsically the happiness of our respective families. We need only suppose, in this case, that when we both confess our respective families spend the ten years in prison, when we both remain silent they spend two years in prison, and so on. In order to generate the dilemma, we do need to presuppose that ideally rational agents can have *different* values or ends that define what they ought to do. We need to presuppose, in other words, the *relativism* that has been defended earlier. The prisoner's dilemma can arise only on the supposition that something can be good for me (my going free, for example) even though it is not good for

13. It would be absurd, of course, to conclude from the truth of this conditional that its being rational for me to confess *causes* it to be rational for you to confess, and even more absurd to suppose that one could somehow infer from this that my confessing causes you to confess and thus has an undesirable effect.

you; something can be a rational end for me even though it is not for you. And so if one thinks that act consequentialist relativism has the consequence that one ought to confess if faced with the prisoner's dilemma *and* one thinks that it is absurd to suppose that ideally rational people can behave in ways that produce for themselves a world inferior to one they could have produced through alternative action, then one might try to use the prisoner's dilemma as a reductio against act consequentialist relativism.

In rejecting act consequentialist relativism, however, one must be clear whether one is rejecting the relativism or the act consequentialism. Since I have already expressed my deep reservations about the intelligibility of the concept of objective value needed to provide an alternative to relativism, my concern in what follows is with alternatives to act consequentialism. Given my response to the voter's paradox, the reader will not be surprised to find that I have no difficulty embracing the view that each individual (of the sort hypothesized) ought to confess even though he will spend a needless eight extra years in prison. I concede that this is a consequence of the view of rationality defended in this book, but I can honestly say that it has never struck me as a terribly counterintuitive consequence. Rather, it has always seemed to me a virtual truism that, given human nature, rational people will unfortunately end up producing for themselves a less-than-ideal world. It is equally obvious that many others reject this supposition, and we should at least examine alternatives to act consequentialism which purport to avoid both the paradoxical consequence of the prisoner's dilemma and the voter's paradox, and at the same time accommodate much more adequately "refined moral intuitions" concerning the virtues of honesty, promise keeping, respect for the lives of innocents, and so on.

Rule Consequentialism

If you want to eliminate the possibility of individuals acting rationally while (actually, probably, possibly) producing for themselves a world worse than one that could have been produced by alternative actions, then it is tempting simply to incorporate the hypothetical consequences of collective action into your criteria defining what one ought to do. And this is the fundamental move made by rule consequentialism in all of its many guises. As we pointed out in Chapter 2, there are as many different versions of rule consequentialism as there are versions of act consequentialism. After one decides that what one ought to do is a function of the correct rules governing certain sorts of behavior, one must make clear one's criteria for evaluating rules. As I use the expression, rule *consequentialism* evaluates rules governing the rationality/ morality of actions by reference to the hypothetical consequences of people in general acting in accord with the rules.[14] Having determined what consequences are to count (have value), one considers the consequences of following one rule rather than an alternative. Just as with act consequentialism, one must decide whether one must take into account actual, probable, or possible consequences of general compliance with a rule. And at least with the concept of rational action, I think the ambiguities discussed earlier arise again with rule utilitarianism. One must still decide, for example, what to make of an agent who acts with the rational but false belief that his action is sanctioned by the correct rules of morality. And if I were a rule utilitarian, I would, no doubt, adopt the suggestion made earlier of recognizing at least a sense in which an agent who acts with the rational belief that his action conforms to the correct rules of morality acts rationally even if his action fails to satisfy the criteria of rationality which define the first-level object of his deliberations. For the sake of the following discussion, I believe it does not matter whether one is evaluating actual consequence, possible consequence, or value adjusted possible consequence rule consequentialism, and for that reason I ignore the very real differences between these views. Indeed, for the most part I shall focus on actual consequence rule consequentialism simply because it is the easiest view to define.

Rule consequentialism is supposed to accommodate our intuitions concerning what one ought to do in some of the situations described above. I ought to vote even though my action considered by itself accomplishes nothing significant because what I ought to do is a function of the correct rule for voting. For simplicity, suppose the two rules are 'Vote' or 'Don't vote'. The consequences of everyone following the former are presumably better than the consequences of everyone following the latter. The voting rule, then, wins the consequentialist battle of rules and defines the correctness of voting. You need a rule governing

14. One can, of course, easily introduce qualifications. One might, for example, consider the consequences of the general observance of a rule to be relevant only if at least a significant number of people are following the rule.

situations like the prisoner's dilemma. Again, suppose the two rules are 'Confess' or 'Remain silent'. The consequences of everyone (the two of us) confessing are worse than the consequences of our remaining silent, and that is why the 'Remain silent' rule wins and entails that we ought to remain silent. Clearly, we would prefer a society in which everyone refrained from littering to one in which everyone littered. Less clearly, we might prefer a society in which everyone kept promises to one in which no one did. This last example, though, illustrates the necessity of becoming much clearer about the rough idea underlying rule consequentialism. In the case of promising, it becomes painfully obvious that a rational person wants a more sophisticated rule than the rule 'Always keep your promise'. Or if she doesn't want a more sophisticated rule, she will at least want to view rules as only prima facie binding with instructions on how to cope with situations in which she gets conflicting instructions from different rules. I promise to meet you for lunch at noon sharp. Walking by the river on my way to meet you, I see a child who has just fallen in and is about to disappear beneath the surface. A quick glance at my watch tells me that I'll never make our noon appointment if I stop to save the child. *Everyone* is going to agree that I ought to forget about my promise in this hypothetical situation, but how does one reconcile this with the rule consequentialist's goal of eliminating the possibility of evaluating an act by looking at its consequences?

As I indicated earlier, one can try to keep one's rules "simple" and introduce a hierarchy of rules or one can allow that rules can become rather sophisticated. In fact, the two strategies are identical. If one says that I am bound by two rules, 'Keep promises' and 'Save lives', where the latter takes precedence over the former, one will need to provide criteria explaining why the latter takes precedence over the former. The criteria will involve hypothetical questions concerning the way the world would be if people broke promises when they could save lives as opposed to keeping promises even when lives are at stake. If the former world would be better, then the 'Save lives' rule takes precedence over the 'Keep promises' rule. But this is surely just a roundabout way of saying that the rule governing promises is something more like 'Keep promises unless you can save lives by breaking them'.

Now most rule consequentialists would be happy to allow that the correct rules governing rationality and morality can become highly complex, can become highly qualified. But this admission carries with it potential ammunition for the rule consequentialist's critics.

To take the most obvious problem first, what is to stop an act consequentialist hiding in rule consequentialism from formulating the relevant rules to his specific advantage? I really don't want to vote, and among the rules I might consider as defining what one ought to do is the rule 'Vote unless your name is Richard Fumerton'. Arguably, the consequences of everyone following that rule are marginally better than the consequences of everyone following the rule 'Vote'. We get the good consequences from general participation in the electoral process with the added benefit of satisfying Fumerton's craving to sit in his easy chair with a nice cold beer and watch the election results on television. Rule utilitarians are going to cry foul here, of course, complaining that the 'rule' does not have the correct form. But we now need criteria for recognizing correctly formed rules. One possibility is to adopt Hare's criteria for defining proper universal imperatives. Rules that define rationality and morality must be properly *general*. And this prohibits the use of proper names, demonstratives, or indexicals in the formulation of a rule. The well-known formal difficulty with this suggestion, of course, is that it is notoriously easy to come up with a perfectly general description that in fact covers only one person.[15] Thus my voting rule can be rephrased: 'Vote in elections unless you have a scar over your left eye that was caused by a puck deflecting off the curved blade of a hockey stick held by a man with his two front teeth missing and a tattoo of an anchor on his right forearm'. I have no doubt that I am the only person who satisfies that description and, consequently, that the rule so formulated has the de facto force of 'Everyone vote but Fumerton'.

One can respond to this problem in a number of different ways. The heroic course would be to stipulate necessary conditions that a rule must satisfy in order to comply with the appropriate sort of "generality," conditions that would rule out "tailor-made" rules of the sort discussed above. The problem is that the generality of a concept is logically unrelated to the number of things that concept applies to, and it is difficult to see how requirements of generality will prevent me from formulating rules that have built-in exceptions for me under some perfectly general description.

If generality isn't the source of the problem, one might simply introduce ad hoc conditions of fairness. One could simply state that a rule cannot make exceptions for one person or group of people unless there

15. In "What Is a Law of Nature?" A. J. Ayer makes the same point in arguing against the effectiveness of similar attempts to require generality of a law of nature.

is some feature of that person or group that relevantly distinguishes him or it from other people or groups. I cannot make an exception for myself in the voting rule even if there is marginally more utility produced by everyone voting but me, because there is no more reason to make the exception for me than for you. Why shouldn't the rule be 'Everyone but Jones vote' since the utility of following that rule would presumably be just as high? The difficulty with this solution is simply that it is not clear why one shouldn't arbitrarily select from among the many equally effective qualified voting rules, all of which are better than the simple 'Everyone vote' rule. Furthermore, if I have egoistic ends or goals, it is not clear that from my perspective the rule 'Everyone but Fumerton vote' isn't *better* than the alternative rules with built-in exceptions.

Of course, one might well appeal to human nature in arguing that, contrary to what first seems to be the case, societies in which everyone followed rules with these sorts of exceptions built in would not really be better than societies in which people followed exceptionless rules. The marginal gains that result from my not voting would be outweighed, one might argue, by the natural resentment people would feel in permitting someone to opt out of a practice that everyone else is committed to. True, perhaps, they shouldn't feel that way as rule utilitarians, but rule utilitarians must cope with human nature as they find it, and our jealousy of people who seem to have things better than we do is a pervasive human trait.

In any event, suppose that there is a solution to the problem of a rule utilitarian bent on finding "biased" rules that win the contest of rules governing a certain sort of behavior. There is another classic attempt to argue against rule consequentialism by showing that in the final analysis it really simply collapses, by its own standards, back into act consequentialism.[16]

16. For a useful detailed discussion of the alleged extensional equivalence of rule and act consequentialism, see Lyons 1965, chaps. 3 and 4. Lyons first argues the extensional equivalence of generalized utilitarianism (utilitarianism that accepts the generalization principle) and act utilitarianism. He then extends the thesis to what he calls *primitive* rule utilitarianism. As I understand Lyons, he may well agree with me when I argue that there is a version of utilitarianism which is conceptually distinct from act utilitarianism. He may recognize that version of rule utilitarianism I shall be discussing as a version of nonprimitive utilitarianism. It is not clear to me, however, for the paradigm nonprimitive rule utilitarianisms that Lyons discusses are versions that prohibit the inclusion of "minimizing-conditions excusing non-conformity" (p. 141). These "ideal" rule utilitarians would not allow the relevant voting rule to make its recommendations vis-à-vis voting contingent on what other people are doing. The argument I present later places

We have already had occasion to note that the rule consequentialist can and no doubt will recognize that plausible rules must be highly qualified. (I have also argued that recognizing a hierarchy of rules is only terminologically different from recognizing that rules must be highly qualified.) Only a lunatic would think that the rule 'Always keep a promise' is the correct rule by the rule consequentialist's criteria. We can surely imagine that things would be better were people to follow the rule 'Always keep a promise unless you can save lives by breaking it'. But this rule, in turn, seems inferior to a rule like 'Always keep a promise unless you can save lives, or help lost children, or stop an armed robbery or . . .' Or what? The list of possible reasons for breaking a promise that we should incorporate into our 'Promising Rule' seems endless. Indeed, when one considers the way in which we intuitively decide whether or not to make a further qualification of the rule, it is difficult to escape the conclusion that we are simply asking ourselves whether things would be better if people broke promises under the relevant circumstances. But then why wouldn't the winning rule for promising, by the rule consequentialist's criteria, be simply 'Always keep a promise unless you get better results by breaking the promise than by keeping it'? Won't such a rule necessarily be such that if people were to follow it the results would be better than if they were to follow some alternative rule? But if this is so, what is the difference between the behavior of a rule consequentialist following the rule 'Always keep a promise unless you can do more good by breaking it than by keeping it' and that of an act consequentialist who decides whether or not to break a promise by trying to decide which action would have the best consequences? And what holds for our promising rule holds also, of course, for the other "rules" we might formulate to govern other aspects of our lives. Why wouldn't the best voting rule, *by the rule consequentialist's criteria*, be the rule 'Vote unless you can get more of value accomplished by not voting'? Surely if such a rule were successfully followed we would necessarily have a better world than if people were to follow the unqualified rule 'Vote'.

The above argument is initially persuasive, and at one time I thought that it effectively demonstrated that rule consequentialism does not provide a coherent alternative to act consequentialism. It now seems to me, however, that a rule consequentialist can prevent his rule from

---

no restrictions on the kinds of qualifications that a rule utilitarian can incorporate into his rule utilitarianism and still concludes that rule utilitarianism is conceptually distinct from act utilitarianism.

collapsing into act consequentialism by taking note of certain ambiguities in the criteria he provides for the correctness of a rule. We can illustrate the point most easily with the example of a rule for voting.

Is it really true that, by the rule consequentialist's criteria, the rule 'Vote unless more of value can be accomplished by not voting' will win out over the unqualified rule 'Vote'? Would more of value result if people followed the former rule than if people followed the latter? Part of the difficulty involved in answering the question concerns the interpretation of the rule and the relevant concept of people following it. The rule could be construed as issuing a directive to the *collective*. Thus the hypothetical question that one asks in evaluating the rule would be, 'What would the world be like if the collective followed the rule "Vote unless more of value results from not voting"?' Trivially, it would seem that more of value would result from the collective following this rule than if they were to follow the unqualified voting rule. But how does an individual follow a rule addressed to a collective? The only thing I can control directly is my own vote. If a rule is to guide my behavior, I need it to prescribe the conditions under which I ought to vote, not just the conditions under which a "collective" ought to vote. If we interpret the rule 'Vote unless more of value results from not voting' in such a way that it is to be distributed among the members that make up the collective, then to follow that rule, *I* must vote unless I can produce more of value by not voting, and you must do the same. But if it is true that as individuals we accomplish nothing of significance by voting but can save ourselves the trouble of voting, then the world in which everyone follows that rule will be a world in which no one votes, a world that, by hypothesis, is worse than the world in which everyone votes.

Suppose we reformulate the voting rule this way: 'Vote unless enough other people are (are not) voting that one's vote will not make a significant difference'. Surely, at least this rule wins out over the straight voting rule, and it will still allow me to stay away from the polls, that is, following it will not produce a result different from that entailed by act consequentialism. In discussing the question, let us ignore sorites problems of vagueness and suppose that we can demarcate the number of people necessary and sufficient for having a "healthy" election. Whether one is successfully following the above rule obviously depends on what other people are doing. I am behaving in accord with the rule provided that enough other people are voting, and consequently I am *justified in believing* that I am acting in accord with the rule provided that I am justified in believing that enough other people are (are not) voting that my vote would not have made the critical difference in making this appear to be a "healthy" election. Now it seems to me that I am *always* justified in believing that my vote would not make such a difference and thus that I am always justified in believing that I am following the above qualified voting rule by not voting. The odds that my vote would have made the critical difference in the health of an election are as low as the odds that my vote would have elected one candidate rather than another. But this very fact suggests a way in which the rule consequentialist can revise his criteria for evaluating alternative rules so that the rule 'Vote unless enough other people are voting that your vote will not make a significant difference' turns out to be inferior to the straight voting rule. One can simply stipulate that the appropriate hypothetical question to ask in evaluating alternative rules governing a certain sort of behavior is, 'What would the world be like if rational people *tried* to follow this rule rather than alternatives?' Indeed, in one sense of following a rule, one *is* following a rule when one tries to behave as the rule prescribes. And one can argue that a world in which everyone tried to follow the above qualified voting rule would be one in which no one voted because everyone would be justified in believing (as I am) that his vote wouldn't make the critical difference in making this a healthy election. But again, by hypothesis, a world in which no one votes is a world that is worse than a world in which everyone votes.

I conclude that rule consequentialism does constitute a genuine alternative to act consequentialism in metaethics and metarationality. But is it an alternative that has anything to recommend it? The question is particularly acute because on the face of it rule consequentialism runs counter to a consequentialist's criteria determining what one ought to do. The original insight behind consequentialism seems straightforward and highly attractive. In the case of rational behavior, one wants to bring about through one's actions the world one values most. If what one values is different from what one judges to be good, then in the case of moral behavior, one wants to bring about through one's actions the best possible world. Modifications of this account are necessary, as we have seen, to take into account considerations of probability, but such modifications do not affect the basic thrust of the view. On a rule consequentialist's theory, however, no matter how sophisticated its presentation, the strange fact remains that I might know that through my actions I can clearly produce more of what I value (more of what is good) even though I (rationally/morally) should not take those actions. So what if it is true that in such situations it would be bad if other people acted in the same way? Provided that I know that my actions do not affect theirs, the question of what would happen if other people acted in a similar way seems utterly irrelevant. I should no more have to consider how the world would be if people were to act in the same way I am acting than I should have to consider how the world would be if people were to act in the opposite way to which I am acting. The world I am interested in is *this* world, and how my actions influence this world is (in part) a function of what other people *are* doing.

Although I cannot consider all of the possible arguments for rule consequentialist accounts of rationality and morality here, I shall close by briefly considering three. The first we might call argument by appeal to "intuition," and we have, in effect, already discussed it. Many rule consequentialists simply argue that their view better accommodates our prephilosophical "intuitions" concerning rational/right conduct. As we have seen, the act consequentialist's critics charge that the view will sanction the rationality/rightness of violations of "conventional" morality more often than is acceptable. We singled out the voter's paradox and prisoner's dilemma for more detailed discussion in this regard. As we said, appeal to prephilosophical "intuition" as a guide to the construction of a philosophical account is notoriously unreliable as a method of argument. One philosopher's unacceptable consequence of a theory of rationality or morality is another philosopher's obvious conclusion. Moreover, one can surely argue that part of the reason we do philosophy is to put ourselves in a position to *reconsider* judgments that we have unreflectively accepted throughout most of our lives. We have been conditioned to accept a great many conclusions about what we ought to do, but the people who condition us may have good reasons to deceive us. I have no objections to the government trying to convince everyone that his vote really does make a significant difference even though I think the position is ludicrous. And I have admitted that as a parent I don't encourage my children to reflect on the possible wisdom of lying (even though I think lying is sometimes wise). Insofar as it is in my power to influence people on these matters, I am not sure that I wouldn't take the same approach with most adults. I suspect people are not very good at figuring out when they ought to be dishonest and are better off unreflectively following the rule 'Tell the truth'. It may even be true that most people would be better off believing that rule consequentialism is true (even though it isn't) because it would make it easier for them to unreflectively follow the rules that they are better off (in general) unreflectively following.

Having said all this, I emphasize again that it is not clear that act consequentialism has all of the consequences its critics point to. The more successful society has been in conditioning me to respond with feelings of uneasiness to the violations of conventional morality, the more I must take into account this causal consequence of my violating conventional morality in deciding whether or not to do it. And the more formal and informal sanctions society imposes on people who violate conventional morality, the more I must worry about the consequences of getting caught. It will not do me a whole lot of good to justify my actions by appeal to act consequentialist considerations if the people I must convince haven't the philosophical sophistication to appreciate these considerations. As we pointed out, the hypothetical situations to which the act consequentialist's critics appeal often involve grossly unrealistic assumptions about what the agent knows about what other people will find out concerning his actions. In evaluating the wisdom of lying, breaking promises, killing innocent people to save lives, and so on, we cannot help but take into account the adjusted value of the possible but unlikely calamitous consequences of our behavior. And this will often be sufficient for us to conclude that, despite the obvious benefits that will certainly result from the hypothetical action, it would in the final analysis be wrong.

If appeal to "intuitions" falls on deaf ears, the act consequentialist's critics may resort to dialectical considerations. In *Impartial Reason,* Darwall tries to convince us that the *normativity* of judgments about rationality requires us to will that our norms of rationality be followed universally. If I judge that I ought to behave in a certain way *because* I judge that behavior to be rational, where the "because" is the "because" of justification, I must also think that anyone else in my situation should act in a similar way. Stripped of its complex terminological disguise, the argument seems to be that, if I choose to act on a principle that makes my act rational, it must be because I have implicitly decided that I want to behave rationally. Rational action has, therefore, value for me, and it has this value regardless of whose action it is that is rational. But in choosing my action-guiding principles of rationality, then I must answer the question, "Does this principle have the property that would justify its being my preference from an impartial perspective that all agents act on it?" (p. 229). We have arrived at the rule consequentialist's conclusion that in deciding how to behave I must consider whether I would want everyone to behave in a similar fashion.

We have, in effect, already objected to the crucial presuppositions of the above argument in our discussion of egoism when we responded to the claim that one cannot want one's own happiness without wanting the happiness of others. We simply made the obvious point that whatever makes me different from you can be the same factor that makes me want my happiness while I am indifferent to yours. If I decide to act rationally, it may follow that in some sense I have decided that I prefer *my* acting rationally to my acting irrationally, but nothing whatsoever follows concerning my desire that you act rationally. I have conceded that it is a trivial analytic truth that, if it is rational for me to act according to certain principles, then it is rational for anyone else relevantly similar to me to act in accordance with those same principles. But as we have had occasion to note several times, it is prima facie absurd to suppose that when I judge that another person would be rational to do X that commits me to *wanting* her to do X. I constantly find myself in competitive situations involving other people in which I quite desperately hope that those people will act irrationally. And unless I have an unrealistically cynical conception of my fellow human beings, I am quite sure that they have a similar attitude toward me.

Darwall, interestingly enough, considers this sort of objection, although he imagines it coming from an egoist. The egoist he considers has decided that it would be rational for him to promote his own self-interest and has conceded that it would be no less rational for others to promote their self-interest. "What the egoist need not admit, they may think, is that an ideally rational agent would prefer that *everyone* promote his or her interest" (p. 227). Darwall objects that this egoist: "is an egoist first and a rationalist second. He begins with a concern for his own interest and accepts the rationality of the self-interested conduct of others as the price for maintaining the rationality of his own self-interested conduct. Such an agent is not . . . concerned first and fundamentally to act rationally" (p. 228). An egoist who believes that his egoistic behavior is rational must admit that anyone relevantly similar to him would be equally rational. This isn't the "price" for being an egoist. It is a trivial tautology, given the obvious interpretation of "relevantly similar". Does an egoist want other egoists to act rationally? Probably not. But does that mean that he is not concerned to act rationally himself? Of course not. One would only reach that conclusion if one believed that one cannot want oneself to act rationally without wanting everyone else to act rationally. But such a conclusion is absurd on the face of it. The only conceivable argument for such a position would be the bad argument for the impossibility of egoistic values which we considered earlier. But if that argument were a good argument, Darwall wouldn't need to secure the necessity of "impartial" reasons through the machinations we have just been considering.

David Gauthier is another philosopher who, though generally sympathetic to the kind of account of rational action I defend, cannot reconcile himself to the inevitability of ideally rational agents in the prisoner's dilemma producing for themselves the second-worst possible outcome. Although Gauthier is not straightforwardly arguing for a rule-governed conception of rational action, he does argue against the view that rational action always involves what he calls *unconstrained maximizing of utility*.[17] More specifically, like Darwall, Gauthier thinks that in situations in which cooperation can yield better results than unconstrained maximizing, it is rational to take account of the interests of other parties. Gauthier argues, in effect, that the practice of maximizing satisfaction of one's desires (ignoring the interests of others except insofar as one has desires concerning them) fails to satisfy a requirement of being *self-supporting* (1975, p. 429). Specifically, he argues that if one assesses the rationality of being a utility maximizer by the criteria of utility maximization, it will, ironically, be irrational to be a utility maximizer. Acting in accord with a principle is not rational, Gauthier appears to argue, if by that principle it would be irrational to choose to act in accord with it. But why is it irrational to choose to be a utility maximizer?[18] Gauthier's argument appears to be that an unconstrained maximizer of utility will not be able to "enter rationally into an agreement to act to bring about an optimal outcome which affords each party to the agreement a utility greater than he would attain acting independently" (1975, p. 429). A constrained maximizer (someone who cooperates with others when the result of cooperation produces better conse-

17. As far as I know, Gauthier first makes the argument in 1975. It is repeated in more detail in his book (1986). In many ways the argument in its earlier form seems clearer to me than what appears to be the same argument expressed in the book.

18. For simplicity I am adopting Gauthier's terminology. I want the reader, however, to interpret maximizing expected utility in the specific way I have indicated earlier in this book.

quences than the result of each acting as utility maximizers) "has in some circumstances some probability of being able to enter into, and carry out, an agreement, whereas the straightforward maximizer has no such probability" (1975, p. 430).

The defect of Gauthier's objection to taking the egocentric perspective in deciding what one rationally ought to do should be obvious. His argument trades on an ambiguity involving the "possibility of entering into agreements". Unconstrained maximizers in the prisoner's dilemma can obviously, in one sense, enter into an agreement to remain silent. They can even read Gauthier's article together and try to convince each other that he is absolutely correct and that consequently they should rationally be constrained maximizers. Having entered into the agreement, the question then becomes: Would it be rational by the principles of unconstrained utility maximizing to be an unconstrained utility maximizer and break the agreement? And the answer seems to be obviously yes. If the person in the next room is a true follower of Gauthier, then by being an unconstrained utility maximizer and breaking my agreement, that is, confessing, I will be better off. If it is someone pretending to accept Gauthier's view, I will still be better off acting as an unconstrained utility maximizer, that is, confessing.

I should emphasize here that this whole discussion presupposes a highly artificial hypothetical situation in which we are assuming that the decision I make in my prisoner's dilemma has no ramifications on my ability to interact with other people in various ways in the future. I build into the hypothesis the highly unrealistic assumption that I know that no one will ever find out what decision I have made and what agreements I have violated in making it. Of course, it *is* to one's advantage in the long run to be able to make agreements and cooperate with other people. If I need you to help me with some task and you agree only on condition that I help you afterward, it is useful for us to have some assurance that we will keep our respective agreements. As Hobbes pointed out, in the absence of any such assurance, it is not clear why a party to such an agreement would ever agree to perform his part of the bargain *first*. Hobbes, of course, suggested that the way to resolve the problem is to create a mechanism, a sovereign, whose own self-interest will involve enforcing contracts with threat of punishment, thus *giving* all parties to an agreement a reason to perform. Hobbes, however, ignored more subtle ways in which one can have reason to perform one's part of an agreement even after the other party has performed first. The most obvious of these is the advantage of being able to make similar agreements with people in the future. One must inductively establish one's honesty if one expects other people to believe that one will do what one says one will do. None of this, of course, has any relevance to a *"pure"* prisoner's dilemma sort of situation in which it is stipulated that any agreement I keep or break has no causal effects on future actions by other people. But in real life, even in a situation like the prisoner's dilemma, one must take into consideration such possible long-term effects. If I make and break an agreement with you to remain silent, and word gets out that I did, no one will make similar agreements like this with me in the future, and this might be an extremely unfortunate consequence of my action.

In his book (1986), and to a lesser extent in his earlier article (1975), Gauthier *sometimes* seems to be arguing only that a rational agent will forgo short-term maximizing for the long-term benefits that come from being able to produce expectations in others necessary for cooperation.[19] With this view, of course, I have no quarrel. Nor should any "unconstrained" maximizer. To be an unconstrained maximizer one does not have to be short-sighted! But for Gauthier's position to constitute a genuine departure from the kind of act consequentialism I defend, he must argue that even in a "pure" prisoner's dilemma I would be irrational to confess. Again, a "pure" prisoner's dilemma is one in which, *by hypothesis,* my behavior on this occasion will have no effects on my future ability to get people to trust me in ways necessary to my being able to make agreements. We may also stipulate that my decision to break any particular agreements I make in this case does not affect my "character" so as to make it more difficult for me to tell the truth in impure types of prisoner's dilemma situations.

In a "pure" prisoner's dilemma, if one *knows* that the other prisoner is an unconstrained utility maximizer (who is also an egoist), one had certainly better confess. Furthermore, I know that if you know that I am an unconstrained maximizer, you will confess. Gauthier may simply be arguing that it is irrational for me to choose to be an unconstrained maximizer because in doing so I have virtually guaranteed that the other

19. It nevertheless seems clear that in the final analysis Gauthier does not want us to understand his argument this way. See, for example, 1986, pp. 169–70.

prisoner will confess, thus guaranteeing at best the second-worst possible outcome for myself. As Darwall points out (p. 196), this argument illicitly assumes that the other prisoner will *know* what principle I have decided to act on. To be sure, he'll find out when I break the agreement to remain silent and he keeps it, but by then it will be too late.

Gauthier is so sympathetic to the basic conception of rationality that I defend (and, indeed, defends it eloquently himself for decision making in which the issue of cooperation does not arise) that it is hard for me to understand why he does not see the futility of trying to avoid the obvious conclusion that ideally rational people can act in ways that guarantee for themselves an outcome worse than they could have achieved had they acted in some other way. Perhaps he is simply engaging in rhetoric designed to produce for himself the optimum outcome should he ever find himself a participant in the prisoner's dilemma! The bottom line, however, must always be this: How could I possibly go wrong being an unconstrained maximizer in a "pure" prisoner's dilemma? My fellow prisoner is either a constrained maximizer or not, a rule consequentialist or not, a Kantian or not, someone who is committed to do valuing the satisfaction of another's values as though they were his own, or not. It just doesn't matter. I am going to end up better off acting as an unconstrained maximizer. Darwall and Gauthier can argue until they are blue in the face and I still know that, regardless of what I might have reason to *say* by way of agreeing with their views, I will be better off being an unconstrained maximizer when it comes to making the critical decision as to whether to confess or remain silent (whether that involves the breaking of some prior agreement or not). Far from lacking self-support, the decision to be an unconstrained maximizer looks as if it is going to maximize my utility regardless of what philosophical views the other prisoner holds and regardless of what actions he takes or fails to take in accord with those views. There is no escaping this conclusion, and it is folly to suppose that, if Gauthier were the other prisoner with me, he could give me some reason to act (as opposed to pretend to agree to act) as a constrained maximizer.

There are no reasons to abandon the act consequentialist conception of rational action defended earlier. I frankly don't care if other people act as rule consequentialists or take some sort of impersonal impartial perspective when it comes to the satisfaction of goals or ends. I'll probably end up better off the more people there are who buy into such views. But if one is a consequentialist at all, if one tries through one's actions to produce the most of what one values, there is surely no alternative to an act consequentialist conception of rational action. And if one is going to tie morality to rationality, one had better not divorce the concept of morally right action from a generic act consequentialist conception of morally right action.

CHAPTER 7

Morality and Rationality

PARALLELS

We have been discussing some issues that arise concerning consequentialist analyses of what one rationally and morally ought to do. And
although it may have been occasionally awkward, we have evaluated
various objections to alternative act consequentialist analyses of rationality and morality without any obvious need to consider the concepts independently. Whether one agrees or disagrees with an attempt
to conceptually link rational action with moral action, one must surely
recognize a remarkable parallel when it comes to the kinds of questions
philosophical accounts of these concepts must answer. This, coupled
with the fact that the same word "ought" is used in expressing both
paradigmatic moral judgments and judgments about the rationality of
action, would surely argue for a close examination of possible conceptual connections between the concept of what a person morally ought
to do and the concept of what a person has the most reason to do.

Even if the reader is not impressed by what seem to me to be obvious
parallels, I should reiterate my overall Humean strategy. As far as I am
concerned, the philosophical *relevance* of moral concepts as concepts
fundamental to decision making rests on the possibility of identifying
the question of what I morally ought to do with the question of what I
have the most reason to do. It is an analytic truth that as a rational agent

I must concern myself with what I have the most reason to do. If it turns out that I might not have the most reason to do what I morally ought to do, then so much the worse for morality. Indeed, if it is possible that morally right and rational action might diverge, then it is unclear why a rational agent should even bother to reflect on questions of morality in deciding what to do, except where moral "rules," particularly the sanctions that society imposes on moral rule breakers, obviously affect the relevant calculations of rationality.[1] I stress, then, the fundamental implications of the move to conceptually divorce morality from rationality. Nothing less than the philosophical relevance of moral concepts as fundamentally *interesting* is at stake. Unless from the egocentric perspective I can identify the question of what I myself ought to do with the question of what I have the most reason to do, it is simply not clear why as a philosopher I should worry about the concept of morality. Indeed, if we divorce the two concepts, it seems to me obvious that we should teach courses in Introduction to Rational Action rather than Introduction to Ethics. The latter course wouldn't address the questions a rational agent needs answered in order to make decisions. The former course would.

Having said all this, I have not forgotten my early admission that the ancient question "Why should one be moral?" seems like a perfectly legitimate "open" question. And if the conclusion I am arguing for is correct, it is obvious that I owe the reader an account of why a question that should be trivial on my view appears to be significant. Such an account is forthcoming.

IDENTIFYING CONCEPTS OF MORALITY AND RATIONALITY

In the introduction to *Individuals,* P. F. Strawson distinguished *revisionary* from *descriptive* metaphysics. When doing revisionary metaphysics, one makes suggestions as to how one can "clean up" one's conceptual framework so as to eliminate various defects of confusion or ambiguity. In doing descriptive metaphysics, one must try to faithfully characterize concepts as they are actually employed. Were I to engage in

---

1. This is essentially the position Glaucon and Adeimentus (playing devil's advocate for Thrasymachus) defend in *The Republic.*

the task of prescribing a metaethical framework within which to discuss ethical issues, I would simply suggest that we define a univocal sense of "ought" which is analyzed in terms of what a person has the most reason to do. Given the analysis of rational action defended earlier in this book, we could conceptually link the fundamental concepts of morality and rationality in the following way (keeping in mind the more detailed analyses offered earlier of the problematic terms):

X is an end for S. = S values X = X is intrinsically good
                            intrinsically.   for S.

S has more reason to choose X
than any of its alternatives $(S$ = X is the morally right thing
rationally ought to do $X)$.   for S to do.

where rational action is defined in terms of value adjusted possible consequences or the relevant justified metabeliefs (see the discussion of derivative concepts of rational action in Chapter 4).

There are, of course, moral concepts not yet interdefined with the concepts employed in the analysis of rational action. The term "good" is rarely actually used to denote the property of intrinsic goodness, and given the adequacy of the above, we could easily define the concept of something being instrumentally good for S in terms of its leading to something intrinsically good for S.[2] There is the further question of how to understand "good" as it is used to describe functionally defined artifacts, a question to which we shall return shortly. A complete analysis of moral concepts would also interdefine such concepts as right action, duty, obligation, morally permissible action, blameworthiness (praiseworthiness), justice, and so on, but I shall concern myself only with the concepts associated with the term "good" and the concepts of what would be right for someone to do, what someone morally ought to do.[3]

The above tentative analyses obviously ignore what I take to be a relatively trivial feature of our concept of a *moral* judgment. It is plausible to argue that the very concept of a moral decision, as opposed to

2. If we were to be more sensitive to ordinary discourse we might say instead that we identify things as instrumentally good when they lead to intrinsic goodness without a great deal of hardship, that is, without producing bad consequences that outweigh the goodness.

3. I am convinced that all other interesting moral concepts can be defined in terms of these fundamental moral concepts.

many other decisions we make concerning what we ought to do, requires that other people take an interest in the outcome of that decision. It may even be true that one describes an action as morally right only if it involves a situation in which there are at least potential conflicts of interest, a situation in which there is a strong probability that people in general will care about what you are going to do. Certainly, the guidelines of what we might call "conventional" morality, the advice we get concerning generosity, courage, honesty, perseverance, loyalty, and so on, are obviously intended to guide us in situations involving interaction with other people where such interaction involves the strong potential for conflict. This is all very vague, of course, but one would be ill-advised to try to make it more precise. Nor is it terribly important. One's decision about which university to attend surely isn't a paradigm moral decision (unless the university is itself morally controversial). But what about one's decision to be a philosopher instead of a medical researcher? I can certainly imagine arguing that this decision is implicitly a moral decision because the well-being of others may well be indirectly affected. By the same token, one's decision to buy a new car implicitly involves a decision to allocate resources one way rather than another and, consequently, could be construed as an ethical decision. One's decision to eat one's boiled eggs from the narrow part down is not a moral decision unless one lives in the land of Lilliput, where people feel quite strongly about such things. Given that people seem willing to kill each other over the most subtle differences between their superstitious religions, it seems to me that there is no telling what people will construe as a matter of moral significance. And unless one can show that the theoretical criteria governing the rationality of decisions are significantly affected by the fact that others take a significant interest in them, it seems to me that we can justifiably neglect this feature of morality.

I have said that if I could prescribe the use of moral terms I would recommend that people use them in the way sketched above. Indeed, it seems to me that there would be far less confusion if we simply discussed issues that relate to justified decision making in terms of the concept of reasons for acting. If wishes were horses, however, beggars would ride, and in fact, the meaning of ethical terms is far too varied and complex to lend itself easily to the above as a description of how we actually use ethical terms. If we were to restrict ourselves to the analysis of *first-person* moral judgments, I think it would be entirely plausible to argue that, whenever I ask myself what I ought to do, I am asking myself what I have the most reason to do where this is defined in terms of value adjusted possible consequences of alternative actions vis-à-vis the satisfaction of my ends. In Chapter 4, however, I noted some ambiguities concerning presuppositions of perspective which creep into the analyses of second- and third-person judgments about the rationality of actions, and I warned that these ambiguities would also be present in the use of the moral "ought". The most obvious of these ambiguities concerns the epistemic perspective presupposed by the judgment. When I assert that Smith ought to do something, the relevant probabilities that, in part, define what he ought to do can be understood relative to Smith's evidence or relative to my evidence. As I argued earlier, when Smith asks my advice as to what he ought to do, it seems obvious to me that *in this context* I am supposed to answer presupposing the probabilities of possible outcomes of his actions relative to *my* body of evidence. On the other hand, if Smith is enlisting my support in a defense of the rationality of some action he took, it is equally obvious that I would be expected to presuppose the relevant probabilities defined relative to his body of evidence. These ambiguities that we noted in the meaning of judgments about rational action must obviously be reflected in an attempt to understand our use of moral concepts.

In addition to the ambiguities of epistemic perspective just discussed, however, there is an ambiguity of perspective which is occasionally reflected in second- and third-person judgments about the rationality of action, but which is much more pronounced when it comes to second- and third-person *moral* judgments. I have argued that my ends are the ultimate court of appeal with respect to what I ought to do and that there is a univocal sense of "ought" that applies to such first-person judgments. I have also argued that there is no way to evaluate one's ends except in terms of one's ends. Only if the having of an end frustrates in various ways other ends can one speak in a derivative sense about one's intrinsic values being irrational. The question is obviously more complicated, however, when it comes to the evaluation of other people's values. One can certainly disapprove of another person's goals or ends even when that person's goals or ends are in "internal harmony." If my neighbor is a masochistic sadist (who enjoys the punishment his sadism reaps), I can find extremely distasteful both his actions and the desires that motivate them even if I recognize that from the perspective of his ends he is acting in a perfectly rational way. And although I wish we didn't do this (because I think it generates needless confusion), I think it is obvious that we do sometimes let our *moral* judgments about what another person ought to do perform the *dual* tasks of assessing the rationality of his action relative to his ends and evaluating his ends, that is, of indicating our approval or disapproval of his ends. And here I use the vague term "indicating" because it really seems to me unimportant whether we say that the judgment *describes* or *expresses* our evaluation of these ends (see the discussion of this issue in Chapter 2).

What is involved in the evaluation of another person's ends? The answer is essentially the same as to any question concerning the evaluation of anything. It is in principle possible to intrinsically value or disvalue the fact that someone has certain ends. I might intrinsically disvalue the fact that a sadist intrinsically values the pain of another person.[4] I suspect, however, that more often we disvalue the values of another person because those values at least indirectly clash with the satisfaction of our own goals or ends. If I value intrinsically the happiness of others, the sadist's desires present an obvious obstacle to the satisfaction of my own goals or ends, at least insofar as there is a significant probability that the sadist will successfully satisfy his sadistic desires.

In addition, then, to the ambiguities of epistemic perspective presupposed by judgments about what a person has the most reason to do, it seems to me that *moral* judgments about the actions of others often (perhaps not always) build into the "ought" of rationality an evaluation of the agent's *ends*. And if one pleases, one can view this as a defining distinction between the "ought" of morality and the "ought" of practical rationality. Note again that the distinction collapses in the case of our first-person evaluations of what we ought to do. We can evaluate another's ends by reference to our own. But we have nothing to which we can appeal in the evaluation of our own ends other than those ends themselves. Again, if I could legislate the use of language, I would recommend against using a moral "ought" to serve the dual purposes of evaluating the rationality of an agent's actions and evaluating that agent's goals or ends. Because the distinction proposed above between a moral "ought" and an "ought" of practical rationality collapses in the case of first-person "ought" judgments, we can accept the distinction

4. Of course, this is a rather implausible characterization of a sadist. Sadists are more likely to be people who get pleasure from knowing that another suffers, where this pleasure is the ultimate goal of their sadistic behavior.

and preserve a connection between our judgments about what we morally ought to do and judgments about what we have the most reason to do. But the use of a dual-purpose "ought" in second- and third-person judgments has the unfortunate result that the truth of our moral judgments may be quite irrelevant to what the person about whom the judgment is made has the most reason to do. If I say that Jones shouldn't do X, meaning not that he would be irrational in doing X but that I disapprove of his goals or ends in doing X, the truth[5] of my assertion would be logically irrelevant to Jones and his considerations about what he ought to do. Of course, if Jones has some reason to care about my attitudes toward his attitudes, there is a sense in which he will take into account my evaluation in calculating the rationality of his actions. But the *content* of my judgment about what Jones shouldn't do will not *contradict* Jones's judgment about what he ought to do. It seems to me that communication would be much simpler if we resolved to *separate* judgments about the rationality of someone's action from our evaluation of the agent and her attitudes. But in doing descriptive metaethics, we must acknowledge, I think, that moral judgments are used to perform the dual function described above.

If the moral "ought" usually does involve evaluation of an agent's goals or ends but the "ought" of rationality does not, we must be careful in placing our metatheories of ethics and practical rationality within the traditional metatheoretical debates discussed in Chapter 2. Judgments about what a person rationally ought to do will be cognitive, descriptive, and naturalistic. And of course, if the denial of an is/ought gap reduces to the above assertion, there will be no is/(rational) ought gap. The view defended is, of course, a relativistic analysis of rational action in the sense analogous to the metaethical relativism discussed in Chapter 2. The goals or ends that (in part) define an agent's rational action are the goals or ends of that person. The subjectivism/objectivism issue is more complicated when it comes to our analysis of rational action. When I defined that distinction in Chapter 2, I said that it is theoretically possible for one to hold that some value judgments are subjective (2) while others are not. On the view I have been defending, my first-person judgment about what I rationally ought to do will be subjective (2) insofar as its truth or falsehood will depend, at least in part, on facts about my psychological states (the facts that define my

5. The noncognitivist who would prefer to think of the judgment as *expressing* disapproval will have to find some other way of putting this.

goals or ends). My judgment about what *you* rationally ought to do, however, are not made true, even in part, by facts about my psychological states except when these judgments reflect probabilities relativized to my body of evidence (see the earlier discussion of this issue).

When it comes to metaethical controversies, our account is essentially the same concerning our first-person "ought" judgments. My judgment about what I morally ought to do is cognitive, descriptive, naturalistic, and subjective (in both senses of subjective). If people were more interested in clarity, they would simply define the ethical concept of goodness relativistically. "Good" would always mean "good for *X*", and the concept of what one morally ought to do would be defined in terms of that relativized concept of goodness. But because in our moral evaluations of what others ought to do we often (perversely, I think) evaluate that agent's actions relative to *our* goals or ends, it is more plausible to characterize our standard use of moral judgments as *subjective (2)* across the board.

"GOOD" AND FUNCTIONALLY DEFINED OBJECTS

This section constitutes something of a digression from the main themes of the book, but it is still relevant to their defense. My primary concern with the concept of goodness has been with the concept of intrinsic goodness. My reason is that I believe it to be the most fundamental ethical concept relevant to decisions about what I (morally) ought to do. Indeed, we could fully analyze the meaning of propositions about what we morally ought to do without invoking any concept of goodness other than the concept of intrinsic goodness. Nevertheless, I would like briefly to explore other uses of the expression "good". We use the word "good" in all kinds of nonmoral contexts. We refer to good cars, knives, liars, assassins, can openers, arguments, golf clubs, paintings, movies, and so on. It argues well for a metaethical theory if it can at least find family resemblances between the meaning of "good" in these contexts and the meaning of "good" in ethical contexts. Someone like Moore, for example, would have a terrible time trying to assimilate the use of "good" as it refers to his objective, nonnatural, simple property in "Knowledge is good" to the use of "good" in "Jones is a good thief". It is not clear how anything like Moore's nonnatural moral goodness is even indirectly referred to in the proposition that Jones is a good thief. One can, of course, simply claim that there are fundamental ambiguities in the use of the symbol "good" and that some of its uses are quite unrelated to others, but such a claim strains our credulity. There is surely some sense in which "good" is operating as a paradigm value term in both the proposition that knowledge is good and the proposition that Jones is a good thief.

On the view I have been defending, the concept of X being intrinsically good for S is defined in terms of X being an end for S. This same concept of a goal or end can be invoked in the analysis of "good" as it is used to describe cars, knives, and thieves. Many artifacts and professions are defined in terms of their purposes, goals, or ends. Other things are not *defined* in terms of what they are used to do, but there is so much agreement between people on their use that it becomes a presupposition of evaluations of such items that they have value only insofar as they can be used to accomplish certain goals or ends. In each case, the proposition that an X is a good F seems clearly to assert a property of X vis-à-vis its ability to accomplish either the defined or the presupposed goals for F's. Thus if a toaster is defined in part as an object used to toast bread, a good one is one that at least accomplishes this task. If a car is defined in part as an object used for transportation, a good car is minimally one that accomplishes this end. A thief is defined as one whose objective is to take things that belong to others, presumably with the further goal of not getting caught, and a good thief, minimally, accomplishes this goal.

The goals or ends associated with other things like paintings, plants, music, breeds of dogs, and so on are not nearly so obvious, and when good is used in these contexts, the person using the term, in effect, implicitly supplies her own goals or ends for the things in question. In some cases, we even attribute to inanimate objects their own goals or ends. Thus it seems obvious to some people that it is bad for a plant if it doesn't get enough sun and water to live and that this is so even if no people take an interest in the survival of this plant. Indeed, one might go so far as to argue that it would be bad for a plant to be deprived of sun and water even if no people existed. I would not deny that we might well talk this way, but I would suggest that when we do so we can best be understood as indulging in a kind of primitive anthropomorphizing. We imagine that the plant "wants" to survive and that this want or end would be frustrated by deprivation of sun and water. Lest the reader complain that this suggestion is rather far-fetched, let me observe that our inclination to anthropomorphize is pervasive. We constantly talk about what ants and bees are "trying" to accomplish through various sorts of behavior. Popular evolutionary accounts even attribute goal-oriented behavior to creatures as primitive as amoebae. All this is perfectly harmless since it can presumably be translated away. But recognizing our persistent habit of projecting our goal-oriented behavior onto other living things can also be used to explain what might otherwise seem to present a difficulty for our goal-oriented analysis of relativized goodness.

I assume that it is obvious how the use of "good" described above bears at least a family resemblance to the concept of goodness in terms of which we have tried to analyze morality and rationality. But the conceptual connections are even more obvious still.

Although we can say that a good thief, knife, car, and so on is one that accomplishes its defined or presupposed function, it is clearly necessary to go beyond this if we are to capture the ordinary use of the term "good". A reliable, safe car that uses little gas still isn't a good car if it is exceedingly ugly and costs two hundred thousand dollars. A thief isn't a good thief if he pays out in expenses two dollars for every dollar he successfully steals. A toaster that takes three hours to brown the bread isn't a good toaster even though it can be successfully used to accomplish the task for which toasters are designed. One wants to say, of course, that a good *F* is one that accomplishes *effectively* the task for which *F*'s are used. But this has all the appearance of a circular analysis of "good". One clearly needs an account of the normative concept of effectiveness. Such an account is readily forthcoming, given the analysis of rationality defended in this book. A good *F* is not simply one that can be successfully used to do the sorts of things *F*'s are used for. A good *F* must be compared to other *F*'s vis-à-vis maximizing satisfaction (minimizing frustration) of our other goals or ends. A *good F*, of course, does not have to be the *best F,* but a good *F* must rank high when it comes to the satisfaction of other goals or ends while accomplishing its own.[6]

6. Richard Feldman has reminded me that it is at best misleading to suggest that all judgments about the goodness and badness of artifacts are comparative. He suggests that we *can* view all products of a certain kind as good even if we view some as better than others. It seems to me that this is compatible with the account I give. In such a case we are probably judging that all products of that kind perform their functions *roughly* the same way and that there are no significant differences among them concerning their impact on our other concerns.

This notion of ranking high is exceedingly vague, but then so is the concept of good as it is used to categorize objects.

As we have argued throughout, goals or ends can vary from person to person, and consequently, the concept of a good *F* must be relativized in just the way that the concept of intrinsic goodness was relativized. A good car for Jones might not be a good car for Smith. A good thief for me to hire might not be a good thief for you to hire. A good movie for me to see might not be a good movie for you to see. If you are a multimillionaire, you might not care about the fifty-thousand-dollar price tag on the Mercedes. I do. If I like the color red, then red is a "good-making" characteristic of cars *for me*. If you don't, it isn't for you. These observations I take to be virtual truisms, but they are truisms that argue for the overall thrust of our analyses of value terms by establishing clear conceptual connections between the use of such terms in significantly different contexts.

Why Should I Be Moral?

We have yet to address one of the most obvious objections to our attempt to conceptually link metatheories of rationality and ethics. If we identify the content of my first-person judgments about what I morally ought to do with the content of my judgments about what I have the most reason to do, how does one account for the seeming significance of the question "Why should I be moral?" As was pointed out in the introduction, if the "ought" or "should" of first-person value judgments really is univocal, then it should be an utterly trivial truth that I should be moral, that is, I should do what I should do. Indeed, it might seem that it is *only* if we bifurcate the sense of "should" by recognizing, for example, a "should" of practical reason distinct from a "should" of morality that we can find a coherent and significant interpretation of the question "Why should I be moral?" With the bifurcated "should", that question could then be understood as the question "Why (rationally) should I do that which I (morally) should do?"

One can, of course, claim that after appropriate philosophical reflection it should become clear to good philosophers that the question "Why should I be moral?" *is* utterly trivial and thus presents no obstacle to an identification of morality and rationality. But it is surely hard to convince oneself that, from the extensive discussion of this issue in

Plato's *Republic* to the present time, so many philosophers have been preoccupied with an utterly trivial issue. If we presuppose the views defended in this book, how can we interpret the question "Why should I be moral?" so that it remains a significant question?

I have unequivocally defended the proposition that the most fundamental "ought" is the "ought" defined in terms of what a person has the most reason to do. The question "Why should I do what I have the most reason to do?" when this "should" is understood in this most fundamental way *is* utterly trivial. It is a tautology that one rationally should do what one has the most reason to do in the sense in which it is a tautology to assert that one epistemically should believe what one has the most reason to believe.

The key to understanding the significance of the crucial question "Why should I be moral?" is essentially straightforward. One simply has to keep in mind the distinction between normative ethics and meta-ethics and acknowledge what seems to me obvious, that in many contexts when people talk about "being moral" they are talking about conforming to some *particular* normative moral code. As an act consequentialist I will, of course, construe a moral code as a system of rules of thumb governing especially our interactions with other people. In the context in which philosophers like Plato try to convince people that they ought to be moral, it seems clear to me that they are trying to convince people that it is rational to live, by and large, in accord with what we might call "conventional morality". Again, conventional morality is a set of normative principles which varies from culture to culture, generation to generation, but one that in western civilization has been remarkably stable for the last two thousand years or so. From childhood to adulthood, through the ages, people have been told that they shouldn't lie, steal, cheat, avoid paying taxes, commit adultery, inflict gratuitous suffering on others, break promises, be ungrateful, be slovenly, be self-indulgent, and so on. Although this advice may be perfectly good, it is certainly not self-evidently correct, and it is natural for intellectually active people to ask themselves whether reason really does always or usually side with *conventional* morality.

When we teach our children the "rules" of conventional morality, we usually put them forth (quite rationally, I argued earlier) as *exceptionless* rules. Interpreted *as such,* it seems to me not only reasonable to ask "Should I abide by the rules of conventional morality?" but reasonable to answer in the negative. Plato himself, while defending the rationality of conventional morality, takes pains to point out to Cephalus and Polemarchus that there are circumstances in which it would be wrong (irrational) to tell the truth or return what you have borrowed, despite the fact that, by and large, one usually should behave in such ways.

In a famous section of *Leviathan,* Hobbes defends a number of natural laws that amount to normative rules prescribing as rational various modes of behavior involving human interaction. For Hobbes, perhaps the most important rule that rational people should follow is the rule "Don't break covenants" (a rule that applies only once the state has come into existence). Operating within a cynical (probably too cynical) egoistic conception of human nature, Hobbes appropriately raises an objection to his view:

> The fool hath said in his heart, there is no such thing as justice; and sometimes also with his tongue, seriously alleging that, every man's conservation and contentment being committed to his own care, there could be no reason why every man might not do what he thought conduced thereunto; and therefore also to make or not make, keep or not keep covenants was not against reason when it conduced to one's benefit. He does not therein deny that there be covenants and that they are sometimes broken, sometimes kept, and that such breach of them may be called injustice and the observance of them justice; but he questions whether injustice, taking away the fear of God—for the same fool hath said in his heart there is no God—may not sometimes stand with that reason which dictates to every man his own good, and particularly then when it conduces to such a benefit as shall put a man in a condition to neglect not only the dispraise and revilings, but also the power of other men.[7]

Hobbes is, of course, raising the question with respect to one aspect of conventional morality, the keeping of covenants, but one can broaden the question to ask why one should pay any attention to any of Hobbes's laws of nature when they run contrary to one's interests. When the smoke clears, Hobbes's answer to the fool (and it is surely clear that he doesn't think the question so foolish after all) really amounts to a refusal to answer the question. Paraphrased liberally (from p. 122), Hobbes

7. *Leviathan,* pp. 120–21. Note here the difference between Hobbes and Rousseau in *The Social Contract.* The latter is widely viewed as having the more subtle and sophisticated social contract theory, but though both Hobbes and Rousseau try (in Rousseau's words) to identify "what interest prescribes with what right prescribes," it never occurs to Rousseau that he should worry about why a rational person should keep a social contract (even if rationally made) when it is no longer in his interest to do so.

argues that, if the state has been set up properly with a powerful enough sovereign whose own self-interest requires him to enforce contracts, it never *will* be in one's self-interest to violate contracts. You cannot rationally gamble that you will get away with this violation of conventional morality—the risks of getting caught will always outweigh any possible advantages of success. As I indicated, this response leaves open the question of whether one should break contracts *if* it is in one's interest to do so. Unlike Hobbes, I do not presuppose that people are by nature egoists, although I suspect the vast majority put their interests and the interests of a few loved ones ahead of all other people. But even so, Hobbes surely points to one good reason why one would be rational to abide by conventional morality. As long as there are laws and sanctions enforcing conventional morality, one must take into account the risk of getting caught violating conventional morality. Is it rational for society to have these laws? Probably. Just as adults don't want children to make too many decisions concerning morality on their own, so, too, the state has an interest in trying to force people to live by rules if it has correctly calculated that people will too often reason poorly when left on their own.[8]

Fear of *state* punishment is relevant only to a subclass of decisions we make concerning whether or not to abide by conventional morality. The state does not enforce all of the moral codes we are encouraged to live by. What reason do we have for abiding by *these* conventions of morality? Given the relativistic conception of rationality defended above, the answer to that question rests largely on human nature. The more egoistic we are, the harder it will be to justify conventional morality. The more we care intrinsically about the well-being of others, the easier it will be. The self-interested can again turn to Hobbes for some plain commonsense advice concerning the rationality of conventional moral behavior. After listing his many laws of nature, Hobbes kindly gives us a summary rule we can use when we can't remember the others, a rule that turns out to be none other than the golden rule: "Do not that to another which you would not have done to yourself" (p. 130). Not surprisingly, given Hobbes's view of human nature, the golden rule turns out to be good egoistic advice. By and large, you

8. In his excellent discussion of the morality of common sense, Sidgwick (1922, Book 4) would also emphasize the stake society has in inculcating *dispositions* to act in certain ways. It may well be true that to bring about stable dispositions one must discourage the making of exceptions that would be otherwise irrational to discourage.

shouldn't be nasty to others because you can expect them to respond in kind, and you won't like it. Though not terribly sophisticated, Hobbes's justification of conventional morality seems to constitute an obvious *consideration* that a rational person will take into account in calculating what to do. The golden rule itself presumably admits of all kinds of exceptions—I assume judges shouldn't worry about punishing criminals even though they wouldn't want to be punished if they were criminals. But when the golden rule does prescribe the same behavior as conventional morality, Hobbes's rationale is often available.

In treating the rule consequentialist's counterexamples to act consequentialism, we discussed some ways in which an act consequentialist could accommodate conventional intuitions about morality from within his act consequentialist framework. We pointed out the necessity of taking into account unlikely, but nevertheless possible, negative results from violating conventional morality in a society that respects it (the Hobbesian rationale for the fool), and the necessity of taking into account the possible negative consequences of having a guilty conscience from behaving in ways that one may have been successfully conditioned not to behave by a society that has its own reason to try to mold its citizens' behavior. If one values intrinsically the well-being of others, or if one is an egoist whose own happiness is causally tied to knowing that others are happy, one will again have reasons to abide by many of those rules of conventional morality which are clearly tied to making others happy. My concern, however, is not to defend conventional morality. If anything, I suspect that far too many people are irrational slaves to the letter of conventional morality. My concern, rather, is to find an interpretation of the question "Why should I be moral?" which is consistent with the historical discussion of that question and which renders it a genuine, significant question. From Plato to the present, it seems to me that philosophers who ask the question "Why should I be moral?" are asking the question "Why should I abide by conventional morality?"—a question that is significant, a question to which many diverse and interesting answers have been offered through the philosophical ages. The question "Why should I be moral?" is, then, like the question "Why should I abide by the rules of etiquette?" or "Should one always abide by the rule of law?" Indeed, just as there is a "should" of conventional morality, there is a "should" of etiquette and a "should" of law. The question "Why should I abide by the rules of etiquette or law?" could be rephrased, "Why should I do what I should do according to Emily Post?" and "Why should I do what I legally should do?" The first "should" in all of these questions constitutes the *fundamental* "should" of practical rationality—the univocal "should" that a rational person employs in asking himself what he should do. The rules of conventional morality, etiquette, and law constitute normative principles whose rationality can certainly be challenged.

One can, of course, argue that the "should" used in prescribing conventional morality is itself *defined* by those conventions. Hare, for example, tries to build into the *meaning* of the moral "ought" principles that I take to be normative. Perhaps one rationally should make decisions only after taking into account how one would react if one were in the affected parties' respective positions, but I do not take this to be an analytic truth. And the cost of making it an analytic truth is to relegate this "should" to an inferior position in the hierarchy of fundamentally significant concepts relevant to decision making. With Hare's view, as with so many other conceptions of morality, one is left with the unanswered question "Why should I be moral?", a question that employs that most fundamental "should" defined in terms of rationality.

So we return once again, and finally, to our original dilemma. It is an analytic truth that if we are to be rational we will do what we rationally ought to do. If the concept of what we morally ought to do is not defined in terms of the concept of what we rationally ought to do, then as rational agents we can safely ignore morality. If we want decisions about what we morally ought to do to be fundamental to rational people making rational choices, we must identify first-person judgments about what we ought to do with judgments about what we have the most reason to do. In this book I have tried to analyze the concept of rational action, the concept that is fundamental to rational people trying to make rational decisions.

References

Aristotle. *Nichomachean Ethics*. In *The Basic Works of Aristotle*, Richard McKeon, ed. New York: Random House, 1941.

Armstrong, David. 1973. *Belief, Truth, and Knowledge*. London: Cambridge University Press.

Audi, Robert. 1983. "An Epistemic Conception of Rationality." *Social Theory and Practice* 9:311–34.

———. 1986. "Acting for Reasons." *Philosophical Review* 95 (4):511–46.

Ayer, A. J. 1952. *Language, Truth, and Logic*. New York: Dover.

———. 1970. "What Is a Law of Nature?" In Brody 1970, pp. 39–54.

Baier, Kurt. 1958. *The Moral Point of View*. Ithaca: Cornell University Press.

Beardsley, Monroe. 1965. "Intrinsic Value." *Philosophy and Phenomenological Research* 26:1–17.

Bloom, A. 1987. *The Closing of the American Mind*. New York: Simon and Schuster.

Brandt, Richard. 1979. *A Theory of the Good and the Right*. Oxford: Clarendon Press.

Brody, B. A., ed. 1970. *Readings in the Philosophy of Science*. Englewood Cliffs, N.J.: Prentice-Hall.

Burks, A. 1977. *Chance, Cause and Reason*. Chicago: University of Chicago Press.

Butchvarov, Panayot. 1982. "That Simple, Indefinable, Nonnatural Property *Good*." *Review of Metaphysics* 36:41–75.

———. 1989. *Skepticism in Ethics*. Bloomington: Indiana University Press.

Chisholm, R. M. 1976. *Person and Object*. LaSalle, Ill.: Open Court.

———. 1977. *Theory of Knowledge*, 2d ed. Englewood Cliffs, N.J.: Prentice-Hall.

———. 1989. *Theory of Knowledge*, 3d ed. Englewood Cliffs, N.J.: Prentice-Hall.

Darwall, Stephen. 1983. *Impartial Reason*. Ithaca: Cornell University Press.

Davidson, Donald, J. C. C. McKinsey, and Patrick Suppes. 1955. "Outlines of a Formal Theory of Value, I." *Philosophy of Science* 22 (April): 140–60.

Donagan, Alan. 1977. *The Theory of Morality*. Chicago: University of Chicago Press.

Dretske, Fred. 1969. *Seeing and Knowing*. London: Routledge and Kegan Paul.

Falk, W. D. 1986. *Ought, Reasons, and Morality*. Ithaca: Cornell University Press.

Feldman, Fred. 1978. *Introductory Ethics*. Englewood Cliffs, N.J.: Prentice-Hall.

Fletcher, Joseph. 1966. *Situation Ethics*. Philadelphia: Westminster Press.

Flew, Antony. 1963. "On the Interpretation of Hume." *Philosophy* 38:178–82.

Foley, Richard. 1987. *The Theory of Epistemic Rationality*. Cambridge, Mass.: Harvard University Press.

Foot, Philippa. 1958–59. "Moral Beliefs." *Proceedings of the Aristotelian Society* 59:83–104.

Frankena, W. K. "The Naturalistic Fallacy." *Mind* 48:464–77.

Fumerton, Richard A. 1976. "Subjunctive Conditionals." *Philosophy of Science* 43:523–38.

——. 1980. "Induction and Reasoning to the Best Explanation." *Philosophy of Science* 47:589–600.

——. 1983. "The Paradox of Analysis." *Philosophy and Phenomenological Research* 43:477–97.

——. 1985. *Metaphysical and Epistemological Problems of Perception*. Lincoln: University of Nebraska Press.

——. 1988. "The Internalism/Externalism Controversy." In *Philosophical Perspectives*, vol. 2. Atascadero, Calif.: Ridgeview, pp. 442–59.

Fumerton, Richard A., and R. Foley. 1982. "Epistemic Indolence." *Mind* 91:38–56.

Gauthier, David. 1975. "Reason and Maximization." *Canadian Journal of Philosophy* (March): 411–33.

——. 1986. *Morals by Agreement*. Oxford: Clarendon Press.

Gauthier, David, ed. 1970. *Morality and Rational Self-Interest*. Englewood Cliffs, N.J.: Prentice-Hall.

Gewirth, Alan. 1978. *Reason and Morality*. Chicago: University of Chicago Press.

Goldman, Alvin. 1979. "What Is Justified Belief?" In Pappas 1979, pp. 1–23.

Hare, R. M. 1952. *The Language of Morals*. London: Oxford University Press.

——. 1963. *Freedom and Reason*. London: Oxford University Press.

——. 1981. *Moral Thinking*. Oxford: Clarendon Press.

——. 1982. "Ethical Theory and Utilitarianism." In Sen and Williams 1982.

Harman, Gilbert. 1977. *The Nature of Morality*. New York: Oxford University Press.

Heald, William. 1985. "The Concept of Pleasure and the Thesis of Hedonism." Ph.D. dissertation, University of Iowa.

Hobbes, Thomas. *Leviathan*, Parts I and II. Indianapolis: Bobbs-Merrill, 1958.

Hodgson, D. H. 1967. *Consequences of Utilitarianism*. Oxford: Clarendon Press.

Hospers, John. 1961. *Human Conduct*. New York: Harcourt, Brace, and World.

Hubin, D. Clayton. 1980. "Prudential Reasons." *Canadian Journal of Philosophy* 10(1): pp. 63–81.

Hume, David. *A Treatise of Human Nature*, ed. L. A. Selby-Bigge. London: Oxford University Press, 1888.

Kalin, Jesse. 1970. "In Defense of Egoism." In Gauthier 1970, pp. 64–87.

Keynes, J. M. 1952. *Treatise on Probability*. London: Macmillan.

Korsgaard, Christine. 1983. "Two Distinctions in Goodness." *Philosophical Review* (April): 169–96.

Kretzmann, Norman. Forthcoming. "A Particular Problem of Creation: Why Would God Create This World?" In MacDonald, forthcoming.

Langford, C. H. 1942. "Moore's Notion of Analysis." In Schilpp 1942, pp. 319–42.

Lyons, David. 1965. *Forms and Limits of Utilitarianism*. Oxford: Clarendon Press.

MacDonald, Scott. "Ultimate Ends in Practical Reasoning." unpublished.

MacDonald, Scott, ed. Forthcoming. *Being and Goodness*. Ithaca: Cornell University Press.

MacIntyre, A. C. 1959. "Hume on 'Is' and 'Ought'." *Philosophical Review* 68:451–68.

Mackie, J. L. 1973. "The Disutility of Act-Utilitarianism." *Philosophical Quarterly* 23 (October): 289–300.

McKinsey, J. C. C. *See* Davidson, Donald.

Medlin, Brian. 1957. "Ultimate Principles and Ethical Egoism." *Australasian Journal of Philosophy* 35:111–18.

Mill, John Stuart. *On Liberty*. New York: Bobbs-Merrill, 1956.

——. *Utilitarianism*. New York: Bobbs-Merrill, 1957.

Moore, G. E. 1899. "The Nature of Judgment." *Mind* 8 (July): 176–93.

——. 1900–01. "Identity." *Proceedings of the Aristotelian Society* 1:103–27.

——. 1903. *Principia Ethica*. Cambridge: Cambridge University Press.

——. 1912. *Ethics*. London: Oxford University Press.

——. 1942. "A Reply to My Critics." In Schilpp, pp. 533–76.

Nagel, Thomas. 1970. *The Possibility of Altruism*. Oxford: Clarendon Press.

Nielsen, Kai. 1970. "Why Should I Be Moral?" In Sellars and Hospers 1970, pp. 747–68.

Nozick, Robert. 1981. *Philosophical Explanations*. Cambridge, Mass.: Harvard University Press.

Pappas, George, ed. 1979. *Justification and Knowledge*. Boston: Reidel.

Parfit, Derek. 1984. *Reasons and Persons*. Oxford: Clarendon Press.

Perry, Ralph Barton. 1926. *General Theory of Value*. Cambridge, Mass.: Harvard University Press.

Plato. *The Republic*, ed. H. D. P. Lee. New York: Penguin, 1958.

Prichard, H. A. 1912. "Does Moral Philosophy Rest on a Mistake?" *Mind* 21:487–99.

Quine, W. V. O. 1953. *From a Logical Point of View*. Cambridge, Mass.: Harvard University Press.

Rawls, John. 1971. *A Theory of Justice*. Cambridge, Mass.: Harvard University Press.

Regan, Donald. 1980. *Utilitarianism and Co-operation*. Oxford: Clarendon Press.

Ross, W. D. 1930. *The Right and the Good*. Oxford: Clarendon Press.

Rousseau, Jean-Jacques. *The Social Contract*. Trans. M. Cranston. New York: Penguin, 1968.

Russell, Bertrand. 1948. *Human Knowledge: Its Scope and Limits*. New York: Simon and Schuster.

Schilpp, P. A., ed. 1942. *The Philosophy of G. E. Moore*. LaSalle, Ill.: Open Court.

Searle, John. 1964. "How to Derive 'Ought' from 'Is'." *Philosophical Review* 73: 43–58.

——. 1983. *Intentionality*. Cambridge: Cambridge University Press.

Sellars, W., and J. Hospers, eds. 1970. *Readings in Ethical Theory*. Englewood Cliffs: Prentice-Hall.

Sen, A. K., and Bernard Williams, eds. 1982. *Utilitarianism and Beyond*. Cambridge: Cambridge University Press.

Shope, Robert. 1978. "The Definition of Rational Desires." *Canadian Journal of Philosophy* 8:329–40.

Sidgwick, Henry. 1922. *The Methods of Ethics*. London: Macmillan.

Singer, Marcus. 1961. *Generalization in Ethics*. New York: Atheneum.

——. 1977. "Actual Consequence Utilitarianism." *Mind* 86:67–77.

Smart, J. J. C. 1956. "Extreme and Restricted Utilitarianism." *Philosophical Quarterly* 6:344–54.

Smart, J. J. C., and Bernard Williams. 1973. *Utilitarianism: For and Against*. Cambridge: Cambridge University Press.

Stevenson, C. L. 1937. "The Emotive Meaning of Ethical Terms." *Mind* 46:14–31.

——. 1942. "Moore's Arguments against Certain Forms of Ethical Naturalism." In Schilpp 1942, pp. 71–90.

——. 1944. *Facts and Values*. New Haven: Yale University Press.

——. 1963. *Ethics and Language*. New Haven: Yale University Press.

Strawson, P. F. 1964. *Individuals*. London: Methuen.

Suppes, Patrick. *See* Davidson, Donald.

Temkin, Jack. 1978. "Actual Consequence Utilitarianism: A Reply to Professor Singer." *Mind* 87:412–14.

Urmson, J. O. 1953. "The Interpretation of the Moral Philosophy of J. S. Mill." *Philosophical Quarterly* 3:33–39.

Warnock, G. J. 1971. *The Object of Morality*. London: Methuen.

Williams, Bernard. *See* Smart and Williams, and Sen and Williams.

Index

between acting rationally and rational action, 93–94, 125–26; distinction between causal and justificatory reasons, 92–93
Rawls, John, 102, 116 n.11
Realism: metaphysical, 20; moral, 20
Regan, Donald, 196 n.9, 202–3
Regress of justification, 12–14
Relative frequency conceptions of probability, 12–15
Relativism, 41–50; anthropological, 22, 41–42; metaethical, 44–50; metaethical cultural, 45–47; metaethical individual, 46–47; situation, 42–44
Ross, W. D., 43 n. 20, 53 n.26
Rousseau, Jean-Jacques, 236 n.7
Rule consequentialism. *See* Consequentialism
Rules of thumb, 174
Rule utilitarianism. *See* Utilitarianism
Russell, Bertrand, 15 n.7

Searle, John, 33 n.11, 97 n.4, 132 n.1
Secondary properties, 36
Shope, Robert, 150 n.13
Sidgwick, Henry, 237 n.8
Singer, Marcus, 51 n.25, 56 n.30, 59 n.34
Skepticism, 21, 105–7, 170–78; in connection with any act consequentialism, 170–78; as a consequence of actual consequence utilitarianism, 105–7

Stevenson, C. L., 24 n.6, 25–26, 40, 77 n.9, 79–82, 86–87; on magnetism, 79–82, 86–87
Strategies, as alternatives, 180–82
Strawson, P. F., 225
Subjectivism. *See* Objectivism/subjectivism
Suppes, Patrick, 135

Teleological/deontological distinction, 54–55. *See also* Consequentialism
Temkin, Jack, 51 n.25
Thrasymachus, 91, 225 n.1

Universalizability, 29, 163–64
Urmson, J. O., 56 n.30
Utilitarianism, 51–59; kinds of generic act utilitarianism, 53–55; kinds of hedonistic act utilitarianism, 51–53; kinds of rule utilitarianism, 55–58

Valuing intrinsically, 94–95, 129–56; arationality of, 143–56; contemplative vs. cognitive valuing, 138–42; dispositional vs. occurrent, 136–38; supervenience of on properties, 151–53. *See also* Ends
Voter's paradox, 200–206, 214–216

Warnock, Geoffrey, 192 n.6
Williams, Bernard, 192 n.6

Library of Congress Cataloging-in-Publication Data
Fumerton, Richard A., 1949–
    Reason and morality: a defense of the egocentric perspective/
Richard A. Fumerton.
        p.   cm.
    Includes bibliographical references.
    ISBN 0-8014-2366-X (alk. paper)
    1. Ethics.   2. Reason.   I. Title.
BJ1012.F85   1990
170'.42—dc20   89-38801